RELIGION IN LIFE AT LOUISBOURG

1713–1758

Three religious groups served the French stronghold of Louisbourg during the eighteenth century. They were the Récollets of Brittany, who acted as parish priests and chaplains; the Brothers of Charity of Saint John of God, who operated the King's Hospital; and the Sisters of the Congregation of Notre-Dame, who conducted the local school for girls.

A.J.B. Johnston establishes the secular and religious contexts of life in Louisbourg, and then traces the mixed fortunes of each of these groups. Drawing on the extensive material in the Archives of the Fortress of Louisbourg, he notes the groups' remarkable persistence in the face of personnel shortages, financial burdens, and conflicts with secular authorities and rival religious bodies. Not the least of their problems was the profound parsimony of the Louisbourgeois who declined to build a parish church or pay a compulsory tithe. Yet despite this independent stance, religion was at the centre of family and community life in Louisbourg, as the author demonstrates in a chapter devoted to the faith, morality, and popular beliefs of the town's inhabitants.

The colourful military history of Louisbourg has been the subject of numerous books and articles, and the economy of Ile Royale has received close attention in recent years. This is the first comprehensive study of the religious aspects of life in this outpost of France's overseas empire. It contributes substantially to the social as well as the religious history of New France.

A.J.B. JOHNSTON is a native of Truro, NS, and since 1977 has been a staff historian at Fortress of Louisbourg National Historic Park.

Religion in Life
at Louisbourg
1713–1758

A.J.B. JOHNSTON

McGill-Queen's University Press

Kingston and Montreal

© McGill-Queen's University Press 1984
ISBN 0-7735-0427-3

Legal deposit second quarter 1984
Bibliothèque nationale du Québec

Printed in Canada

Canadian Cataloguing in Publication Data

Johnston, A. J. B.
    Religion in life at Louisbourg, 1713–1758
    Bibliography: p.
    Includes index.
    ISBN 0-7735-0427-3
    1. Louisbourg (N.S.) – Religious life and customs.
    2. Louisbourg (N.S.) – Church history. 3. Catholic
    Church – Nova Scotia – Louisbourg – History. I. Title.
    BX1424.L68J63 1984   282.71695   C84-098071-X

This book has been published with the help of a grant from the Canadian Federation for the
Humanities, using funds provided by the Social Sciences and Humanities Research Council
of Canada.

Cover View of Louisbourg, 1731, by Verrier *fils* (*Bibliothèque nationale, Cartes et Plans,
GeC. 5019)*

To my father, James A.L. Johnston, and stepmother,

Elizabeth Langille, and to the memory of my mother,

Clarissa A. Bayly

Contents

Figures

Tables

Acknowledgments

My greatest debt is to the Fortress of Louisbourg project itself, especially to the dozens of researchers who have preceded me and whose finding aids, note cards, and unpublished reports I have used in writing this study. Too many historians have contributed to the Louisbourg project to name all of them, but the ones whose work I found particularly helpful must be mentioned: B.A. Balcom, Brenda Dunn, Christopher Moore, Gilles Proulx, and Barbara Schmeisser. I am equally indebted to my current colleagues, Kenneth Donovan, Eric Krause, T.D. MacLean, and William O'Shea, whose suggestions, criticism, and general support have added much to this study. I would also like to thank Roger Ruel for drawing the graphs and charts, Art Fennell and Glenn Langille for the photography, and Isabel Levy for typing and retyping the manuscript so often in such a professional manner. Special thanks are in order for Cornelius Jaenen and Claudette Lacelle for their close reading and helpful criticism of the study at the manuscript stage.

An earlier version of chapter 3, then entitled "The Frères de la Charité and the Louisbourg Hôpital du Roi," was published by the Canadian Catholic Historical Association in its *Study Sessions* 48 (1981): 5–25.

Ile Royale, 1742 *Bibliothèque nationale, Cartes et Plans, 131-2–6*

Louisbourg and vicinity, 1729 *Bibliothèque nationale, Cabinet des Estampes, Vd. 20a-44*

Plan of Louisbourg, 1742 *Archives nationales, Outre Mer, DFC, IV-198c*

View of Louisbourg, 1731 *Bibliothèque nationale, Cartes et Plans, GeC. 5019*

Church emplacement and Récollet property *Collection du Ministère de la Défense, Archives du Génie, Vincennes-14-1-22*

Proposed church *Archives nationales, Outre Mer, Atlas Moreau de S. Mery, F3-290, no. 42*

Chapelle de Saint-Louis *Parks Canada photo*

Plan of the Hôpital du Roi *Archives nationales, Outre Mer, DFC, IV-154*

St Marguerite Bourgeoys *Centre Marguerite Bourgeoys, Montreal; photo, Armour Landry*

Madonna and child *Glenn Langille photo*

Crosses, crucifixes, and medals *Glenn Langille photo*

Holy-water basins *Glenn Langille photo*

Illustrations from Picart, *The Ceremonies and Customs of the Various Nations of the Known World*, vol. 2 *Courtesy Harvard College Library*

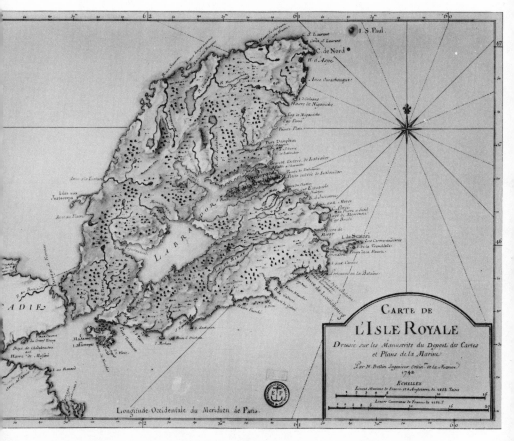

Ile Royale, 1742. Nicholas Bellin's map shows the concentration of French settlements along the eastern and southern coasts of Cape Breton.

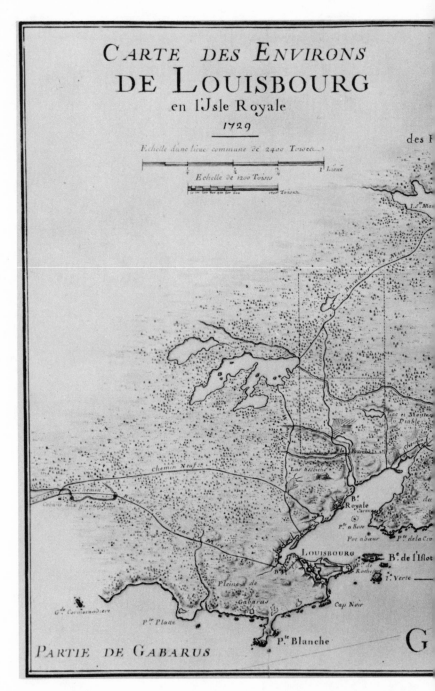

Louisbourg and vicinity, 1729. Before 1731 only the settlements closest to Louisbourg were served by the Récollets of Brittany, who in that year assumed responsibility for every parish on the island.

Barachoir de lange

R.ᵉ de Miré

B. du Colombe

PARTIE DE LA BAYE DE MIRE

B. de Pontarly

Pᵗᵉ d'Jsidore

Ba. de Pontif

charite

B. de Miré

ᵉ habit. de la charité

le Jacobin

le Caputin

Pᵗᵉ aux Pigeons

Pᵗᵉ aux Oiseaux

Tour à chaux

ne

bitation de De Catalogue

en defrichem.ᵗ

Menadou

G. Cormorandiere

Pᵗᵉ Cormorane

Cap Menadou

C. du Cap

SCATARI E

Ance de Menadou

C. de lance

Pᵗᵉ et Batture de Menadou

Pᵗᵉ Montag.ᵉ remarquable pour latterage des Vau.x

Pᵗ Laurembec

la Baleine

I. aux Canes

Laurembec

du Petit

Pleine

Laurembec

Cap Vert

Islea aux Morceaux les bateaux

Pᵗ du Sud

Isto du Nord

la Madelaine

Cap Laurembec

Bat.ᵉ de Laurembec

Pᵗᵉ Basse?

Pᵗᵉ aux Chais

Batture de Porte-nove

Porte-nove

ANDE MER

Levée en 1729 Par le S.ʳ Boucher Ingenieur du Roy

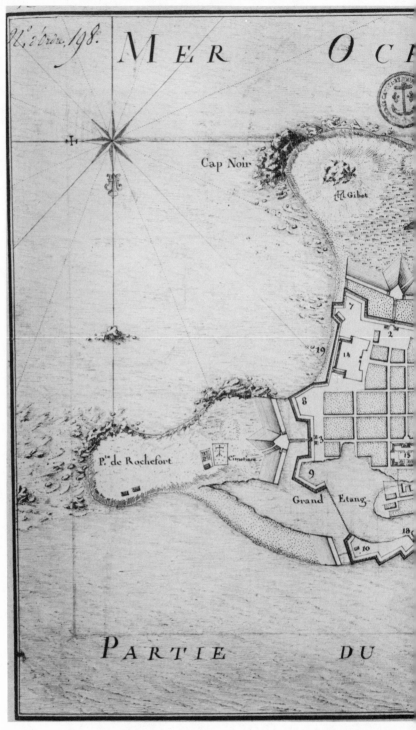

Plan of Louisbourg, 1742. Shown here are the property of the Récollets of Brittany (16), the King's Hospital, run by the Brothers of Charity (13), and the property of the Congregation of Notre-Dame (17).

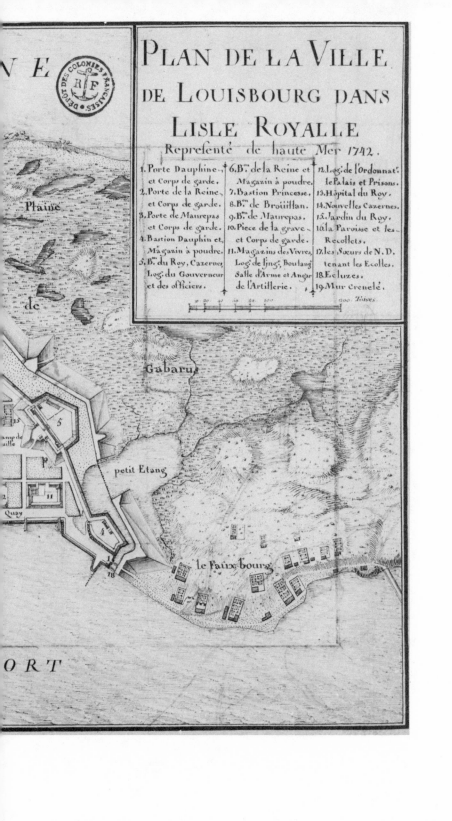

Plan de la Ville de Louisbourg dans Lisle Royalle

Representé de haute Mer 1742.

1. Porte Dauphine, et Corps de garde.
2. Porte de la Reine, et Corps de garde.
3. Porte de Maurepas et Corps de garde.
4. Bastion Dauphin et Magazin à poudre.
5. B.on du Roy, Cazerne, Log.t du Gouverneur et des officiers.
6. B.on de la Reine et Magazin à poudre.
7. Bastion Princesse.
8. B.on de Brouillan.
9. B.on de Maurepas.
10. Piece de la grave et Corps de garde.
11. Magazins des Vivres, Log.t de s[in]g.rs Boulang, Sale d'Arme et Ang.ar de l'Artillerie.
12. Log.t de l'Ordonnat.r le Palais et Prisons.
13. Hôpital du Roy.
14. Nouvelles Cazernes.
15. Jardin du Roy.
16. la Paroisse et les Recollets.
17. les Sœurs de N.D. tenant les Ecolles.
18. Ecluzes.
19. Mur Crenelé.

N E

Plaine

de

Gabaru

petit Etang

le Faux bourg

Camp de ville

Quay

ORT

View of Louisbourg, 1731. A detail from the painting by Verrier *fils*. Though a number of the features depicted were still in the planning stage, the overall representation is considered accurate. Dominating the skyline are (*left*) the King's Hospital and (*right*) the King's Bastion barracks.

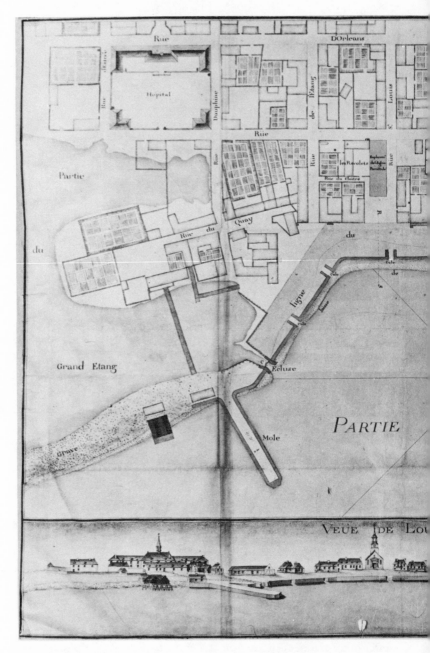

Church emplacement and Récollet property. The emplacement for a parish
church was at the corner of rues Royalle and St Louis, where a portion of the
foundation was laid in 1721. Never completed, the proposed church is depicted

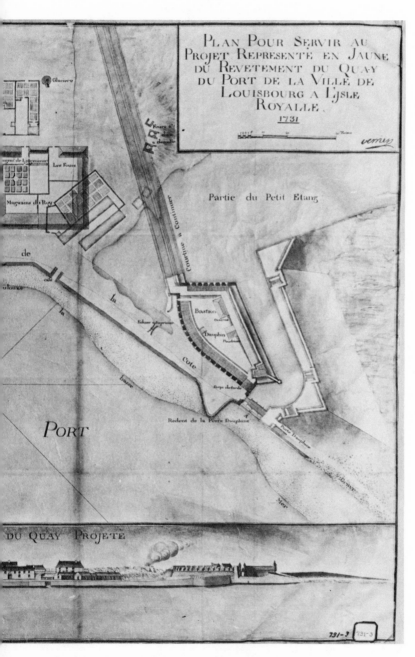

in the view of Louisbourg accompanying this plan. The adjacent lot contained the residence and chapel of the Récollets of Brittany; from 1724 to the mid-1730s this Chapelle de Sainte-Claire served as the town's second parish church.

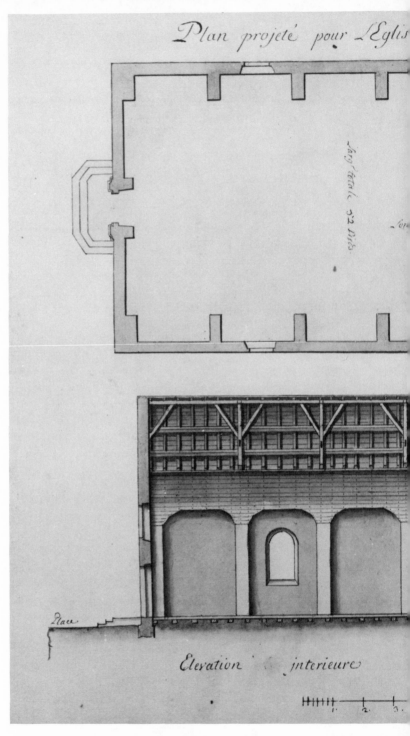

Proposed church (c.1737). This is undoubtedly the plan *ingénieur du roi* Etienne Verrier was asked to produce in 1737 for submission to the minister of marine in the hope of obtaining royal funds to build a parish church for Louisbourg.

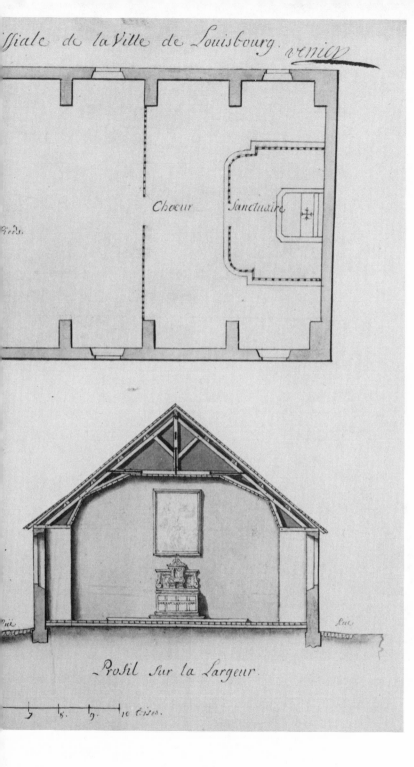

...ssiale de la Ville de Louisbourg. *venier*

Choeur Sanctuaire

Pieds

Profil sur la Largeur.

Chapelle de Saint-Louis (reconstruction). Located in the barracks of the King's Bastion, this military chapel served as Louisbourg's parish church from the mid-1730s until the evacuation of 1745 and again from 1749 to 1758.

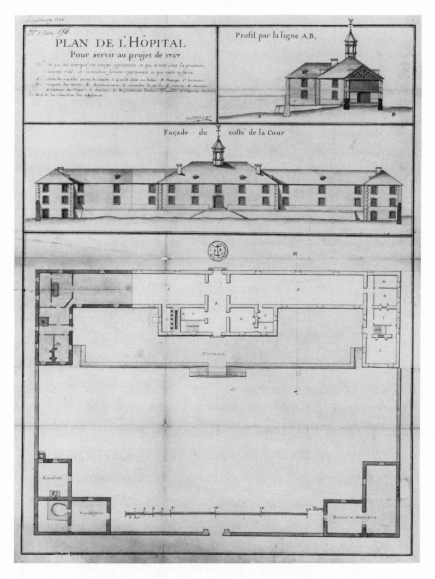

Plan of the Hôpital du Roi. The ground floor layout shows the chapel, wards, latrines, morgue, dispensary, and living quarters for the brothers; other buildings, at the bottom of the plan, contained the laundry, bakery, and stables.

Récollet friar (opposite above) and (below) Brother of Charity of the Order of Saint John of God, from *Histoire des ordres monastiques religieux et militaires*, vol. 7 (1718). (Above) St Marguerite Bourgeoys (1620–1700). Sister St Renée's 1904 painting depicts the foundress of the Congregation of Notre-Dame instructing girls at one of the schools she established in New France.

Madonna and child (above). This small ivory statue, about 10 centimetres high, was found during excavation of a casemate in the King's Bastion. Rosary (below). On one side of the cross is a representation of the Crucifixion; on the other, the Assumption of the Blessed Virgin.

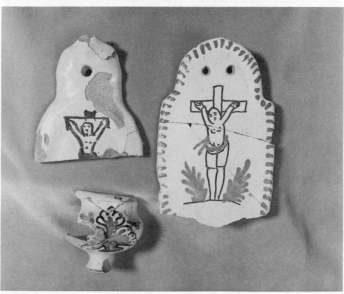

Crosses, crucifixes, and medals (above). The upraised arms on the crucifix on the right are thought to reveal a Jansenist influence. The medal on the right, found on the property of the Sisters of the Congregation, bears the inscription "Catherine de Bologne." The two figures on the largest medal are believed to represent St Anne and the Blessed Virgin. Holy-water basins (below). These fragments of two *bénitiers* were discovered by archaeologists during the Louisbourg reconstruction project.

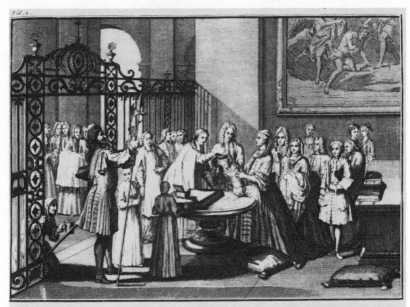

BAPTISM ADMINISTRED
by a PRIEST.

LE BAPTEME ADMINISTRE par
un PRETRE.

BAPTISM ADMINISTRED
by a MIDWIFE.

LE BAPTEME ADMINISTRE par
la SAGE-FEMME.

Baptism, from Picart, *The Ceremonies and Customs of the Various Nations of the Known World*, vol. 2 (1734). Though ideally the sacrament was to be administered by a priest, in church, high infant mortality rates meant that midwives always had to be prepared to baptize the newborn.

COMMUNION. *La COMMUNION.*

The CEREMONY *of* MARRIAGE. *Ceremonie de* MARIAGE.

Communion and marriage (Picart, *Ceremonies and Customs*, vol. 2). First communion was a turning point in a young person's life. Marriage, some years later, was an even more important step, for it had not only a religious dimension but might have economic and social repercussions as well.

CONFESSION. ‖ La CONFESSION.

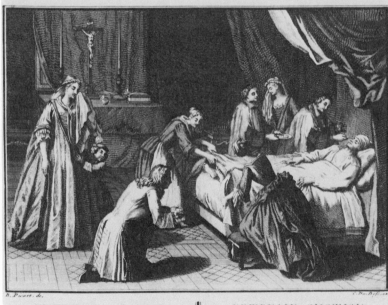

B. Picart. de.   E. Du Bosc. sc.

EXTREME UNCTION. ‖ EXTREME ONCTION.

Confession and extreme unction (Picart, *Ceremonies and Customs*, vol. 2).
Reconciliation with God, through confession, was to be achieved at least once a
year, at Easter, and preferably more often. A "good death" included three sacraments: confession, communion, and extreme unction.

RELIGION IN LIFE AT LOUISBOURG

1713–1758

Introduction

Historians writing about eighteenth-century Louisbourg have traditionally looked at the town through secular eyes. In the nineteenth and early twentieth centuries the focus was on military history, principally the sieges of 1745 and 1758, with Louisbourg being seen as one of the main stages where the dramatic Anglo-French struggle for North America was acted out.[1] In recent decades there has been a shift away from the sieges, which after all occupied only four months of the town's forty-five year life span, and toward economic and social histories of the community. Inspired or funded by the massive research and reconstruction project at the Fortress of Louisbourg National Historic Park, which began in 1961, historians have produced studies of Louisbourg's merchants and their international trading links, of its role in the North Atlantic cod fishery, of its place in French public construction in the Atlantic region, of the composition and activities of its peacetime garrison and of the many aspects of family life there.[2] Slowly, a comprehensive view of the eighteenth-century settlement is emerging. Yet, to date, there has been little acknowledgment that the community, overwhelmingly French and Catholic, also had a spiritual dimension.[3] That is, that it was a parish as well as a commercial centre and a fortified town, with three religious orders, four chapels, and several thousand inhabitants, each with his or her own unique religious needs.

To understand the religious situation at Louisbourg one must first be familiar with the secular context within which its inhabitants and its *religieux* found themselves. The settlement was established by the French in 1713, following their loss of Acadia and Newfoundland to the British by the terms of the Treaty of Utrecht. Louisbourg was but one of many harbours on Cape Breton (renamed Ile Royale) which were settled by the French, yet from the very beginning it was the most populous and important of them all. In 1717 it was selected to become the administrative centre for the colony of Ile Royale, which also included Ile Saint-Jean

(Prince Edward Island). Though Ile Royale formed part of the larger colony of New France, because of its isolation from Québec it was largely administered as a separate colony. The local royal officials, the governor and com-missaire-ordonnateur, corresponded directly with the minister of marine, who held the responsibility for France's overseas colonies as well as its navy, rather than through the governor-general and intendant at Québec.

Louisbourg's primacy within the colony of Ile Royale stemmed from a combination of geographic and economic factors. The harbour was large, well shaped (with a narrow opening which made it defensible as well as a safe haven from storms), and it was close to both the offshore cod banks and the transatlantic trade routes. The fishery, by itself, generated enormous wealth. The annual value of the Ile Royale cod catch, most of which was exported through Louisbourg, ranged between 2.5 to 3.5 million *livres* for the period 1718 to 1741. It declined thereafter, but still remained close to or above two million *livres* a year.[4] Building upon these massive exports of cod, as well as its excellent location (jutting out into the North Atlantic), Louisbourg quickly emerged as a major trading and trans-shipment centre. By the 1720s, well over a hundred ships a year from France, the West Indies, New England, Canada, and Acadia entered the port to unload their goods and take on return cargoes of cod and other commodities. As a result, a flourishing merchant community developed in the town, drawing people and investment from other regions.[5]

The third important sector of the Louisbourg economy was government expenditure. Once the decision was taken to transform the settlement into a major fortified town and naval base, large amounts of royal funds were expended there annually. In the process, Louisbourg was given a system of bastioned fortifications and detached batteries that ranked among the most elaborate on the continent; huge public buildings like the King's Bastion barracks, Hôpital du Roi, and King's storehouse; as well as North America's second lighthouse and a careening wharf. The cost for these public works was high (between four and five million *livres* for the fortifications, about 16 million *livres* on other expenditures), and much of the money, in hard currency, circulated at Louisbourg.[6]

With its economic advantages, Louisbourg enjoyed rapid growth. By 1737, its permanent civilian population had increased tenfold, from 149 in 1713 to 1,463 in 1737. By the 1740s, there were likely 2,000 permanent civilian residents in the town and its suburbs, along with 650 to 700 soldiers who formed the garrison. In addition, there were hundreds of sailors and seasonal fishermen who came to reside, visit, or work in the port each summer. During the 1750s, Louisbourg's population swelled even more, perhaps as high as 10,000 by 1758, as additional soldiers and civilians

FIGURE 1
Louisbourg Population, Selected Years

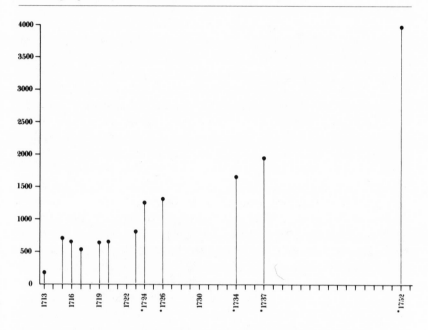

* Includes military population.

came to live there. Within the colonial North American context, Louisbourg was a major settlement.[7]

Who were the people of Louisbourg, or indeed of the larger colony of Ile
Royale?[8] In several ways they were quite different from the inhabitants of
other parts of New France. To begin with, there were almost no farmers
or fur traders, nor was a seigneurial system ever introduced. Instead,
Louisbourg was a town of fishermen, sailors, merchants, innkeepers,
tradesmen, and royal officials. And, of course, soldiers. Generally, the military population formed about one-quarter of the total populace, though on
the eve of the siege of 1758 it numbered well over one-half. Because of
the military presence, as well as the large number of seasonal fishermen,
there was always a marked imbalance in the sexes. In the 1720s, adult
males outnumbered adult females eight or ten to one. The gap decreased
somewhat as the years went by, but even leaving out the military population, the ratio of adult males to females was never lower than three to one.
This demographic fact had far-reaching effects, on specific matters such as

the age at which young people married, and possibly on more general aspects such as the moral standards which prevailed in the community.

The very "newness" of Louisbourg also set it apart from eighteenth-century Acadia and Canada. There had been French settlements on Cape Breton in the seventeenth century, but they had been small, short-lived, and well before the founding of Ile Royale. Unlike Acadia and Canada where many families had been associated with a given town or village for three or four generations, at Louisbourg, until the 1740s and 1750s, the residents were mostly recent immigrants. In the beginning their emotional and cultural ties lay elsewhere and their religious and other customs varied according to their places of origin. It would take time and common experiences to bring about feelings of attachment and a sense of local identity.

In the very early years of Louisbourg's history the largest group of settlers came from Plaisance (Placentia), Newfoundland, having relocated to the new colony in 1713.[9] Through the years that followed, the Placentia group, and their children, formed a core group in the community, with its most prominent members becoming dominant fishing proprietors, merchants, and civil officials. As Louisbourg began to develop into a fishing and trading centre, and concomitantly was selected to become the fortified stronghold of the colony of Ile Royale, hundreds of immigrants began to arrive from France. First of all, there were the fishermen (Bretons, Normans, and Basques). Some chose to live year round, others on a seasonal basis only. Then there were the merchants and financiers, many of whom had their start as fishing proprietors (habitant-pêcheurs). Next, tradesmen and labourers had either to be brought from France or induced by high wages to come by themselves to build the growing town and its fortifications. Finally, there were the soldiers, most of whom were French-born and would stay in Louisbourg only as long as their enlistment required.

Nothing indicates the preponderance of Frenchmen in the town better than the fact that 77 per cent (181 of 233) of the men to marry in Louisbourg during the period to 1745, were natives of France. Ranking far behind were grooms from Acadia, Canada, and Newfoundland, each at around 5 per cent. The female population balanced the situation somewhat as most came from colonial backgrounds. Of the Louisbourg brides before 1745, the largest group, comprising 37 per cent and of necessity quite young, were natives of Ile Royale itself, followed by women from Newfoundland, Canada, Acadia, and, last of all, France.[10]

To return briefly to the origins in France of the Louisbourg grooms, one sees there were roughly an equal number (about 19 per cent) from each of the areas of Brittany, Normandy, and Guienne-Gascony. The four western provinces of Poitou, Aunis, Angoulême, and Saintonge contributed a combined total of 10 per cent, while the Ile de France region followed with slightly less than 7 per cent.[11] Louisbourg, therefore, like Canada and Acadia, received the bulk of its French immigrants from the north, west, and southwest of France. At the level of provincial origins, however, there were some notable differences. On a percentage basis, there were at Louisbourg considerably more Bretons and Gascons and fewer Normans and people from the Ile de France region than was the case in Canada. Available figures for Acadia indicate the situation there was quite similar to that at Louisbourg, though there were more emigrants from Picardy and Ile de France among the Acadians than in the capital of Ile Royale.[12]

Although most of Louisbourg's inhabitants were of French extraction, from either France or New France, the town did contain a significant number of people from completely different ethnic backgrounds. The most numerous were the Basques. Exactly how many Basque fishermen lived at Louisbourg, or at least resided there on a seasonal basis, is impossible to tell from the census material. Neither the names nor the places of origin of the fishing population are recorded. In the only extant list that does provide that kind of information, a 1752 document on the winter fishery, nearly one-half of the 199 men wintering in Ile Royale outports were from the largely Basque dioceses of Bayonne and St Jean de Luz.[13] During the more active summer fishery (May to September), there would have been many more Basques in the colony, perhaps as many as 200 to 300 in Louisbourg alone. When ashore, these men stayed in their fishing proprietors' *cabanes* that lined the north shore of the harbour. Though the Basques shared a common religious faith, differences in language and culture kept them largely apart from the French majority. Interpreters had to be used in the court cases in which they were involved, and conflicts between Frenchmen and Basques were not uncommon.

The next largest minority were the Swiss and German soldiers of the Karrer Regiment, who helped garrison Louisbourg from 1722 to 1745. Initially, there were only 50 of them, but that was raised to 100 in 1724 and to 150 in 1741. Because they lived within the fortress walls, either in the barracks or in private dwellings, and wore distinctive uniforms, the presence of these foreigners was likely far more conspicuous to the average French inhabitant than that of the Basques, who lived and worked around and across the harbour. More importantly, many of the Karrer soldiers were Protestant, a fact which undoubtedly disturbed a portion of the French Catholic majority. In 1724, Governor Saint-Ovide warned the minister of marine that France's Micmac allies regarded the Protestant troops "as suspects." Three years later, the governor complained that the Karrer officers refused to lead their soldiers in the *fête-Dieu* (Corpus

Christi) procession in the town. The minister, however, was unsympathetic to such complaints, believing that the utility of having the Karrer Regiment in the colony outweighed any problems they created on account of religion.[14] How many residents were able to adopt a similarly broad perspective is unknown.

There were other Protestants in Louisbourg besides those in the Karrer Regiment, including two Huguenot merchants who had business connections with the town. There were also the Protestant residents of English, Irish, and Scottish backgrounds. For all of these people, being of a different religious faith had its drawbacks, including possible social ostracization and the certainty of not being buried in consecrated ground. Such realities led over forty Louisbourg Protestants, Karrer soldier and civilian alike, to convert to Roman Catholicism between 1722 and 1758. Whether or not the Protestants who did not choose to convert met secretly to practise their faith, or if they developed some sense of group solidarity, is not known.[15]

Of the various non-French nationalities at Louisbourg, those which probably fitted most easily into the local society were the Irish Catholics. Most of the forty or fifty whose names appear in the parish records worked as servants in French households, but there were a few who possessed tradesmen skills. Indeed, there were even Irish priests on Ile Royale. One, identified as Abbé Byrne, served as a missionary to the Micmacs in 1733–4, a second was in the town in 1744, while a third, Timothée Lynch, married an Irish couple at Louisbourg in 1754.[16] For religious as well as other reasons, these Irish Catholics felt more at home in Louisbourg than in comparable English settlements in North America; at least if one can judge by the eight Irish families en route from Newfoundland to Halifax who jumped ship in Louisbourg in 1750 seeking the freedom to practise their religion.[17]

Two other groups worthy of mention are blacks and Micmacs. There were nearly two dozen black slaves baptized at Louisbourg, and there were doubtless many more who had already been baptized in the French West Indies before being shipped north. There were also a few "free blacks" in the town, one of whom became an apprentice baker and another who purchased the freedom of a local slave in order to marry her.[18] As for Micmacs, these military allies were rarely seen in the town. The southern part of the island, particularly the Port Toulouse (St Peter's) and Bras d'Or Lakes region, was their normal area for hunting and fishing. There they had their own chapel and their own missionary, the best known of whom was Abbé Pierre Maillard who arrived in the colony in 1735. Nonetheless, the occasional baptism of a native child, the entry into domestic service of a young Micmac girl, and the infrequent visits of their scouts or chiefs, testify that Micmacs did sometimes come to Louisbourg. The only time in which their presence would have been particularly noticeable, however, was in 1757, when as a defensive precaution against a feared British assault over 100 Micmacs and Malecite were accommodated in and near the town throughout the summer. The cost of the stay to the French treasury was high, over 60,000 *livres* for arms, tobacco, and assorted merchandise, but such expenses were regarded as a good investment to keep an ally friendly to their cause. An outdoor mass at Gabarus Bay in July, said in Micmac by Abbé Maillard, attracted a large crowd of curious French onlookers, who were "edified by the propriety and composure with which the natives addressed their prayers to the Lord." The missionaries to the Micmacs, notably Maillard in Cape Breton and Jean-Louis LeLoutre in mainland Nova Scotia, were regular visitors to Louisbourg, spending a week or so in the town each year to discuss with royal officials matters of mutual concern.[19] (The efforts of these missionaries among the native population fall outside this study, which concentrates on religious life at Louisbourg.)

To summarize in very general terms, eighteenth-century Louisbourg may be described as follows: politically, it was the *de facto* administrative centre for France in the area known as Atlantic Canada; economically, its strength lay in the fishery, international trade, and large-scale royal expenditures; socially, it was a garrison town with males greatly outnumbering females; culturally, it was obviously French, but because of trade and immigration patterns, and other factors (most notably the presence of the Karrer Regiment and large numbers of Basques) the port had a definitely cosmopolitan air. As for religion, most of the population was of course Roman Catholic, though there was a significant Protestant presence, particularly during the period up to 1745.

The study which follows is an attempt to answer some basic questions about religion at Louisbourg: such as who the religious were and what they did, how closely the priests and parishioners followed the precepts laid down by the church, and to what degree the commercial and military orientations of Louisbourg might have influenced the religious life and morality of the civilian inhabitants. Did, for instance, the presence of large numbers of unmarried soldiers and fishermen tend to undermine the influence of the *religieux* among the residents, or indeed were the religious themselves, because of the distance from their ecclesiastical superiors, less rigorous in exercising their ministry at Louisbourg than in other settlements in New France?

The kinds of questions which can be asked about religious life in eighteenth-century Louisbourg are of course largely determined by the extant sources. The documentation on the French occupation of Louisbourg is massive, at times overwhelming, but in the sphere of religion there are some unfortunate gaps. The parish records (baptisms, marriages, and burials), for instance, for the first decade of Louisbourg's history did not survive, making analysis of certain aspects of life during that early period all but impossible. Thereafter, the records appear to be complete, with the exception of the period between July 1745 and July 1749 when the inhabitants were in exile in France. Another shortcoming is the general absence of letters or memoirs written by the Louisbourg religious themselves, documents which would have expressed their own views on the many difficulties they encountered. This lack is particularly noticeable when one attempts to explain the various controversies between religious and civil officials, or simply among the different religious groups. Invariably, the sources one must rely on are those of the opposing side, either the correspondence of royal officials (both in the colony and in France) or of the bishop of Québec or one of his vicars-general (again both in the colony and in France). Only occasionally is one able to hear the arguments and viewpoints of the local religious in their own words.[20] Still another drawback is the complete lack of any documents on such things as parish finances, school attendance, and communion and confession records.

Notwithstanding these shortcomings, one can still obtain a comprehensive picture of religion at Louisbourg, principally by using these sources: parish records for thirty-two years of the town's history, correspondence and financial records of royal officials from 1713 to 1758, reports and letters of the bishops and their vicars-general, census data, court records, wills, and inventories. Also useful are the hundreds of historic maps and plans of the town, the accounts written by various besiegers and prisoners, and the archaeological evidence uncovered during the 1960s and 1970s.

1 Religion and Ile Royale

Marriage of good design
Of Church and Lily Divine.
If one or the other should part,
Each will feel it in his heart.[1]

The waning days of the summer of 1713 witnessed the beginning of what was to be a final chapter in the story of France's colonization of North America. On 23 July, roughly three months after France had officially ceded mainland Nova Scotia and Newfoundland to Great Britain, an expedition of about 250 people set sail aboard the *Semslack* from Plaisance (Placentia, Newfoundland). They were entrusted with the mission of founding a new colony. Their destination was Cape Breton, an island whose population at the time was a single Frenchman and twenty-five to thirty Micmac families. Directed by the minister of marine to settle in a location suitable for exploiting the bountiful fishery and developing the commercial potential of the island, the expedition spent several weeks exploring different anchorages.

When the time came to make an establishment before the advent of winter those in command selected a commodious harbour on the eastern coastline known as Havre à l'Anglois. On 2 September 1713 a landing party went ashore, formally claiming the island for Louis XIV. Details of the "Prise de possession" were not recorded but the Récollet father in the landing party, Dominique de la Marche, undoubtedly offered prayers to bless and solemnize the birth of the latest French colony, and a cross may even have been raised on the shore of the harbour. Initially called Port St Louis, the location's name was later changed to Louisbourg. The island and colony of which Louisbourg would later become capital was designated Ile Royale.[2]

The impetus for the settlement of Ile Royale clearly grew out of economic and commercial considerations. The minister of marine, who held responsibility for France's overseas empire, expected the island to become much more than just a new home for relocating French subjects. The hope was that the colony would rapidly develop into a major fishing base and an important trading and transshipment centre.[3]

Apparent as the economic motives behind the founding of Ile Royale were, French officials always maintained that the promotion of religion was the first object of the colony.[4] From a twentieth-century perspective one may be tempted to dismiss such assertions as no more than rhetoric, as an outdated carry-over from the zealous days of sixteenth-century New World missionary activity. But one must resist that temptation. Although an exaggeration, the statement that religion was the "first object" of French colonies does point to a fundamental truth. The stability of French society, on either side of the Atlantic, depended in part on the secure ideological and moral underpinning supplied by religion. The most basic concepts of the era, loyalty to the king, respect for order, acceptance of a hierarchical social structure, and feelings of a sense of community, were both fostered and reinforced by the teachings and practices of the contemporary French Roman Catholic Church.

The Religious Context
There is little doubt that secular officials in France and in Ile Royale recognized the important place which religion held in their society. Time and again governors, commissaires-ordonnateurs, and ministers of marine intervened in religious controversies which threatened to disturb what they termed the "tranquillity" of the society. In the case of Ile Royale the concern for religious matters began even before the colony was founded. Meeting the spiritual needs of the colonists was given top priority during preparations for the 1713 settlement of Cape Breton. With letters to the governor-general of New France, to the superior of the Récollets in Canada, and to the commander of the *Semslack* expedition, the minister of marine directed that *religieux* be included in the settlement party. Realizing that the early days of the new colony would be filled with hardship, the minister specified that each religious selected should be "an accommodating man of good spirit." Furthermore, he stressed that regular church services should commence as soon as possible after landing. In the minister's words, that was the best way to bring "the blessings of Heaven upon the new establishment."[5]

There were two main functions which religion was expected to fulfil in colonial society. First, and most obviously, it was to help meet the emotional, psychological, and spiritual needs of the inhabitants. So well understood were people's spiritual needs that vessels going on long voyages with a crew of forty or more were required by the king to carry a chaplain.[6]

Similarly, large settlements ashore without benefit of clergy were inconceivable. People could not be deprived of sacraments and spiritual comfort. If they were, they died, as a colonial military officer put it, "like beasts in the forest."[7]

The second function of religion was as a binding social force. During the early years on Ile Royale the view that religion brought the community together and deterred deviant behaviour was particularly strong. In 1714 the minister of marine informed the commissaire-ordonnateur that religious influences came before formal justice in helping to prevent and suppress disorder.[8] The link between religion and social control was perhaps best expressed in 1720 by the colony's second governor, Saint-Ovide de Brouillan: "I am striving to make the inhabitants live in both Religion and Obedience to the King, and to preserve harmony among them; treating them with Kindness yet punishing them severely when they merit it."[9] The connection which Governor Saint-Ovide made between religion, obedience to the king, and social harmony is perhaps most easily understood in terms of the distinctive nature of the contemporary French Roman Catholic Church.

The Catholic church in eighteenth-century France was an independent "national" church whose ties to the monarchy were as strong as those to the pope in Rome. The politico-religious doctrine which justified that arrangement was known as *gallicanisme*[10] (hence the French church came to be known as the Gallican church). By the eighteenth century *gallicanisme* consisted of an assertion that the popes held no temporal authority over French kings and a conviction that even in spiritual matters the authority of Rome was strictly limited in France, as prescribed by the canons and customs of the kingdom. According to the defenders of the doctrine the special rights and liberties of the Gallican church dated from the period when France had first converted to Christianity. Since then, for over a thousand years, those rights and privileges had been carefully safeguarded by French kings, parlements, and bishops. By the fifteenth century, the Gallican position was that decisions by councils of bishops had supremacy over those of popes, that there could be no papal intervention in the selection of French bishops, and that revenue would no longer be sent to Rome. A century later, in 1516, French prelates and the pope reached a new agreement, the Concordat of Bologna. Under the terms of the Concordat the right of the king to appoint the bishops and abbots of France was reaffirmed, thereby strengthening his hand in dispensing patronage and in controlling politically sensitive religious issues.[11] The French in turn agreed to send a portion of their ecclesiastical income to Rome. Both those principles were still in effect two hundred years later, at the time of the founding of Ile Royale.

The church in New France, of which Ile Royale was a part, was "an extension of the Gallican Church," but in an unusual way. The bishop of Québec held ecclesiastical jurisdiction over all French possessions in North America and yet had "neither seat nor vote in the Assembly of the French clergy."[12] Moreover, the bishop was directly subordinate to Rome, not to an archbishop in France. In spite of those peculiarities, however, the diocese was very much part of the Gallican establishment. The bishop was named by the king, took an oath of loyalty to the monarch, was paid out of the royal treasury, and was in regular correspondence with the minister of marine and his colonial officials.[13]

As for the royal officials, they were partially dependent on the church because only practising Catholics could hold public posts. Before being given a position an individual had to obtain a certificate from his curé testifying that he was at least twenty-five years old and that his morals, way of life, and adherence to the Roman Catholic faith were acceptable.[14] The relationship between royal officials and the bishop of Québec (or his representative) was relatively harmonious in the eighteenth century, in comparison with the sometimes turbulent situation in the seventeenth century. Indeed, eighteenth-century ecclesiastics and religieux were more inclined to quarrel among themselves than with representatives of the king.[15] The grounds for such harmony between church and state seems to have lain in the principles of gallicanisme, which each side shared. As Guy Frégault expressed it: "The men of the State were Catholics, the men of the Church served the State."[16]

For the most part, the theory of gallicanisme had little impact on the religious life of ordinary subjects. It was more a matter of concern to churchmen, jurists, and scholars. But on a practical level there were definite implications for the close ties between church and state. Not only were parish records legal documents of the civil estate, but curés regularly read royal edicts and proclamations from their pulpits. Another area where gallicanisme likely influenced the common people was in their perception of the king. In the popular mind the king's "religious" role went far beyond naming the country's bishops. Each succeeding monarch proudly retained the centuries-old titles of "fils aîné de l'Eglise" ("eldest son of the Church") and "le Roi très-chrétien,"[17] titles which had been accorded by Rome because France had been the first nation to embrace Christianity. That heritage, combined with the anointing which took place at the king's coronation and the influence which he had in spiritual affairs, caused the monarch to be widely regarded as a "sacred personage ... as a father to his people."[18] Church and state worked together to cultivate that idea as it was to their mutual advantage. On the one hand, the king gained a powerful ally for his absolutist cause through his support of gallicanisme and his

TABLE 1

Expenditures on Public Ceremonies, Selected Years
(to nearest *livre tournois*)

	1738–9	1740–1	1749	1750	1751	1752
Fête de Saint-Louis	1,176	472	262	162	672	1,542
Fête-Dieu et de l'octave	1,080	94		142	282	428
Arrival of Governor	463	215			182	
Funeral of duc d'Anville			388			
Fête of Commandant			126	135		182
Fête of Ordonnateur				126	117	
Birth of duc de Bourgogne						4,038

SOURCES: AN, Colonies, C11B, vol. 21, fols. 157–57v., Estat de la Consommation, 1 octobre 1738 à 1 octobre 1739; ibid., vol. 23, fols. 180–80v., 1 octobre 1740 à 1 octobre 1741; ibid., vol. 27, fols. 266–9, 30 septembre 1751; ibid., vol. 32, fols. 169–70v., Prévost, 30 septembre 1752.

control over the appointment of prelates; on the other hand, the principles of *gallicanisme* depended in part on the concept of a paternalistic, quasi-divine monarch.

On Ile Royale the most striking manifestation of the close ties between the monarchy and the church were the celebrations each August on the *fête de Saint-Louis*. A feast day commemorating the thirteenth-century king of France (Louis IX) who had been canonized for his saintliness and for his crusades to the Holy Land was the perfect occasion for fostering loyalty to the monarchy. As a king, Louis IX was renowned for his strong and fair rule; as Saint-Louis he was a patron of the cathedral at Québec and "our protector in Heaven."[19] The unique qualities of the saint-king, as a father to his people in both this world and the next, made the *Jour de Saint-Louis* a day on which patriotism and piety became nearly indistinguishable.

Royal officials on Ile Royale did all they could to make the festivities as spectacular as possible. Artillery salutes during the day, and evening bonfires, each of which was paid for out of the colonial budget, helped to make the *fête de Saint-Louis* a memorable day. Year in, year out, the amount spent on the Saint-Louis celebrations outstripped the sums spent on nearly every other comparable public occasion (see Table 1). The most lavish expenditure on record occurred in 1752 when 1,542 *livres* were spent on artillery salutes.

The nature of those salutes in 1752 illustrates clearly how a celebration of the French monarchy was an integral part of the *fête de Saint-Louis*.

TABLE 2
Church Calendar, Diocese of Québec, 1694–1744

Holy Days [Fixed]	Date	Fasting (Vigils)	Abstinence
			every Friday and Saturday, except from Christmas to the Purification
Circumcision	1 January		
Epiphany	6 January		
Presentation / Purification	2 February		
St Mathias, Apostle	24 February (25 February in Leap Year)		
St Joseph, First Patron of Colony	19 March		
Incarnation / Annunciation	25 March		
			St Mark's Day (25 April)
St Philip and St James, Apostles	1 May		
St John the Baptist	24 June	23 June	
St Peter and St Paul, Apostles	29 June	28 June	
St James, Apostle	25 July		
St Anne	26 July		
St Lawrence, Deacon and Martyr	10 August	9 August	
Assumption of Holy Virgin	15 August	14 August	
St Bartholomew, Apostle	24 August		
St Louis, Second Patron of Cathedral	25 August		
Birth of Holy Virgin	8 September		
St Matthew, Apostle	21 September	20 September	
St Michael, Archangel	29 September		
St Simon and St Jude, Apostles	28 October		

	Date	Fasting (Vigils)
All Saints	1 November	31 October
St Andrew, Apostle	30 November	29 November
St Francis Xavier, Second Patron of Colony	3 December	
Conception of Holy Virgin, First Patron of Cathedral	8 December	
St Thomas, Apostle	21 December	
Birth of Jesus Christ	25 December	24 December
St Stephen, First Martyr	26 December	
St John, Apostle and Evangelist	27 December	

Holy Days (Moveable)	Date	Fasting (Vigils)	Abstinence
Easter, and two days following	spring	all of Lent, except Sundays	Sundays of Lent
	spring		Rogations
Ascension	spring	Vigil of Pentecost	
Pentecost, and two days following	spring	Ember Days after Pentecost	
Holy Sacrament (Corpus Christi), with octave	spring		
Patron of the Parish	probably 2 August at Louisbourg, Parish of Notre Dame des Anges		
	fall	Ember Days after Holy Cross Day (14 September)	
	winter	Ember Days after third Sunday in Advent	

SOURCES: Saint-Vallier, *Rituel du diocèse de Québec*; Henri Têtu and C.-O. Gagnon, eds., *Mandements, lettres pastorales et circulaires des évêques de Québec* 1: 335–6.

The fête began, probably at dawn, with a twenty-one gun salute to announce the day. That salute was followed later in the day by twenty-one guns for the health of Louis XV, nineteen guns for the health of the queen, and seventeen guns for the entire royal family. A final twenty-one gun salute was fired during a Te Deum service in the chapel which served as Louisbourg's parish church (and which incidentally was named after Saint-Louis).[20]

The different Te Deums sung at Louisbourg provide another indication of the degree to which the temporal and spiritual worlds of eighteenth-century Frenchmen were united.[21] On at least eleven occasions officials called for the singing of the ancient Latin hymn of thanksgiving to celebrate temporal good fortune. The most typical cause of rejoicing was either a military victory (taking of Fontarabie, 1719; victories in Germany, 1734; capture of Canso, 1744; taking of Minorca and Fort St Philippe, 1756)[22] or some blessing bestowed on the royal family. Into the latter category fell such events as the recovery of health of young Louis XV in 1721, his coronation in 1722, and the birth of legitimate royal offspring in 1727, 1729, and 1751.[23]

In accordance with the wishes of the minister of marine, the Te Deum services held in the Louisbourg parish church were attended by all members of the Conseil Supérieur and followed by artillery salutes, ceremonial bonfires, and general rejoicing. The bonfires (feux de joie) were to be ignited by the representatives of both church and state, with the parish priest, governor, and commissaire-ordonnateur each having his own torch.[24] The Te Deum celebrations typically included toasts to the royal family and a general illumination of the town from people's houses. As part of the festivities following the Te Deums for the birth of the duc de Bourgogne (1752) and the convalescence of the dauphin (1753), the commandant of Ile Royale, the comte de Raymond, sought to engender a special attachment to the royal family by distributing wine from his own cellar among the soldiers and ordinary people of the town.[25]

Religious life on Ile Royale, of course, encompassed much more than the occasional Te Deum and the annual "Jour de Saint-Louis." As part of the diocese of the bishop of Québec the colony would have followed, until 1745, the church calendar set down by Bishop Saint-Vallier in 1694.[26] There were thirty-seven holy days of obligation on the calendar, all of which were to be dedicated to mass and prayers (see Table 2). Any leisure time on such days, according to a late seventeenth-century French writer, was to be spent visiting "the sick, the poor, the afflicted," or having "sober & modest meals," or participating in "games & diversions that are honest & beneficial to themselves."[27] The addition of fifty-two Sundays to the total meant that theoretically there was one-quarter of the year given over to devotion rather than to work and other temporal pursuits.

In recognition of the fact that Ile Royale's prosperity depended on its fishery, Bishop Saint-Vallier authorized, in 1716, departures from the diocesan calendar during the months when fishing activity was at its peak. To the men who went to sea the bishop gave special permission to fish on several of the June, July, and August fêtes. For the remaining summer holy days, those considered to be more important, fishing was also permitted but only if the men attended mass before setting sail.[28]

A similar concern for the practical requirements of life in a new colony manifested itself years later in connection with the work on the fortifications. The building season on Ile Royale was short enough to begin with (in 1718 it was estimated to be five months, included in which there were twenty-two Sundays, eighteen fêtes, and twenty days of poor weather on which no work could be done), so when local officials were confronted with a pressing need to make progress on the fortifications, as they were in 1742 and 1756, they ordered construction work to continue on Sundays and feast days.[29] There is no indication whether or not the bishop was aware of these departures from the church calendar, but he likely would have understood and approved. In late 1744, pressured by Versailles to reduce the number of lost working days and concerned himself about the transgressions which some colonists were being forced to commit on holy days of obligation, Bishop Pontbriand transferred nineteen of the fêtes to the nearest Sunday (see Table 3).[30] The shorter church calendar was in effect on Ile Royale throughout the period from 1749 to 1758.

The fêtes of the church calendar appear to have been "deeply engrained in popular awareness." In court cases, correspondence, and probably in conversation people used holy days as reference points for other events. Uncertain about the precise date of some occurrence, people could usually remember that it took place relatively close to this or that feast day, thereby giving an approximate date. The recall of holy days as benchmarks in the passage of time "does not prove Catholic devotion, for the day off work" may have been the remembered aspect.[31] Certainly that was the opinion of the late eighteenth-century commentator on Paris life, the cynical Louis-Sébastien Mercier: "It is noteworthy that in Catholic States Sundays are nearly everywhere days of disorders ... of drunkenness and debauchery."[32] An exaggeration, to be sure, but there is ample evidence from France and Canada to support the contention that Sundays and feast days were often characterized by excessive drinking and rowdy behaviour.[33]

Louisbourg suffered from the same excesses, at least on occasion. Commissaire-ordonnateur Soubras stated in 1719 that at Louisbourg the hours of divine service on the most solemn feast days were the times "selected for the most outrageous debauchery."[34] No details were provided but the

TABLE 3
Adjustments to Church Calendar, Diocese of Québec, 1744

Holy Days	New Date	Fasting (Vigils)
Presentation / Purification	1st Sunday in February	
St Mathias	1st Sunday after 19 February	
St Joseph	1st Sunday after 13 March	
St Philip and St James	1st Sunday in May	
St John the Baptist	1st Sunday after 20 June	Saturday
St James	1st Sunday after 16 July	
St Anne	1st Sunday after 23 July	
St Lawrence	1st Sunday after 6 August	Saturday
St Bartholomew	1st Sunday after 15 August	
St Louis	1st Sunday after 22 August	
Birth of Holy Virgin	2nd Sunday in September	
St Matthew	1st Sunday after 16 September	Saturday
St Michael	1st Sunday after 23 September	
Fête des Reliques	2nd Sunday in October	
Notre Dame de la Victoire	1st Sunday after 17 October	
St Simon and St Jude	1st Sunday after 24 October	
St Andrew	1st Sunday after 29 November	Saturday
St Francis Xavier	Sunday before conception of Holy Virgin	
St Thomas	Sunday before Christmas	

SOURCES: Henri Têtu and C-O. Gagnon, eds., *Mandements, lettres pastorales et circu-laires des évêques de Québec* 2: 40–3, 24 novembre 1744.

most common vice was undoubtedly drunkenness; visitors to the English fishing settlements of Newfoundland during the same period reported that there were more "Strong Liquors" sold on Sundays than on any other day and that in some harbours there might be as many as two hundred men "drunk of a sabath day."[35] The Louisbourg officials took steps to reduce or eliminate such behaviour in their community by declaring in 1720 that all cabarets had to be closed during the mass. Thereafter the situation improved, although it was found necessary to reissue ordinances containing that clause in 1734, 1735, 1741, 1742, and 1749.[36] A few, and perhaps there were only a few, cabaret owners who violated the regulation were fined for their transgressions, as were ship captains who neglected to fly all their flags on Sundays and feast days, as they were required to do.[37] Government action on these matters offers yet another example of how the state offered its support to the church.

Notwithstanding the presence of some individuals who preferred drink to devotion, religion was at the centre of family and community life at Louisbourg. Mass was a social occasion as well as a religious event, as it gave people a chance to catch up on news, spread gossip, or simply be seen. After the service the congregation was frequently greeted by announcements of coming auctions or estate sales, while on the way home (or to a cabaret) they might encounter vendors peddling their wares.[38] As for the Catholic faith itself, from baptism to burial the Louisbourgeois participated in a wide range of activities which conveyed one fundamental message: salvation could be achieved only through the Roman, Catholic, and Apostolic Church. As an article of faith it was probably taken for granted simply because it was so self-evident. Virtually everyone in the community except the Protestant soldiers in the Karrer Regiment shared the same tenets, performed the same duties. Of course, some aspects of the popular faith likely had little to do with the official teachings of the contemporary church. In eighteenth-century France, and presumably in Louisbourg, folk customs and superstitions based on magical rather than Christian principles continued to hold an important place in the hearts and minds of the ordinary people. On Ile Royale, however, there would probably have been few customs peculiar to the island because the colony was so new; it had no martyrs or shrines of its own, nor any long traditions associated with the area. Whatever folk beliefs there were would have come from the colonists' native regions.

At the level of the individual, there was of course a variation in the intensity of faith. For some citizens in provincial towns in France the principal motivation for attending high mass was, so it has been alleged, to "make display of their rank." Symptomatic of that attitude was competition for a prominent position within the parish church, a phenomenon a Jesuit wit described as "pew mania."[39] In Louisbourg there were undoubtedly a number of inhabitants whose piety was more displayed than felt. Nonetheless the point remains: whether for status or for salvation, it was essential to be perceived by the rest of the community as an orthodox Roman Catholic.

For literate colonists religious faith could manifest itself in the books they acquired. Complete figures on book ownership are unobtainable, but the available data reveal how pervasive interest in religious matters was.[40] Over 35 per cent (191 of 524) of the books described as sold or purchased in the Louisbourg documentation were works of a religious or philosophical nature. As for the titles mentioned in people's inventories after death, religious books were the second most numerous (43 of 216) after science texts. Perhaps more importantly, they are the only category of work to be found in all social levels, from fishermen to tradesmen to merchants to royal officials. Prayer books were the most common, with others on the lives of the saints, moral theology, and so on. One title which stands out from the list of religious and philosophical works is Blaise Pascal's *Pen-*

sées. A book of Jansenist speculation and doubt, the *Pensées* was viewed with a jaundiced eye by the church. Nonetheless, there were copies of the work in Louisbourg, in the homes of two local merchants. Besides books, other objects of a religious dimension in people's homes included holy water basins, crosses, crucifixes, paintings (two of the Holy Shroud in one household; two of St Pierre and St Paul in another), reliquaries, plaster figures (two of Christ mentioned in different inventories), and, of course, rosaries.[41]

Important as religion was for some people in personal and social terms, the church as an institution did not have a pronounced impact on Ile Royale society. In that regard the situation on the island was quite different from that in Canada, particularly at Québec. To begin with there was no clerical representation on the Louisbourg Conseil Supérieur, as there was in Canada. Second, there was no major church edifice in the capital of Ile Royale. The most impressive and architecturally significant buildings in the town belonged to the king and were dedicated to temporal functions. The town's parish church was always located in simple chapels; first the Chapelle de Sainte-Claire of the Récollets and then the Chapelle de Saint-Louis in the King's Bastion barracks. Third, the people of Ile Royale paid no compulsory tithe. In France the common rate was one-thirteenth. In Canada it was one-twenty-sixth. At Louisbourg contributions to the church were strictly voluntary. Finally, none of the bishops of the diocese of Québec ever found time to visit Ile Royale. That is not to say that they forgot about the island: there was the 1716 direction on feast days, a pastoral letter in 1756,[42] and regular attention to the colony's spiritual welfare through correspondence. But it was a remote administration, totally dependent on the reports of the local vicars-general (*grands-vicaires*), representatives to whom a degree of ecclesiastical authority was delegated.

The difficulties faced by the different bishops of Québec in communicating with their vicars-general on Ile Royale, as well as with those in Nova Scotia and Louisiana, led to the establishment in 1734 of a senior vicar-general in France who was given direct responsibility over ecclesiastical matters in those areas. The man chosen was Pierre de la Rue, Abbé de l'Isle-Dieu. From the date of his appointment until the end of the French regime, Abbé de l'Isle-Dieu acted as the bishop of Québec's liaison with Rome, the French court, the minister of marine and the *grands-vicaires* in the remote colonies.[43] The vast distance in time and space between the *religieux* on Ile Royale and their ecclesiastical superiors in France and Québec inevitably led to problems, the most noteworthy of which appears to have been occasional laxness among some of the religious serving the colonists.

The involvement of religious in the history of the colony commenced at the founding of Ile Royale in 1713 and continued until 1758. By 1717 two orders were officially established on the island, while a representative from a third religious community arrived in 1727. Each of those communities looked after a different sphere of colonial life; each played a major role in shaping the nature and character of society on Ile Royale.

The Coming of the Religieux

The first religious to come to the new colony of the Ile Royale were Dominique de la Marche and Jean Capistran, friars of the province of Paris in the Récollet order. Following a request from the minister of marine they sailed from Canada to Cape Breton to join the settlement party from Plaisance.[44] La Marche, who had earlier done mission work at Detroit and lectured on philosophy at the Québec convent, participated in the "prise de possession" on 2 September 1713. Capistran was likely there as well, as an observer. One assumes that the ceremonial aspects of the "prise de possession" were brief since there were weeks of arduous labour ahead. Winter was close at hand and there was much to be done to house the settlers, but their spiritual needs were not forgotten. In the largest building (93 *pieds* by 20 *pieds*) erected at Louisbourg that fall space was provided for an interim church and accommodation for the Récollets.[45]

The following year, again in accordance with the wishes of the minister of marine, religious belonging to the Récollet province of Brittany arrived on Ile Royale. This second group of Récollets (Gratien Raoul is the only one whose name is known) sailed from Plaisance, accompanying the additional contingent of French colonists who came from Newfoundland in 1714.

The minister's reasoning in requesting *religieux* from two different Récollet provinces was based on simple logic. Ile Royale was to be settled by French subjects relocating from the English colonies of Nova Scotia and Newfoundland. The Acadians of the former region had been served for years by the Paris Récollets while the parishioners of the latter region had been served by the Brittany Récollets since 1701. The minister thought it prudent to offer the settlers parish priests from the same Récollet provinces with which they had been familiar in their former homes. In that way he hoped to minimize some of the reluctance the subjects might feel about relocating to Ile Royale.

The provision of such dual religious representation was regarded only as an interim arrangement. The minister instructed the governor and commissaire-ordonnateur of the colony to keep a close eye on the situation and to recommend which province they thought would be "the most suitable and agreeable to the inhabitants."[46] The bishop of Québec, Saint-Vallier, cooperated in the matter by naming two vicars-general, Dominique de la Marche of the Paris Récollets and Gratien Raoul of the Brittany Récollets.

The arrangement whereby the two groups of friars shared a joint responsibility for the spiritual life of the colony did not prove to be very peaceful. Even though they served different groups, with the Brittany friars looking after the settlers from Newfoundland and visiting fishing crews and the Paris Récollets serving the king's chapel and relocated Acadians, conflicts between the rivals were inevitable. The members of the two provinces had different outlooks, customs, approaches, and, probably most important of all, different superiors.[47]

After slightly more than a year of observing the situation the first governor of Ile Royale, Philippe de Pastour de Costebelle, informed the officials in France that he thought the Brittany Récollets were more suitable for the colony than their counterparts of the province of Paris. Costebelle acknowledged that the latter group was not without merit but it was his opinion that the Récollets of Brittany possessed the virtues most needed in the colony. They had "a popular and inimitable apostolic zeal for the arduous missionary work they were obligated to do in all the harbours scattered along the coast."[48] Governor Costebelle's assessment of the two provinces was probably coloured by previous events as much as by current behaviour. As a longtime resident of Plaisance, Costebelle remembered that the Newfoundland parish had once been abandoned by the Récollets of Paris and then served satisfactorily by the Brittany friars.[49] The memory of that episode must have helped Costebelle make up his mind as to which group of religious was better suited to Ile Royale.

In France the officials of the Conseil de Marine accepted Governor Costebelle's analysis and quickly took action. By late March 1716 the Conseil had announced that the Récollets of Brittany would replace those of the province of Paris in nearly every settlement on Ile Royale. The sole exception was to be in the Port Toulouse (St Peter's) area where relocated Acadians were to continue to have the Paris Récollets as their parish priests.[50] In May 1716, patent letters were drawn up officially establishing the Récollets of the province of Brittany in the colony.[51] The alacrity with which officials in France acted on Costebelle's recommendation must have pleased the governor. It soon became evident, however, that there were others in New France who were not so happy with the turn of events.

The commissaire-ordonnateur of Ile Royale, Pierre Auguste de Soubras, protested that dual religious representation should have been maintained for a longer period of time. While Soubras argued for a return to the status quo it is clear that he had more repsect for the Récollets of Paris than for those of Brittany. In a letter to the Conseil de Marine he expressed his opinion that the typical Brittany friar "has no other merit than his habit, hardly impresses and generates more contempt than respect." By way of contrast, the commissaire felt that the superior of the Paris Récollets, Dominique de la Marche, was "a man of genius, active, adroit, and fitted to direct and manage minds." Soubras described the current situation in the colony as an "Ecclesiastical war."[52]

Whatever impact the commissaire-ordonnateur's comments had on the Conseil de Marine, the steps taken by the bishop of Québec certainly had more. In a series of letters to all parties involved, Bishop Saint-Vallier expressed his anger over the change that had been made.[53] The bishop pointed out that since Ile Royale was within his diocese decisions concerning who would serve the parishes on the island could not be made without his participation and consent. Annoyed by the infringement on his authority, Saint-Vallier's irritation was all the greater because he held the Récollets of Brittany in low esteem. He stated that he had allowed them to serve in Newfoundland because there had been no other alternative. As for Ile Royale, it was the bishop's belief that the Brittany Récollets had been restrained from impious and unacceptable conduct only by the example of the "more controlled and much more instructed" Récollets of Paris. Mentioned as a particular failing of the Brittany friars was their tendency to socialize with heavy-drinking sea captains, merchants, and fishermen.

The bishop of Québec was so opposed to the replacement of Paris *religieux* by those of Brittany that he refused to give the latter permission to act as parish priests in some communities. Saint-Vallier's own solution to the situation was to effect a clear division of responsibilities between the two provinces. In August 1716 he divided the colony into three spheres of religious responsibility, based on where the principal settlements were at the time. Two of the areas, Port Dauphin (Englishtown) and Port Toulouse were given to the Récollets of Paris. The other, Louisbourg and its dependencies, were to be served by the Récollets of Brittany.[54]

Confronted by the bishop of Québec's strong stand on the issue, the Conseil de Marine cancelled the patent letters of 1716 and issued a new set in May 1717 which established each of the Récollet provinces in the areas accorded them by Saint-Vallier.[55] The bishop was undoubtedly relieved that the controversy was over, especially since secular officials of the Ministry of Marine had accepted his solution. Nonetheless, nothing had been written or done during the dispute to allay his fears about the alleged weaknesses of the Récollets of Brittany. Those prejudices were to surface again in later religious controversies on the island.

Where two Récollet provinces held responsibility for the spiritual welfare of the inhabitants of Ile Royale, the care of their physical well-being was given to another religious order, the Brothers of Charity of the Order of Saint John of God, known popularly in the colony as simply the Brothers of Charity. In March 1716, two and one-half years after the founding of the colony, the Conseil de Marine requested the superior of the Brothers of Charity to select a few religious to take charge of the hospitals in the colony.[56] At the time there were only makeshift hospitals in the main settlements on the island, which colonial officials wanted to see in well-trained hands.[57] Details were worked out with the Brothers of Saint John of God and in April 1716 "Lettres patentes" were drawn up establishing the order on Ile Royale.[58] That summer, aboard a ship which also carried five Récollets of Brittany, four Brothers of Charity sailed to the colony.[59]

When the brothers arrived at Ile Royale they were sent to Port Dauphin, which was the colonial capital at the time. To their disappointment they were not given an evacuated barracks for their use, as had been promised, but the house of an inhabitant.[60] Living conditions there were certainly unhealthy. A midwinter account stated that the Brothers of Charity were "reduced to soldiers' rations and without any wine" and that the situation for the patients was extremely poor. Soldiers were lying, and dying, on no more than wooden bedframes, without the benefit of either straw mattresses or blankets.[61] The following year, 1717, all but one of the brothers left Port Dauphin for the larger community at Louisbourg, where they were given a surplus government building to use as a hospital.[62] Two years later Louisbourg was chosen to become the principal settlement of Ile Royale. The single brother who had remained in Port Dauphin, Frère Félix,[63] soon moved, bringing together all of the Brothers of Charity in the new capital.

The hospital at Louisbourg operated by the brothers during the early 1720s was situated on the north shore of the harbour. Criticism of that facility surfaced shortly after work on the fortifications began, with the main complaint being that the facility was too far (one-half league by land, one-quarter league by sea) from the construction area. Since the greatest number of accidents and injuries, some of which often required immediate attention, occurred in fortifications work, the governor and commissaire-ordonnateur argued that a new hospital should be built in a more suitable location. The Conseil de Marine agreed and in 1721 work on a new facility, the Hôpital du Roi, began on the centrally located Block 13 of Louisbourg.[64]

Construction of the new hospital lasted throughout the 1720s. In 1730, after the slate roof was put on and windows and stoves installed, it was finally ready to admit patients.[65] The Hôpital du Roi was the second largest building in Louisbourg with an elegant spire similar to the one on the barracks. With four large wards containing about twenty-five beds each, its own chapel, apothecary, bakery, kitchen, laundry, latrines, and morgue, the hospital was an impressive and needed addition to the growing town. Right from the beginning the largest single group of patients treated there were soldiers from the garrison. Sailors, civilians, prisoners, and others were also cared for, but generally in much smaller numbers. The move into the Hôpital du Roi necessitated the sending of a fifth Brother of Charity to the colony. One acted as the prior or superior and the others served as sacristan, surgeon, pharmacist, and nurse.

Largely because the Brothers of Charity had no competition in their sphere of concern, their early years in the colony were not characterized by the kind of controversy which surrounded the establishment of the two Récollet groups. The brothers' stay in Louisbourg, however, was not without contention. The disputes in which they became involved were usually over the cost and quality of health care or alleged wrongdoings by some of the brothers. The first of those major conflicts arose in the mid-1720s after the Brothers of Charity had been on the island for a decade.

The final group of religious to serve in colonial Louisbourg was a community of women, the Sisters of the Congregation of Notre-Dame. Founded in Canada in the seventeenth century by St Marguerite Bourgeoys, the Congregation was dedicated to providing a rudimentary yet religiously sound education to girls. Unlike the Brothers of Charity and the Récollets, the *religieuses* did not come to Ile Royale at the request of officials within the Ministry of Marine. Nor indeed did the first sister to sail to the colony leave with the blessing of her superior in the mother house at Montréal. Rather, the Congregation of Notre-Dame was established on the island solely on the initiative of the bishop of Québec, who chose to ignore the expressed wishes of both the minister and the superior of the Congregation. For a religious community it was an unusual beginning, the consequences of which were felt for years afterward.

The independence shown by the bishop of Québec in sending a sister of the Congregation of Notre-Dame to Louisbourg is understandable given the situation on Ile Royale at the time. Since 1724 Bishop Saint-Vallier had pressed the minister of marine, the Comte de Maurepas, to support the idea of sending several teaching sisters to Louisbourg to establish a school. At that point the educational opportunities in the town were extremely limited.[66] The minister's response to the proposal was that the time was not yet right for such a step.[67] The following year the governor and commissaire-ordonnateur of the colony added their support to the bishop's plan. Once again the Comte de Maurepas rejected the idea as premature. To his way of thinking "we must wait until the settlement is fortified and more populated."[68]

The minister's reluctance to send a few nuns to Louisbourg before the town was fortified was apparently based on a parsimonious concern about the additional burden they would place on the king's treasury. As for waiting until the population of Louisbourg increased, by 1726 there were already over 300 children in the town, not including the ones in domestic service.[69] The proponents of the plan to send Sisters of the Congregation to Louisbourg must have wondered how many children there would have to be before the minister would support the proposal. In the bishop's eyes any unnecessary delay was unacceptable. He believed that there were girls growing up in Louisbourg who were ignorant of the basic principles of Roman Catholicism and who possessed "bad morals."[70] As a result Bishop Saint-Vallier at last took the matter entirely into his own hands. In 1727 he convinced one of the sisters from the Congregation of Notre-Dame, fifty-five-year-old Marguerite Roy (Sœur de la Conception) to go to Ile Royale without the sanction of her superior in the mother-house.[71] Assisted by two lay people who accompanied her from Canada, Roy opened a school at Louisbourg in October 1727.

The parents in the town with the inclination and income to have their daughters educated were evidently delighted by the arrival of a bona fide teacher. By mid-December, twenty-two students were enrolled and more were expected.[72] All of the students were undoubtedly girls. In some locations in Canada the bishop of Québec gave the Congregation special permission to admit boys to their schools,[73] but there is nothing to indicate that boys ever attended the sisters' school in Louisbourg.

Marguerite Roy remained in Louisbourg for nearly seven years. During that period her piety and zeal won her the affection and admiration of the inhabitants.[74] When she finally left in 1734 it was not of her own choosing nor that of the colonists.[75] Rather, the sister was compelled to leave because a new bishop of Québec (her supporter Saint-Vallier having died) had been convinced by the superior of the Congregation of Notre-Dame that she was not suitable to head the teaching mission on Ile Royale. Three sisters were sent to replace her in the fall of 1733 and two more and a novice arrived in the following year.[76] Like Marguerite Roy, the sisters that followed her to Ile Royale repeatedly drew praise from the colonists for their devotion and self-sacrifice.[77] They also earned the inhabitants' pity for the many hardships they had to endure in Louisbourg. Financial difficulties combined with sheer bad luck made their stay on Ile Royale as much a tale of adversity as accomplishment.

The problems which beset the Congregation of Notre-Dame at Louisbourg were similar in kind to but more burdensome in degree than those which confronted either the Récollets or the Brothers of Charity. From time to time the continued presence of the sisters in the colony seemed doubtful because of the extreme hardship they faced. As it turned out, the Congregation remained attached to the Louisbourg residents right to the end, accompanying them in 1758 to France, where the last sister died in 1766.[78] While the difficulties of the Sisters of the Congregation were the must severe, the Récollets and the Brothers of Charity certainly had their own problems to overcome. Those problems, and how they were handled by the secular officials in charge of the colony, form the subject of the next three chapters.

2 Curés and Chaplains: The Récollets of Brittany

... they commonly say here [in Canada], by way of proverb, that a hatchet is sufficient to sketch out a recollet; a priest cannot be made without a chisel; but a Jesuit absolutely requires the pencil; to show how much one surpasses the others.

Peter Kalm, *Travels into North America* (1749)[1]

The spiritual welfare of the people of Louisbourg was in the hands of Récollet friars. From the date of the town's founding in 1713 to its ultimate fall in 1758, Récollets served Louisbourg's civil and military populations as their curés and chaplains. In both capacities their goal was the same: to direct people's behaviour and consciences so as to lead them closer to morally acceptable behaviour in this world and toward salvation in the next.

Being involved in the religious life of a new colony was nothing unusual for the Récollets. The spiritual needs of Champlain's settlement at Québec had been met by four Récollets, the first missionaries to go to that part of New France.[2] Over the years that followed they served in Acadia and Newfoundland as well as in Canada. In the colony of Ile Royale, which included Ile Saint-Jean (Prince Edward Island), Récollet friars provided religious services and spiritual comfort to several thousand inhabitants located in numerous scattered settlements. The largest settlement was of course at Louisbourg, whose parish was known as Notre Dame des Anges. By the 1730s there were normally four friars at Louisbourg: a curé (or parish priest) for the civilians and three chaplains to meet the specific needs of the patients in the King's Hospital and of the soldiers in the barracks and Royal Battery.

The history of the Récollets as a distinct religious group began in the sixteenth century when they developed as a branch within the Franciscan order (or Ordre des Frères Mineurs). From the beginning they patterned their lives as closely as possible on that of the order's thirteenth-century founder, St Francis of Assisi. Indeed, the very name "Récollet" was given to them because of their attempt to harken back to the original Franciscan spirit. They were known for their mendicant ways and were identified by their brown or grey homespun habits, bare feet, and sandals or clogs.

By the mid-eighteenth century there were nearly 150 Récollet convents in France, each with its own superior or *gardien*. These were grouped into seven different administrative units called provinces. Overall responsibility for each province lay with a provincial (*ministre provincial*).[3] Until 1731 there were friars from two Récollet provinces serving on Ile Royale. The Récollets of Paris were located in the Port Dauphin and Port Toulouse areas and the Récollets of Brittany served Louisbourg and its nearby outports. When the Paris Récollets decided to withdraw in 1731, their rivals from the province of Brittany assumed the responsibility for all parishes on the island.[4]

The distance of the provincials from Ile Royale made it imperative that selected local friars be given supervisory responsibilities over all the other Récollets. The individuals so chosen were known as commissaires (*commissaires provinciaux*). Generally, the superior of the mission at Louisbourg was named as commissaire for the Récollets of Brittany. Quite often, but not always, the friar named commissaire was also chosen by the bishop of Québec to be a vicar-general (*grand-vicaire*). In that capacity he was given ecclesiastical authority over the parish priests of Ile Royale (compare Figs. 2 and 3).

In theory an individual could hold the dual responsibilities of commissaire and vicar-general without difficulty. The spheres of administrative concern should have been complementary. The commissaire was to ensure that the rules of the Franciscan order were followed by the local friars. The bishop's vicar-general was charged with overseeing the parishes in the colony, as well as with performing on the bishop's behalf such duties as dispensing with marriage banns. In practice, however, there were often times when it must have been difficult to hold both titles. Conflicts between the two superiors, bishop and provincial, were both frequent and bitter.

At the centre of virtually every conflict was a single issue: the quality of the Récollets serving on Ile Royale. Supporters of the Récollets always spoke of their simple piety and ability to communicate with ordinary people, traits that had led Louis XIV to name the friars as chaplains for his troops and aboard naval vessels.[5] At Louisbourg, the popularity of the Récollets among the common people is perhaps best illustrated by Governor Costebelle's remark that it was "the common voice" that had requested the Brittany friars. It was an affection that the Récollets repaid, as in 1720 when the local superior, probably Bruno Sauvé, lamented that

FIGURE 2
Diocese of Quebec: Parishes on Ile Royale and Ile Saint-Jean (1750s)

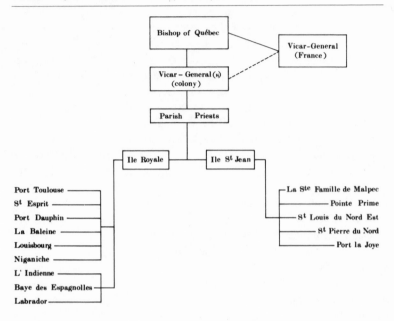

FIGURE 3
Récollets of Brittany: Locations Served (1750s)

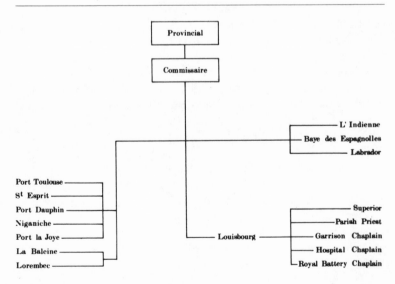

numerous poor families in the original settlement had been forced to relocate on account of the decision to lay out the town according to a formal grid plan.[6]

People who preferred their clergy to be well educated and somewhat aloof from parishioners, however, were often disappointed with the Récollets. The Swedish botanist Peter Kalm obviously heard negative remarks about the friars on his travels through Canada in 1749. Kalm was told that the Récollets "do not endeavour to choose cunning fellows amongst them, but take all they can get. They do not torment their brains with much learning; and I have been assured, that after they have put on their monastic habit, they do not study to increase their knowledge, but forget even what little they knew before."[7]

Not all critics generalized so broadly about the Récollets. As became apparent in the 1716–17 dispute on Ile Royale over where the Brittany and Paris Récollets were to serve in the colony, some people perceived fundamental differences between provinces of the same order. Of the two groups serving Ile Royale the Récollets of Brittany were the only ones criticized for their lack of education and lax morals.[8] Four decades later complaints about the personal shortcomings of the Brittany friars were still being made, at least in some circles. One critic was Thomas Pichon, who wrote in the late 1750s that the Récollets "set a bad example to the common people, especially by their intemperance and ignorance."[9]

Derogatory remarks about the flaws and frailties of the Louisbourg friars must be seen in the proper perspective. In France in the late seventeenth and early eighteenth centuries, there were also complaints about the general ignorance of priests, about the occasional neglect to wear a cassock (even during mass), and about the extreme sociability of some clergymen, to the point of excessive drinking and participating in parishioners' immoral conduct.[10] That similar behaviour might have sometimes surfaced among the Récollets at Louisbourg, a garrison town and bustling seaport, is not too surprising.

How many Récollets were guilty of failings or lapses is not known, nor perhaps was it an important consideration for most of the parishioners. When a secular priest arrived in Louisbourg in the fall of 1718 the inhabitants of the town became alarmed that he had come to replace their beloved friars. A petition signed by more than thirty people was submitted to the governor and commissaire-ordonnateur requesting that the Récollets of Brittany remain as their parish priests. The petitioners affectionately described the Récollets as their "true and legitimate pastors" and claimed that the inhabitants of Plaisance and Louisbourg had been edified by "their wise conduct and good examples."[11] On this occasion the fears of the Louisbourgeois appear to have been groundless. There is no evidence to suggest that the secular priest's arrival in town was linked with any plan to take the parish away from the Récollets, but that is not to say that such an idea never occurred to those who disapproved of Louisbourg's Brittany friars. That idea was to surface repeatedly in the town's history, beginning in the mid-1720s.

One of the factors motivating people to sign the petition in support of the Récollets was the understandable desire to have a church to attend. The only church or chapel in the town in 1718 was located in part of a large building (93 *pieds* by 20 *pieds*) close to the waterfront. Though the structure had been erected in 1713 with royal funds, by 1718 the Récollets appear to have assumed ownership, at least in the eyes of the inhabitants, who feared that if the parish were handed over to secular priests the friars would no longer allow the chapel to be used as the town's church.

It was probably partly in response to that concern, as well as out of a simple desire to have a major church edifice in the town, that the first official proposal to build a new church was made. In 1720 Commissaire-ordonnateur Jacques-Ange Le Normant de Mézy submitted the project to the Conseil de Marine for consideration.[12] By way of introduction to the subject Mézy put forth the view that colonists were unlike the typical citizens of France. They did not feel attached to the settlements where they lived; rather, they came to colonies out of "avarice" and while there "they think only of their own personal interests." The commissaire-ordonnateur disapproved of such self-interest and argued that the construction of public edifices, such as a parish church, might help to settle the colonists in their communities and foster sentiments of pride and belonging.

To illustrate his point Mézy described the situation in Louisbourg concerning the need for a place to worship. He claimed that there was hardly a stable in France that was not "more beautiful and more clean" than the structure currently used as a church. On a number of occasions he and Governor Saint-Ovide had assembled the inhabitants in the hope of convincing them to contribute toward the construction of a new parish church and presbytery. But, according to Mézy, the parishioners "promise much but give little." The Récollets blamed the churchwardens (*marguilliers*) for the lack of public interest in the project and the churchwardens stated that it was useless to collect for a new church since the friars would send the money to France for their convents there. The commissaire-ordonnateur added that there seemed to have been some truth in the latter complaints. It was said, by Governor Saint-Ovide and several of the principal residents of the town, that the Récollets "have always carried away considerable sums," with the figure for 1720 reaching 4,000 *livres*.

Convinced that the colonists would never construct a church at Louisbourg on their own initiative, Mézy urged the Conseil de Marine to reimpose a compulsory tax on the fishing industry. In 1715 a tax of a *quintal* (48.95 kilograms) of cod per shallop had been collected with an eye to offsetting hospital costs on Ile Royale. Though such a tax had been collected at Plaisance, the merchants and fishermen of Louisbourg protested until the tax was lifted in 1716. The commissaire-ordonnateur maintained that the time had come to reimpose the tax to pay for the public edifices the town needed. In addition, he hoped that skilled tradesmen (masons and carpenters) might be sent to the colony to erect the required structures.

While Mézy was awaiting the official response to his suggestions, the chief engineer at Louisbourg, Jean-François de Verville, apparently decided to begin work on the project. In December 1721 the governor and commissaire-ordonnateur reported that Verville had laid a portion of the foundation for the proposed church and presbytery in the lots on Block 3 set aside for those structures.[13] But the construction was stopped by Saint-Ovide and Mézy when the Récollets sought to place a copper plaque in the foundation that made mention of their order. The royal officials interpreted the action as an attempt by the friars to appropriate the church and rectorship of Louisbourg to their order in perpetuity. Worried that the king would not remain the patron of the new church, and thus have control over naming who would serve the parish, Saint-Ovide and Mézy had felt obliged to stop all work on the structure. They urged Versailles to provide the funds to build at least the chancel (*choeur*). They argued that the cost would be relatively small, but the control thereby gained by the king would be essential. As for the copper plaque, it was withdrawn and two medals (one bronze, one silver) bearing the profile of Louis XV on one side and a conjectural view of Louisbourg on the other were placed in the foundations in its place.[14]

The officials in France agreed that it was desirable to have a new parish church and presbytery in Louisbourg, yet they did not attach the same importance to it that Mézy did. They decided to reintroduce the annual tax on the fishery in 1722, as had been recommended by the commissaire-ordonnateur in 1720. Initially, however, the proceeds were to go exclusively towards the construction of the Hôpital du Roi. Only after the hospital was completed was the revenue to be used for a church and priest's residence.[15]

Anyone who was hopeful of having a parish church eventually erected at Louisbourg through the collection of the tithe (*dîme*) on the fishery was soon disappointed. Protests over the tax surfaced quickly, as had happened in 1715, and in 1723 the tithe was discontinued for the second and final time.[16]

With the project for funding the construction of a parish church set aside, attention seems to have shifted to the adjacent land on Block 3 which had been granted to the Récollets of Brittany in 1717. During the early 1720s a residence and chapel belonging to the friars were brought to completion on this property (Lot C). Possibly the structure which became the residence was built upon the presbytery foundation which Verville had laid in 1721. Similarly, the tax money (a total of 1,700 livres 13 sols) which had been collected during 1722 and 1723 may also have been used to help pay for the Récollet buildings, since permission had been given to use the funds on construction of a parish church.[17]

While the Récollet chapel was being built, the old church on the waterfront continued to be used. In 1723, and probably in early 1724, religious services were still being held there.[18] Those services were likely shifted to the new chapel during the spring of 1724. The first indication of the chapel, the Chapelle de Sainte-Claire, being used as the town's parish church appears on a parish record entry for 12 April 1724.[19] The building on the waterfront which had housed Louisbourg's first church was removed sometime between 1724 and 1726 to make way for a private dwelling.[20]

The Récollet chapel served as the Louisbourg parish church for roughly a decade. Then, in the mid-1730s, the parish church function was transferred from there to the barracks or garrison chapel, the Chapelle de Saint-Louis. The change was apparently made following a request by the friars.[21] Whether the Récollet chapel had suffered from its decade of continued use by hundreds of parishioners or whether the religieux simply found it too inconvenient and inappropriate to have a parish church in a small chapel is not known.

Around the time that parish church functions were moved the question of the need for a permanent full-sized church came to the fore again. On this occasion the issue was raised by a secular priest, Jean Lyon de Saint-Ferréol, curé of Québec at the time, who visited Louisbourg in the fall of 1735 on his way to France. In a subsequent report, which was to be forwarded to the minister of marine, Lyon recommended several measures which he considered necessary to improve the quality of religious life on Ile Royale.[22] First and foremost he urged that a parish church be built with royal funds. In marshalling his arguments for such an undertaking, Lyon reiterated most of the points which had been made by others before him. To begin with, he stated that the inhabitants could not afford to build a large church by themselves. Since the garrison chapel served as the parish church at the time, the residents were showing neither interest in contributing to its upkeep nor in paying customary church charges, nor even in electing churchwardens. They left all financial and maintenance responsibilities to the Récollets and to royal officials in the town. Perhaps the most important drawback of using the Chapelle de Saint-Louis as the parish church was that it was too small to accommodate large numbers of parishioners. The visiting vicar-general found the situation deplorable and urged that a new church be built by the king, using funds from the fortifications allotment. Lyon's expectation was that if a sum of money from the royal treasury was committed to the project, the inhabitants would willingly contribute. Without a royal commitment, he correctly foresaw that the people would do nothing.

The commitment which Lyon de Saint-Ferréol argued for was not forthcoming. In January 1737 the minister of marine explained to the Récollet provincial that the current situation simply did not permit the king to undertake any new expenditures. Three months later the minister mentioned to the governor and commissaire-ordonnateur the possibility of additional funds for a church, but first he requested that they send him a plan, a cost estimate, and an indication of what the inhabitants could contribute. The chief engineer at Louisbourg, Etienne Verrier, produced the requested plan and estimate during 1737 and in January 1738 they were forwarded for the minister's consideration. The commissaire-ordonnateur, Le Normant, wrote that the cost could be reduced if the inhabitants contributed materials and labour to the project, but he advised against that approach. In his opinion the structure would be superior if constructed entirely by a hired entrepreneur.[23]

The projected cost (10,200 livres from the inhabitants; 11,780 livres from the king) of a parish church for Louisbourg was apparently more than the officials in France were willing to consider. In the spring of 1738 the minister notified the governor and commissaire-ordonnateur that it was not yet the appropriate time to erect a large church. The fortifications of the town would have to be completed first. The local officials duly informed the residents of Louisbourg of that decision, but they may have held out the possibility that at some point in the future a church might be built.

It was with that goal in mind that the governor and commissaire-ordonnateur again pointed out to the minister that a new church was "absolutely necessary because of the size of the Louisbourg population and the fact that the barracks chapel is too small and inconvenient."[24]

Notwithstanding any promises or hopes expressed in the 1730s, Louisbourg was never to have the proposed parish church. The project came up for discussion from time to time but it was always dropped because of the reluctance to act of either the royal officials or the local residents. As Abbé de l'Isle-Dieu, the bishop's vicar-general in France, commented in 1756, circumstances were just not right at Louisbourg for the construction of a parish church and presbytery, "neither on the part of the court who would not contribute to it, nor on the part of the residents, who are more preoccupied with their positions than with the building of a church."[25]

The criticism that the inhabitants of Louisbourg were unwilling to contribute toward the construction of a church, that they refused to look beyond their own self-interest, was by 1756 a familiar complaint. And to a degree perhaps, an accurate assessment. What other town of its size, with a combined civilian and military population by the 1740s and early 1750s of from 2,000 to 4,000 permanent residents, was without a parish church?[26] Residents in neighbouring settlements one-tenth the size of Louisbourg, like La Baleine and Lorembec, succeeded in building their own churches by deciding among themselves what each person would contribute to the project.[27] A similar approach could easily have been adopted in the capital of Ile Royale, which had both a larger and a wealthier population. Bishop Dosquet's estimate that the parishioners of Louisbourg could annually donate 5,000 to 6,000 *livres* to the church[28] may have been high, but it nonetheless suggests that the citizens were probably capable of paying for the construction of a parish church, had they been so inclined.

The reasons why the Louisbourgeois did not undertake the building of a church are unclear. Contemporary critics always spoke of a lack of community spirit or of a tendency toward parsimony, though it is difficult to see why such qualities would have had a stronger hold on the Louisbourg populace than on that of other towns. A more likely explanation is one which takes into account the distinctive situation at Louisbourg. Louisbourg's economy was based principally on private ventures in the cod fishery and merchant trade,[29] yet the most significant buildings and features in the town were those built at royal expense – the fortifications, the barracks, the hospital, the Magasin du Roi, the official residences, the town gates, the quay wall, the sea batteries, and the lighthouse. With so many public structures and edifices having been erected out of royal funds, perhaps the inhabitants came to feel that the king should build them a church as well. Indeed, that very approach was suggested on a number of occasions, both by local officials and visiting religious officials. As it turned out the king and his ministers did not commit the required funds, but they never ruled out the possibility that they might do so in the future. Apparently encouraged by that prospect, the citizens of Louisbourg made no noticeable effort after 1721 to build their own church.

To return to 1724, when the Récollet chapel became the community church, the curé of Louisbourg was then a friar named Claude Sanquer. As was frequently the case for Louisbourg's parish priests, Sanquer was also the superior of the town's Récollet mission, commissaire of all the other Brittany friars in the colony, and a vicar-general of the bishop of Québec.[30] Towards the end of the summer of 1724, Bénin Le Dorz, a friar recently arrived from France, assumed Sanquer's duties as curé, superior, and vicar-general.[31]

Whatever his virtues, Bénin Le Dorz seems to have had a weakness for alcohol. In either 1724 or 1725 he sailed to Québec to discuss his spiritual responsibilities on Ile Royale with Bishop Saint-Vallier. During that visit the bishop reprimanded Le Dorz for his tendency to appear intoxicated in public in the company of his fellow friars. Apparently as a result of Saint-Vallier's dissatisfaction with Le Dorz's actions the friar ceased to be one of the bishop's vicars-general.[32] The Récollet duly promised to correct his behaviour in the future. Notwithstanding Le Dorz's promise, the bishop was informed in 1726 that the friar had not reformed. The Récollet superior "has continued, and continues still to become intoxicated and in that state to dance and do other excessive things."[33]

Scandalous as Le Dorz's erratic behaviour was, the bishop felt that the friar had done even worse by giving clerical sanction to three prohibited marriages.[34] The first was the marriage of a Protestant, Baron de l'Espérance, a lieutenant in the Karrer Regiment, to Marguerite Dangeac, daughter of another officer in the garrison. While the wedding appears to have been a magnificent social occasion with both governor and commissaire-ordonnateur in attendance,[35] it was nonetheless unacceptable in the eyes of the church. Le Dorz should have made Baron de l'Espérance become a convert to Roman Catholicism before the marriage. De l'Espérance ultimately was converted, but not until 1731.[36]

The second marriage, between local merchant Michel Daccarette and Catherine Gonillon, violated the church's strictures against marrying close relatives of a deceased spouse.[37] The bride was the sister of Daccarette's late wife Jeanne Gonillon. Not only was the marriage carried out under the authority of an invalid dispensation from Rome but there were rumours that Daccarette had given the Récollets 1,000 écus so that the wedding could take place.[38]

The third marriage brought to the bishop's attention was one in which the couple had not gone to confession before receiving the marriage sacrament. Le Dorz's explanation was that he had thought such confession unnecessary if all three banns were published. To Bishop Saint-Vallier it was yet another example of Le Dorz's "deplorable ignorance."[39]

When the bishop heard the reports of marriage irregularities and moral laxity among the Récollets he decided that the situation on Ile Royale warranted immediate action. He chose two secular priests in Québec, Joachim Fornel and Jean-Baptiste Brault, to go to Louisbourg as his new vicars-general.[40] Fornel seems to have been the only one actually to make the voyage to the island, carrying with him the power to suspend the undisciplined Le Dorz and to take the Louisbourg parish entirely out of the hands of the Brittany friars. The bishop conceded that they could retain their functions as military chaplains and remain in the more isolated parishes where there was less to fear from their scandalous behaviour.[41]

After the bishop's representative arrived in Louisbourg and the purpose of his visit was made known, the governor and commissaire-ordonnateur interceded on behalf of Le Dorz and the Récollets of Brittany.[42] The colonial officials acknowledged that the Récollets could not act as curés without the approval of the bishop of Québec but they maintained that the parish could not be taken away from the friars without the consent of the king, who had given them their *lettres patentes* a decade earlier. Abbé Fornel indicated that he understood the position and that he would do nothing to disrupt the parish until after a decision on the issue had come from the French court.[43]

A little over a week later, Fornel suddenly acted. At the end of high mass on the first Sunday in November 1726, he suspended Bénin Le Dorz as curé. Fornel named the military chaplain, Isidore Caulet, as the new parish priest, but Caulet refused the appointment. Le Dorz, who was still the superior of Récollets in and around Louisbourg, responded to Fornel's action by stating that he would withdraw the friars from the nearby settlements and send them back to France. This declaration deeply upset the inhabitants of La Baleine, L'Indienne, and Scatary, who would in that event be without parish priests. Governor Saint-Ovide intervened by compelling Le Dorz to leave the Récollet missionaries where they were. In an attempt to rectify the situation in Louisbourg, the governor called together Fornel, Commissaire-ordonnateur Mézy, and four or five of the principal citizens of the town. After weighing the matter carefully, Fornel decided to reinstate Bénin Le Dorz as curé and to await a decision from France.[44] Fornel himself sailed for France to lobby for a decision in favour of secular priests. The initial stage of the controversy was over. The next stage was fought through correspondence directed towards the minister of marine, who had the responsibility of resolving the issue.

The minister, the comte de Maurepas, received letter after letter during the fall and winter of 1726–7 from those concerned on either side. The basic argument of those opposed to the Récollets was that the Louisbourg parish was being poorly served by the friars and that the introduction of secular priests would be a great improvement. Bishop Saint-Vallier, who contended that except for Gratien Raoul all the Brittany Récollets sent to the colony were "reprehensibles," was the strongest proponent of that view.[45] But it was a perspective shared by the commissaire-ordonnateur of Ile Royale. To the standard criticism of the laxness of the Récollets, Mézy added the charge that the friars' first concern seemed to be to collect money in Louisbourg for their convents in France. The figure alleged to have already left the colony was 6,000 *livres*.[46]

Opposing the views of Mézy and the bishop were those who wished to see the Brittany Récollets retain the parish at Louisbourg. These people put forward two arguments. First, the complaints about the friars, Le Dorz in particular, were exaggerated and it was wrong to condemn the entire province for one man's mistakes.[47] Second, a changeover to secular priests would lead to additional expense and inconvenience for the colonists. That contention was based on a belief that if the largest and most prosperous parish, Louisbourg, was taken away from the Récollets, they would no longer allow their chapel to be used as the town's parish church and they would withdraw the friars from the outport communities. It was those two possibilities which motivated the inhabitants of Louisbourg, L'Indienne, and Scatary to submit petitions in support of the Récollets of Brittany.[48]

In the end, the minister of marine sided with the apparent wishes of the inhabitants.[49] He decided that the Récollets would continue to serve the Louisbourg parish as well as the nearby outports. In communicating his decision to the principals in the dispute, the comte de Maurepas made it clear that he hoped such controversies could be avoided in the future. To the critics of the Brittany Récollets, Maurepas wrote that though it might be desirable to introduce seculars the time was not yet right. A spirit of cooperation with the friars was therefore essential.[50] To the Récollets, the minister offered support, along with a reminder that the controversy might not have arisen had the provincial been more careful in the selection of friars for Ile Royale. Henceforth the provincial was to send to the colony only those Récollets "who edify the people by their morals and good conduct."[51]

For a few years after the minister's decision there was no further talk of replacing the Récollets at Louisbourg. The man who had been at the centre of the controversy, Bénin Le Dorz, was recalled to France in 1727. In December of that same year the most critical and influential opponent of the friars from Brittany, Bishop Saint-Vallier, passed away.[52] His successor, Louis François Duplessis de Mornay, never visited to New France during his six years as bishop,[53] so he was not inclined to pursue the matter. The man who replaced Le Dorz as curé of Louisbourg and superior of the Récollets of Brittany was Michel-Ange Le Duff, formerly a missionary at La Baleine.[54] While the Brittany Récollets retained the parish of Louisbourg, there was not an immediate return to the earlier status quo. Unlike his predecessors Le Duff was not named a vicar-general. Instead, in 1727 and 1728 a friar of the Récollets of Paris, Joseph Denys, was given ecclesiastical authority over both the Paris and Brittany friars.[55] However much it might have irritated Le Duff to have a Paris Récollet overseeing him and the other Brittany Récollets,[56] he did nothing to jeopardize his province's stay in Louisbourg. Careful to avoid the errors of Le Dorz, Le Duff always made sure that he obtained the vicar-general's approval before proceeding with any marriages requiring dispensations of banns.[57]

Michael-Ange Le Duff did not remain long as Louisbourg's curé. He found himself, after having been in the colony for a little over three years, completely worn down by the harsh climate, poor diet, and hard work. Extracts from a plaintive letter to his superior in France, written in November 1727, present an excellent picture of the conditions under which the Ile Royale Récollets exercised their ministry:

> In the first letters which I had the honor of writing to Your Reverence, ... I took the liberty of explaining to Your Reverence the infirmity with which God has been afflicting me since I have been in the colony, and which I can only ascribe to the fatigues I have endured in the ice and snow and to the wretched food we have here, since throughout the year we are obliged to eat no flesh, and fresh meat is rare and very expensive. All these fatigues have so altered my health and exhausted my strength that I now find myself suffering from a very considerable hernia. Concerning it, I have consulted the Reverend Fathers of Charity and the surgeon major of the city, who have told me that this infirmity proceeded from the fatigues and the travels we are obliged to undertake in a country where the winters are very long and very hard, all the more as I am not of a strong constitution or robust temperament. I earnestly entreat Your Reverence to have some regard for the infirmities with which the Lord is afflicting me.[58]

Le Duff received his wish shortly thereafter, returning to France in 1728.

The friar first suggested to replace Le Duff was Gratien Raoul, who had been in the colony during the first few years of the settlement. As the only Récollet of Brittany whom Bishop Saint-Vallier held in high regard, Raoul's name was apparently put forward by the minister of marine as a means of winning the confidence of the bishop.[59] The idea seems to have been dropped after news of Saint-Vallier's death reached France in 1728. Instead of Raoul the Récollet selected by the provincial to become his commissaire in the colony was Zacharie Caradec.[60]

Caradec was a small, vigorous man full of integrity and zeal,[61] though in the eyes of some people his zealousness was undoubtedly perceived as the meddling of an intolerant cleric. To illustrate, following a 1725 voyage to Louisbourg aboard La Victoire, a king's ship upon which he was serving as chaplain, Caradec voiced strong criticism of the conduct of the ship's officers. His complaints brought his name to the attention of the minister of marine and led to an investigation of the *La Victoire*'s officers.[62] Three years later, when he came to Louisbourg as its curé, Caradec had not changed. He was still willing and perhaps even eager, to confront temporal authorities in the name of religion and morality.

Unlike his predecessors, who tended to share parish duties with the other friars (that is, the chaplains) in the town, Zacharie Caradec personally officiated at nearly every marriage, baptism, and burial during his years as curé. It was probably as a result of his obvious dedication and earnestness that he was named a vicar-general of the bishop of Québec in the fall of 1728.[63]

Caradec seems to have taken his responsibilities as the bishop's representative very seriously. In accordance with diocesan policy he carried out a thorough inspection of the Louisbourg parish in February 1730, the only such inspection recorded in the town's history. He questioned schoolmasters and midwives to determine their suitability for the positions they held; he inspected the sacristy and parish records to make sure they were in order; and he spoke to the assembled parishioners on how parish business should be conducted.

Until Caradec arrived in Louisbourg there had never been a vestry (*fabrique*) established in the parish to take care of church revenue and maintenance. Indeed, before 1721 there do not appear to have been any churchwardens (*marguilliers*) in the town. Commissaire-ordonnateur Mézy, in December 1720, seems to have been the first person to propose that churchwardens be selected, and his suggestion came seven years after the founding of the town. Mézy believed that two would be sufficient, each of whom was to serve a two-year term. The positions were nonpaying but the commissaire-ordonnateur expected that the two men would be suitably compensated in terms of honour and status. He envisioned them being accorded a prominent pew in the parish church, as was customary in France, and being given seats on the Conseil Supérieur. The first churchwardens were probably chosen by parishioners in March 1721, acting upon Mézy's suggestion.[64] How long *marguilliers* continued to be selected in the parish is unknown; there seem to have been none in the town by 1742.[65]

The fact that it had apparently taken action by the financial administrator of the colony to bring about the selection of Louisbourg's first churchwardens suggests a certain lack of interest in parish affairs on the part of the residents of the town. The situation obviously improved little in the decade that followed, as demonstrated by the lack of a formal vestry in the community at the time of Zacharie Caradec's inspection of the parish in 1730. The inhabitants explained their attitude to Caradec by pointing out that the town did not have its own parish church, but used the Récollet chapel on Block 3 as a substitute. Without their own parish church, they saw no need for a vestry. They simply left the collection of revenue and upkeep entirely to the friars. Caradec disapproved of the irregular situation and set out to rectify it on his terms. He called for the election of three additional churchwardens, there being only one at the time, to look after the business of the parish. To reward the church-wardens for their service to the community, Caradec decided that each one would hold a pole supporting the dais carried in religious processions.[66] That decision, combined with a related effort to increase church revenue, soon gave birth to a hotly debated controversy with Zacharie Caradec right at the centre.

The dispute began when visiting ship captains learned that in Louis-bourg's religious processions the churchwardens were henceforth to carry all four poles of the dais. Up until that time it had been the practice, first at Plaisance and then at Louisbourg, that two of the poles were held by ship captains. Since this was an age and a society in which customs and privileges were guarded extremely carefully, the break with tradition deeply upset the captains. Their irritation grew when Caradec proposed that all visiting fishing crews be taxed at the rate of 40 sols per man. They protested in the most effective way they could, by ceasing to pay the traditional tithe (dîme) of a quintal (48.95 kilograms) of cod per shallop.

By 1730 payment of the tithe on Ile Royale was customary yet nonethe-less voluntary. In 1715 and 1722 attempts had been made to collect the tax on a compulsory basis, but each time the measure had been greeted with protest and then lifted.[67] The residents had not objected to the uses to which the money would be put (initially it was to help offset hospital and health care and later it was to pay for the construction of a parish church and presbytery). Rather, they complained that the colony was still in its infancy and they were not yet able to pay a compulsory tithe. A similar argument had been used in seventeenth-century Canada to have the tithe there, which was compulsory, lowered from one-thirteenth, the common rate in France, to one-twenty-sixth of one's income.[68]

During precisely the same period that Zacharie Caradec was attempting to reorganize the Louisbourg parish and to generate additional revenue for the church on Ile Royale, Pierre-Hermann Dosquet, first as coadjutor and then as bishop of Québec, was seeking to convince the minister of marine to restore the tithe in Canada to the rate of one-thirteenth.[69] Conceivably, the actions of the two men may have been related. Caradec was Dosquet's vicar-general and some of the Récollet's innovations at Louisbourg may well have been suggested, or at least supported, by his ecclesiastical supe-rior. Dosquet's efforts, like those of Caradec, were ultimately doomed to failure, and for basically the same reason: neither Canada nor Ile Royale was judged by the minister to be sufficiently developed to justify increasing the financial burden on their colonists.

When the ship captains and fishermen who visited Louisbourg seasonally arrived in port, they refused to pay the customary tithe, both because of the change in the town's religious processions and the proposal to tax each crew at 40 *sols* per man. Their refusal infuriated Zacharie Caradec. He responded by insisting that a few individuals be imprisoned. The situation was exacerbated and the governor and commissaire-ordonnateur found themselves unable to handle the growing strife. Consequently, they sought the intervention of the minister of marine.[70]

The minister ruled that the payment of the tithe was simply a traditional donation, not a tax that could be enforced. Therefore the clergy could use only "the voice of exhortation" to encourage contributions to the parish,[71] a highly unlikely prospect given the animosity which existed between the two sides. He further directed the colonial officials to find some way to conciliate the factions and bring the conflict to an end. Interestingly enough, the initial reports of the dispute did not affect the comte de Maurepas' confidence in Caradec. Indeed, in 1731 he interceded with the provincial of the Récollets of Brittany so that Caradec would not be replaced on Ile Royale as planned. In the minister's opinion, Zacharie Caradec "has reestablished order and discipline among the Religious."[72]

Caradec attempted to deflect criticism over the tithe question from himself by denying that he had ever suggested that visiting ship captains should be forced to pay it. He explained that it was the permanent residents of Louisbourg who rented beach properties, flakes, and fishing boats to visiting crews whom he wanted to see contribute to their parish.[73] Unfortunately for Caradec, here again such compulsion had no legal justification.[74]

It is worth noting that Governor Saint-Ovide sympathized with Caradec in his struggle to increase church revenue. In 1731 the governor observed that Ile Royale was perhaps the only place in the world where parishioners did not pay a tithe to their parish priests.[75] Two years later he stated that the problem at Louisbourg was not in convincing visiting mariners to make donations to the church, it was in overcoming the parsimony of the residents of the town. Saint-Ovide explained to the minister that the inhabitants gave nothing "for all the trouble the curés take to administer the sacraments, perform their curial functions and instruct their children in their faith."[76]

Saint-Ovide was exaggerating when he wrote that none of the residents paid the voluntary tithe; some of them did.[77] Yet he was obviously irritated at the many who did not pay, or else who paid only in part or in a grudging manner. The attitude which he decried seems to have been basically the same one Commissaire-ordonnateur Mézy had noted a decade earlier; that is, the inclination of the colonists to put their own interests ahead of those of the community at large. Needless to say the people of Ile Royale were not the only ones guilty of such self-interest and lack of charity when it came to giving to the church. During the same era, royal officials and bishops in Canada were repeatedly complaining about the reluctance or failure of the parishioners there to pay the tithe.[78]

The controversy over the payment of the tithe began in 1730 and lasted until 1733, when it was decided to give back to the visiting ship captains their positions of prominence in Louisbourg's religious processions. That suggestion, the obvious solution, was first put forward by the commissaire-ordonnateur.[79] By October 1733 an acceptable compromise had been reached, whereby "the most senior Captains" were given the right to carry two flambeaux (torches or candlesticks) in the processions.[80] As for Zacharie Caradec and his plans for the parish, the damage had been done. Caradec had alienated so many people in Louisbourg that it became essential that his provincial recall him to France.[81] In mid-1733 a friar named Hippolyte Herp was sent to the colony to assume the duties as curé of Louisbourg and superior of the Récollet mission there. Caradec retained his titles as commissaire and vicar-general until 1734, when he returned to one of the Récollet convents in Brittany.[82]

When Caradec left the colony, Hippolyte Herp took over the responsibilities as commissaire. During Caradec's years at Louisbourg those responsibilities had increased significantly. In 1730 the Récollets of Paris had indicated their desire to withdraw from Port Dauphin, Port Toulouse, and other settlements on the island. Initiated by the Paris Récollets, the withdrawal was approved by the minister of marine and new lettres patentes were issued in July 1731, giving the Récollets of Brittany the right to serve every parish in the colony.[83] All but one parish appears to have been handed over to the Brittany friars by 1732. The exception was at Niganiche where Jean Capistran stayed on after reaching an agreement with the Récollets of Brittany.[84]

The spread of the Brittany Récollets into new areas was not welcomed by the coadjutor of the diocese, Pierre-Hermann Dosquet. A Belgian, Dosquet had supported a proposal that Récollets from the province of St André in Flanders be asked to take over the missions vacated by the Paris Récollets.[85] When that idea was rejected, Dosquet countered with the suggestion that a secular vicar-general be established at Louisbourg, who would hold authority over all the missions and parishes of Ile Royale, Ile Saint-Jean, and Nova Scotia.[86] The merit of the proposal, from the coadjutor's point of view, was that it would centralize and strengthen the bishop of Québec's control over the more remote areas of his diocese. The governor-general and intendant of New France lent their support to the scheme because they believed that a secular vicar-general might have a closer attachment to and greater appreciation of the interests of the state than a Récollet.[87] The difficulty with the idea was in funding it. The minister of marine would consider neither taking the income from the parish of Louisbourg away from the Récollet nor providing additional funding out of the king's treasury.[88] Already committed to heavy state expenditures on Ile Royale, the minister felt obliged to be parsimonious when it came to additional expenses in the religious sphere.

Hippolyte Herp's two years in Louisbourg appear to have been relatively tranquil. His hours were probably taken up for the most part with routine parish business and with his supervisory and administrative responsibilities over all the other Récollets. The most unusual episode during Herp's stay in Louisbourg was a case of alleged incest. The birth of an illegitimate child to Pierre Santier and Servanne Bonnier in September 1734 scandalized the town, and probably Herp in particular, until it was discovered that the young couple involved were not first cousins but more distant relatives.[89]

Another issue which surfaced during Herp's stay in Louisbourg was the request of Basque fishermen for a priest who could speak their language. It was an old issue on Ile Royale, and like the similar question of providing German-speaking priests for the Catholic soldiers of the Karrer Regiment, it was never satisfactorily resolved. At the time of the founding of the colony the comte de Pontchartrain had identified the need for a Basque-speaking Récollet so that the hundreds of Basque fishermen who made the transatlantic voyage each year would have their spiritual needs met. Pontchartrain hoped that a Basque-speaking friar from the Récollet convent in St Jean de Luz, a town close to the Basque region of France, might be found and persuaded to go to the new colony. Not only was none found but in 1715 the bishop's vicar general on Ile Royale expelled a Basque priest, Sr Dordos, who had previously served the fishermen at Plaisance for years. The specific reasons for the expulsion were not given but the suggestion was that Dordos had been guilty of "conduct that was too licentious and inappropriate." The Basque ship captains and their crews naturally protested the absence of any priest who could provide spiritual advice and comfort while they were in the colony. By May 1718 a priest from Bayonne, Dirigouyen d'hauteville, was found who was willing to sail to Ile Royale "to administer the Sacraments to Basque sailors who stay there to fish."[90]

How long the priest sent out in 1718 remained in the colony is not known. By 1733, and probably earlier, the Basque fishermen were again without anyone who could give them "Spiritual Succour." On their behalf the merchants of St Jean de Luz submitted a petition to the king asking for a Basque priest to be dispatched to the colony as a salaried king's chaplain, with the freedom to minister to fishermen all over the island. The idea was rejected both on account of the expense involved and because the preferred solution was to find a Récollet from St Jean de Luz who spoke Basque.

The Récollet commissaire Hippolyte Herp appears to have been less than enthusiastic about the idea of sending a Récollet from a province other than Brittany to the colony. The governor and commissaire-ordonnateur reported to the minister in October 1733 that it would cause discord on Ile Royale if that were to happen. Besides, in their opinion and probably also in Herp's, there was no need to send anyone special to the island. There were Récollet missionaries at Niganiche and St Esprit who had already learned enough Basque "to give confessions and fulfil the other functions of their Ministry."[91] That answer seemed to satisfy the minister of marine and the subject was dropped. Whether or not the Basque fishermen were contented with the situation, in particular the absence of a priest in Louisbourg who spoke their language, is of course another question. Perhaps eventually they took matters into their own hands and arranged to have priests accompany their spring voyages to Ile Royale. A reference in a 1737 Louisbourg court case to a "Basque priest" in the town suggests that may have been the case.[92]

The similar issue of providing priests for the Catholics in the Karrer Regiment was first identified by the minister of marine in 1738, though the need had perhaps existed since the Swiss and German troops had come to Louisbourg in 1722. In 1738 the minister wrote to the provincial of the Récollets of Brittany, explaining that there were several Karrer soldiers at Louisbourg of the Catholic faith who did not understand French, and therefore were without spiritual comfort. Informed that there was a Récollet in Normandy who spoke German, the minister asked the Brittany provincial to inquire if the friar in question could come to Ile Royale. The provincial was apparently reluctant to pursue the matter for the comte de Maurepas had to write again, pointing out that the German-speaking Récollet was to be on the same footing as the other friars; he was not to be the chaplain of the Karrer Regiment. The provincial seems to have agreed to this arrangement, though he may not have been committed to the idea for in the end no German-speaking Récollet was ever sent to Louisbourg.[93]

Hippolyte Herp sailed from Ile Royale in 1735 and his responsibilities were taken over by Etienne Le Goff. Le Goff had been in the colony since 1729, serving at Louisbourg, La Baleine, St Esprit, and Niganiche. On the basis of his years in the disparate settlements in the colony, Le Goff would have been thoroughly familiar with the difficulties experienced by inhabitants and curés alike. That experience, combined with his apparent administrative ability (he would be named provincial of the Brittany Récollets in 1742), made him an excellent choice as the commissaire of the Ile Royale and Ile Saint-Jean Récollets. The bishop of Québec obviously held Le Goff in high regard for the friar was named vicar-general, a title which had not been bestowed on Hippolyte Herp.[94] According to the commissaire-ordonnateur of Ile Royale, Le Normant, Etienne Le Goff was a remarkable man whom the colony was fortunate to have. Le Normant described the friar as mild yet firm, with all the virtues one could ask for in a person responsible for the spiritual affairs of the colony.[95]

Considering his high opinion of Le Goff, Le Normant became understandably dismayed when he discovered during a trip to France that Zacharie Caradec was soon to go back to Ile Royale in his former capacities. Describing Caradec as headstrong and unpopular, the commissaire-ordonnateur used his influence with the minister of marine to prevent Caradec's departure in 1735.[96] But Caradec was not without influential friends of his own, in particular the bishop of Québec and Governor Saint-Ovide. Finally, in 1737, the provincial of the Récollets of Brittany received the minister's permission to send the friar back to the colony. In giving his approval the comte de Maurepas noted that Caradec's zeal was never in doubt, only his ability to conduct himself so as to please everyone in the colony.[97]

In spite of assurances to the contrary, Caradec quickly stirred up opposition in the colony. He began by sending Etienne Le Goff to Niganiche to become the curé there. Unpopular though that action may have been, at least Caradec, as the new superior and commissaire of the Récollets, had the authority to relocate other friars. However, he erred technically, claimed Le Normant, when he adopted the title of vicar-general without having the appropriate papers. Moreover, again in Le Normant's opinion, Caradec irritated parishioners by alternating different friars as Louisbourg's curé, before at last settling on Athanase Guégot as the new parish priest. In general, asserted the commissaire-ordonnateur, Zacharie Caradec alienated people by his haughty and malevolent ways.[98]

Although Le Normant made it sound as if most inhabitants were annoyed by Caradec's return, it is impossible to know how widespread popular resentment really was. To be sure, not everyone would have been disenchanted with the Récollet commissaire. Pierre Maillard, the missionary to the Micmacs of Ile Royale, claimed in the fall of 1738 that the Récollets were showing improvement in many areas.[99] Caradec was not mentioned by name, but it stands to reason that as commissaire at the time he would have been largely responsible for the improvement mentioned by Maillard.

One person who definitely was annoyed with Caradec was Jean-Pierre Roma, the director of a fishing venture on Ile Saint-Jean. Roma and Caradec had clashed during the Récollet's previous stay in the colony over the suitability of a particular priest at Roma's settlement[100] and each one appears to have retained a grudge against the other. According to Roma, Caradec was instrumental in 1737 in deterring two girls from France from proceeding to Ile Saint-Jean, as had been arranged by Roma. The girls in turn persuaded three of Roma's men and a cooper to stay in Louisbourg. Roma requested the commissaire-ordonnateur to take action against Caradec and to return his people to him.[101]

By relaying such complaints to the minister of marine, Le Normant did the best he could to assist Roma and generally to undermine Caradec. The comte de Maurepas' initial reaction was, as usual, to act as a conciliator. On the one hand, he notified the provincial of the Récollets of Brittany that Zacharie Caradec would be withdrawn from the colony unless he showed "more moderation and prudence in the exercise of his ministry." On the other hand, the minister directed Le Normant to cooperate with the friar and not to seek disputes.[102] Whatever attempts were made to effect a rapprochement, they failed. In November 1738 Maurepas informed the provincial that Caradec absolutely had to be recalled from Ile Royale to preserve "the tranquillity in that Colony, where he wants to meddle in everything."[103] The following spring the minister relented to the extent of offering the provincial the possibility of Caradec staying at Louisbourg if he moderated his approach.[104] The possibility was not explored. During the summer of 1739 Zacharie Caradec left Ile Royale for the final time.

For the third time in a little more than a decade, first with Bénin Le Dorz and then twice with Zacharie Caradec, a Récollet of Brittany had been recalled to France in the midst of a controversy. Although there are similarities in the handling of the disputes, most noticeably the conciliating role played by the minister of marine, the contrasts are even more striking. With Le Dorz the criticism had come principally from the bishop of Québec concerning moral laxity and the dereliction of clerical duties. The inhabitants of Louisbourg and adjacent settlements appear to have been generally satisfied with Le Dorz. In contrast, with Caradec the complaints were of overzealousness and vindictiveness and came not from the bishop but from some of the inhabitants. It was said that Caradec did not possess "a flexible enough spirit,"[105] an ironic complaint considering the protests about Le Dorz's laxness. As for the bishop of Québec, he was apparently among Zacharie Caradec's supporters. Involved in his own attempt to generate additional church revenue, the bishop was probably more than sympathetic to Caradec's stand on the tithe and on related issues.[106]

On the evidence of the Le Dorz and Caradec controversies it seems that the bishops of Québec and the inhabitants of Ile Royale had quite dissimilar perspectives on what constituted a good curé or a well-run parish. To the minister of marine, who was charged with keeping the tranquillity of the colony, those conflicting perspectives must have made him despair of there ever being religious peace on Ile Royale.

It was not long before there was more discord. Zacharie Caradec's successor as commissaire and as vicar-general was the Louisbourg curé Athanase Guégot. A missionary and parish priest on Ile Royale and Ile Saint-Jean since 1731,[107] Guégot had the experience to oversee the spiritual affairs of the colonists. But apparently he did not have the ability, at least in the opinion of the sixth bishop of Québec, Henri-Marie Dubreil de Pontbriand. Bishop Pontbriand named Pierre Maillard, the missionary to the Micmacs of Ile Royale, his principal vicar-general on the island.[108] Guégot was also named a vicar-general, yet he was subordinate to Maillard.[109]

By 1742 the Récollets had come to resent being under Maillard's ecclesiastical jurisdiction, although there is no indication of any particularly contentious issues. Perhaps the general criticism expressed a few years earlier by Maillard, that the friars were complacent towards "the disorders and irregularities of the colony,"[110] was voiced more openly. In any case, the Récollets complained of Maillard's interference to the local officials and to their provincial, the former Louisbourg curé Etienne Le Goff. Having served in the colony for eleven years, Le Goff undoubtedly listened to the complaints of his friars with great sympathy. He relayed their concerns to the only person who could change the situation, the minister of marine.

In similar fashion Ile Royale's commandant, Jean-Baptiste Le Prévost Duquesnel, and commissaire-ordonnateur, François Bigot, passed on to the minister the Récollet view of Abbé Maillard. In general, that view was that the abbé was unjustifiably meddling in Récollet affairs and thereby causing the friars to lose face in front of their parishioners. For the sake of peace in the colony the Récollets asked for Maillard's recall. Duquesnel and Bigot agreed, adding that since Maillard had taken up his responsibilities as the bishop's vicar-general he had lost sight of some of the duties the king expected of him as a missionary to the Micmacs.[111]

The different complaints about Pierre Maillard, in particular the allegation that he was neglecting the Micmacs, led the comte de Maurepas to issue stern warnings that the situation must improve or Maillard would be replaced. Bishop Pontbriand and his vicar-general in France, Abbé de l'Isle-Dieu, disagreed forcefully with the minister's interpretation of the situation. The bishop asserted that Maillard had done nothing wrong; the Récollets simply wanted to be "independent." As a compromise Pontbriand proposed in 1743 that there would be two vicars-general: Maillard and the Récollet commissaire Athanase Guégot. In the event of a disagreement they were to write the bishop for a decision. In effect, it was a return to the policy of dual ecclesiastical representation that had existed when the Récollets of Paris had been in the colony. The minister of marine hoped the arrangement would end the religious strife on Ile Royale, but he made it clear that if it did not, Abbé Pierre Maillard would definitely be withdrawn.[112]

The division of responsibilities appears to have pacified both sides. In early 1745 the minister expressed his contentment that the controversy had ended.[113] Maurepas' remarks on the matter probably never reached the colony. In May and June 1745 a military expedition of 4,000 provincials from New England supported by a British and colonial fleet of over 100 vessels besieged and blockaded Louisbourg. The siege would last approximately six weeks and throughout it the Récollets ministered to the spiritual needs of the inhabitants. At times the friars were close to the action. On 13 May, during the preparations to withdraw from the Royal Battery, the chaplain there, Felix Nizan, suffered burns to his face when his habit caught on fire.[114] Near the end of the month the Chapelle de Saint-Louis, which served as the Louisbourg parish church, was badly damaged in the bombardment of the town. Thereafter the Récollets held daily services in the chapel of the Hôpital du Roi. On 3 June a shot fired from the English-held Royal Battery smashed through the wall of that chapel.[115]

The New Englanders took possession of the town on 28 June, entering through the Queen's Gate with "Colours ... flying the Drums Beating Trumpets Sounding Flutes & Viols Playing." Though the town was now occupied by a Protestant army, the articles of capitulation stipulated that until deportation the Louisbourgeois were to "enjoy the free exercise of their religion." Parish life resumed with the first baptism since the beginning of the siege taking place in the hospital chapel. In all, nineteen baptisms occurred before the final departure of the French from Louisbourg, nearly all of which were officiated at by Récollet Calixte Kerriou. Similarly, each of the five marriages held before the evacuation in late July 1745 was probably sanctified in the hospital chapel. Members of the occupying army occasionally went to the hospital to observe the French inhabitants at worship. One curious but unsympathetic onlooker recorded his thoughts on 22 July: "This Day I went into the Hospital to See the French People Say Mass. I Could'ent help wondring to See Gentlemen who were men of Learning ... So Led Aside as to worship Images, to Bow Down to A Cross of wood, and to See So many of all Ranks Seemingly Devout. when we've Reason to think They never had any Communion with God Through the Course of their Lives. Being Ever So Strict in the Practice of their Religion." The observer took pleasure in noting, ten days later, that "the Friers and Priests being gone the french Left of Worshiping in the Hospital." The New Englanders immediately took over the chapel for their own use.[116]

The evacuation of the French colonists from Ile Royale stretched over a couple of weeks, so it was not possible for all the Récollets to sail together. Indeed, there was one Récollet friar who did not return to France at all. Juvénal Adam, who was perhaps on Ile Saint-Jean in 1745, made it safely to Québec that summer, where he remained until his death in 1748.[117] The last two to leave Louisbourg were Angélique Collin and Alexis Guillou. Until their departure they said mass every day, with Guillou acting as the interim curé.[118] Remaining in or near Louisbourg after most of the inhabitants left was a group of over forty French men, women, and children. Whether they chose to stay, or were asked to by the English is unknown. At least one of them, Jean-Baptiste Guion, worked for the English as a pilot during the period of occupation. Besides this group, it was estimated that there were another 250 French "still out in the country concealing themselves to prevent their being sent to France, to wch they are very averse."[119]

Legend has it that the capitulation of Louisbourg led to a notorious act of vandalism on French church property by Parson Samuel Moody, General Pepperrell's chaplain. Moody is said to have taken his axe to the altar and statues of the barracks chapel, in fulfilment of a vow he had made before he left New England. Sometime later, Moody, who was over seventy at the time, gave the first Protestant sermon to be heard in the town. There would be many more sermons offered in the weeks and months ahead, twice daily on Sundays, as the New Englanders undertook what was to be a lengthy and devastating occupation. In the beginning the sermons were exultant, celebrating a victory not just of English over French, but also of righteous Protestants over ungodly "Papists." Typically, in a morning prayer meeting at the Citadel (the King's Bastion barracks) on 18 July, Parson Moody spoke on the theme "Sit on my Right Hand, Untill I make thine enemies thy footstool." That afternoon Rector Elisha Williams sounded a similar note, elaborating on: "Remember His Marvellous works which He hath done His wonders." An anonymous diarist recorded what was likely a common feeling among those in attendance. "Hardly any Can tell what Joy it was – to See God worshiped ... where Anti Christ had [been worshipped] ... I must Confess it Seem'd to me Like what wee read in the 126 Psalm 1 verse" ("When the Lord restored the fortunes of Zion, we were like those who dream").[120]

The initial thrill of victory soon waned for the New Englanders. Denied what they considered to be their rightful share of booty and forced to garrison a town they had wished only to conquer, the mood of the troops altered drastically. Expressions of self-congratulation gave way to fits of depression and bouts of heavy drinking. These factors, combined with inadequate rations and housing, gave birth to talk of mutiny and brought an unprecedented wave of disease and death to the town. An epidemic of dysentery ("bloody fluxes") and other diseases swept through the troops. One soldier lamented in late September that "it's an Awful and Disstressing time with Us in this Citty ... [especially] when I Call to Mind what God has Done for Us Heretofore." It would get much worse. Whereas only about 100 provincials had died during the siege (and only slightly more than 50 French), approximately 1,200 would pass away before the winter of 1745–6 was over.[121]

The subsequent years of the English occupation of Louisbourg were much less tragic. The problems of the first year were solved, or at least minimized, by improved provisioning, the replacement of New England troops by British ones, and the repair and new construction of various buildings. One of the structures given attention during this period was the barracks chapel, which had served as the French community's parish church. The inside roof of the chapel, damaged during the siege, was repaired and two galleries were installed, probably on either side of the altar. In addition, "proper Seats and Pews" were placed in the nave. What was there before this renovation is not known, but there were probably simple benches as seen in Richard Short's well-known drawing of the Récollet church in Québec in 1759. The "Seats and Pews" introduced by the English would later be dismantled by the French when they returned to Louisbourg in 1749, with the wood being used for floor repairs and a temporary altar.[122]

To return to the story of the Louisbourg Récollets, they had no sooner reached Rochefort in 1745 when talk began of replacing them on Ile Royale, should the colony be returned to France. Like his predecessors Pontbriand wanted to substitute secular priests for the friars. He argued that it was only a matter of time before seculars would be sent to Louisbourg so the switch might as well be made right away, before the town was reoccupied. The bishop was opposed on that view by commissaire-ordonnateur François Bigot, who argued that the Récollets should be returned to Ile Royale with Athanase Guégot once again as the superior. The minister of marine chose to follow Bigot's advice rather than that of the bishop.[123] When the Treaty of Aix-la-Chapelle (1748) handed Cape Breton back to France, it was decided that the Récollets would once again provide the curés and chaplains for the island. But the proposal to replace the friars with seculars did not die with that decision. Throughout the entire second French occupation (1749–58) the bishop and his vicar-general in France persisted in trying to persuade the minister to have seculars serve the colonial parishes, particularly Louisbourg. Those attempts and the rationale behind them form the dominant theme in the story of the Récollets of Brittany's final decade on Ile Royale.

The French settlements on Ile Royale were reestablished during the summer of 1749. Among the approximately 3,200 colonists and soldiers who sailed to the island that year were six Récollets of Brittany, four of whom had previously served in the colony. Returning as curé of Louisbourg and as superior and commissaire of all the other friars was Athanase Guégot. He was accompanied by the chaplains for the barracks, hospital, and Royal Battery, as well as two other friars destined to serve in outport communities and three servants.[124] Their voyage to Louisbourg was apparently not an easy one. Upon arrival in late August, Guégot wrote to his superior at Morlaix, in Brittany: "We were on the water for two months, where I was so ill that I made a kind of vow to never again cross the sea." Not all voyages to Isle Royale were as vexing or as long, as for instance Récollet Chérubin Ropert's 32-day crossing in the spring of 1752. Yet they could also be much longer. Another friar, Julian Moisson, reported in July 1752 that he had been at sea for 91 days, and that it had been 127 days since he had left Brittany.[125]

At the time of the reoccupation of Louisbourg in 1749, the Récollets' ministry to the settlers began even as they lay anchored in the harbour awaiting the English evacuation. Between the arrival of the French ships in late June and the taking possession of the town on 23 July, there were at least five deaths among the French. In each case the corpse was taken ashore and buried in consecrated ground by Récollet chaplain Isidore Caulet.

Within a few days of the English withdrawal normal parish activities began anew. The Chapelle de Saint-Louis, with its English additions of galleries and "Seats and Pews," although the latter were soon removed, again became a centre of community life. Among the first religious acts was the baptism of a three-month-old girl left behind by the English. In the weeks that followed the Récollets found themselves busier than they had ever been in the colony's history. During their first four months back at Louisbourg there were more marriages (twenty-seven) in the town than in any previous entire year. Likewise, the fifty baptisms they officiated at before the end of the year far surpassed the number recorded in any comparable period earlier in the colony's history. Burials too were at a record high, excepting the period of the 1732–3 smallpox epidemic.[126]

Hectic as the first few months of resettlement were, the parish workload was not shared equally among the Récollets. Almost every marriage, baptism, and burial was performed by the same man, military chaplain Isidore Caulet.[127] An aged, slightly deaf friar, with two decades of service at Louisbourg, Caulet was by 1749 a beloved institution in the town.[128] Popular and capable, he was usually excluded from the denunciations of the Récollets which were to be renewed in the 1750s.

The conditions in which the Récollets lived and worked during the 1750s were far from ideal. Chérubin Ropert, who arrived in the colony in June 1752, described Louisbourg as a "place of exile." That assessment was undoubtedly coloured by the unsatisfactory state of his accommodation. The Récollet residence was "completely dilapidated, without provisions"; the order had to rent another house in town (for 400 livres), in which Ropert had a room in the attic that was "exposed to the four winds." Moreover, there was not even a bed for him on his arrival; "luckily for me I had bought one in France" before departing. Other essential purchases made before the voyage included a mattress and cover, three pairs of stockings, two pairs of shoes, two pairs of breeches, six pairs of undershorts, twelve handkerchiefs, a coat, a cap, and three tunicles.[129]

The poor housing conditions in which the Louisbourg Récollets seem to have lived, combined with the by then customary personnel shortages, must be taken into account when one reads the criticism of the Ile Royale friars during the 1750s. The loudest complaints were made by Abbé de l'Isle-Dieu, the bishop of Québec's vicar-general for New France. Reflecting the pessimism he felt about the situation of the church generally in New France, Isle-Dieu almost never found anything praiseworthy about the Récollets. Indeed, after they returned to the island in 1749 the vicar-general wrote to his bishop that it was probably unreasonable to expect improved behaviour from the friars.[130] Shortly thereafter, he claimed that the Récollets had met his worst expectations.

Typical of Isle-Dieu's view of the friars was his description of the Louisbourg curé and Récollet commissaire, Athanase Guégot, as a man with "no talent, no speaking ability and perhaps also little goodwill."[131] To further his goal of having the Récollets replaced by secular priests, the abbé forwarded in May 1751 a memoir on behalf of Bishop Pontbriand to the new minister of marine, Antoine-Louis Rouillé. In that document Isle-Dieu presented the many reasons why the Récollets of Brittany deserved to be recalled.

To begin with, there were not enough friars in the colony. There were only six, whereas, the abbé estimated, twelve would be needed if all sizeable settlements were to be served properly. Second, the ones already on the island were generally of extremely poor quality. They neglected or performed badly virtually every parish duty. Third, there were reports that the superior was lax in allowing friars in the smaller settlements to give dispensations to their parishioners in return for money payments. Fourth, the Récollets resisted taking directions from the bishop's vicar-general, Abbé Maillard, and followed instructions only from their own commissaire and provincial. Finally, they had ignored Bishop Pontbriand's explicit request that they forward to Isle-Dieu annual reports on the state of their parishes and missions. In the light of these numerous failings Abbé de l'Isle-Dieu argued that all of the friars, except those in the traditional Récollet role of military chaplain, be withdrawn and replaced by secular priests. In the vicar-general's opinion, seculars would not only be far superior but also less of a burden on the royal treasury. As Isle-Dieu put it, "six secular priests would do more work than nine Récollets."[132]

Abbé de l'Isle-Dieu's assessment of the Récollets of Brittany was echoed in January 1752 by that of the commandant of Ile Royale, the comte de Raymond. Like the vicar-general, Raymond complained that there were too few friars and that those who were in the colony were largely unsatisfactory. Those Récollets "who led irregular lives and whose ignorance was too pronounced" needed to be recalled and at least ten new friars sent out. Better still, in the commandant's opinion, would be to have all the parishes served by secular priests. Of the Récollets, Raymond could imagine retaining only Isidore Caulet. He described the aging military chaplain as a "good priest, very charitable and with good morals, a man to keep."[133]

Unwilling to explore the possibility of introducing secular priests in the parishes of Ile Royale, the minister of marine did the next best thing. He relayed the concerns of Raymond and Isle-Dieu to the provincial of the Récollets of Brittany, together with his own admonition to increase the quantity and quality of friars serving the colony. The best the provincial could do in 1752 appears to have been to send out two or three new friars, with Candide Fournier to replace Athanase Guégot as superior and commissaire. In a move to allay some of Bishop Pontbriand's fears about the Brittany Récollets, Guégot's successor, Fournier, was instructed to sail directly to Québec to meet the bishop and be accorded proper authorization as a vicar-general.[134] Fournier was a new face to the bishop but not to the inhabitants of Ile Royale. From 1734 to 1739 he had served in the colony at Louisbourg, La Baleine, and Laurembec.[135] As the preparations to send Candide Fournier to the colony were being made, Athanase Guégot died at Louisbourg, in February 1752.[136] Abbé Maillard, in his capacity as vicar-general, named Isidore Caulet as the interim parish priest.[137]

As a result of Fournier's voyage to Québec he did not reach Louisbourg until late summer.[138] Delayed though he was, at least when he arrived it was as a full vicar-general of Bishop Pontbriand. Not long after his arrival he was called upon to exercise his ecclesiastical powers. On a single day in early October 1752 there were fifteen marriages held in the Chapelle de Saint-Louis. At the request of the comte de Raymond, for each couple Fournier and Maillard jointly dispensed with two of the three wedding banns normally required.[139]

As curé of Louisbourg, Fournier seems to have made a good impression. The comte de Raymond praised him as an excellent speaker whose sermons were always well attended.[140] The parishioners probably hoped that Fournier, aged forty-five, would remain in the community for years to come. But it was not to be. On 8 November, about two months after his arrival, Candide Fournier passed away, "with edification and resignation to the will of God." The following day he was buried beneath the floor of the hospital chapel.[141] For the second time in ten months the people of Louisbourg had lost a parish priest through death. Given that there were already too few friars in the colony, Fournier's passing was undoubtedly keenly felt. To the Récollets, the loss of their superior and commissaire rendered them "like bodies without souls," there being no one very suitable to direct them. Isidore Caulet filled in again as curé and superior but without the required abilities for either position.[142] Thus, nearly two years after Abbé de l'Isle-Dieu had articulated the need for more and better friars on Ile Royale, the situation had not only not improved, but it had probably worsened.

Woeful though the state of religious affairs was in the colony in mid-January 1753, the inhabitants of Louisbourg had their attention shifted from that concern to a much more controversial matter when a case of alleged profanation occurred in the Chapelle de Saint-Louis. Profanation was regarded by both church and state as an extremely serious crime in the eighteenth century. According to the king's ordinance of 1728 on military crimes, soldiers who swore or blasphemed were to have their tongues pierced by a hot iron; those who stole from a church were to be hanged and strangled; those who profaned holy objects while stealing were to be burnt at the stake.[143] The punishments for civilians guilty of such crimes were not as cut and dried, but they could be equally harsh.

The alleged profanation case at Louisbourg involved a civilian drifter named Yacinthe Gabriel Le Bon.[144] Aged thirty-three at the time of the incident, Le Bon had sailed to Louisbourg from Brittany in 1752 without any trade but with the hope of teaching the colonists and their children "how to read and write and also arithmetic." Yet he never got around to doing any teaching, opting instead to work at sea for a short while and then at cutting firewood in the forest. Finally, "not being able to earn his keep otherwise," he thought about becoming a soldier. For all of his apparent irresolution, Le Bon seems to have been a religious man. On Christmas Eve, 1752, he helped the chapel verger (bedeau) set up the parish church for the midnight service, even staying afterward to extinguish the candles. Three and a half weeks later, however, he would return to the chapel in a drunken state to commit "attrocious acts" that would shock the Louisbourg community.

On the night of 16 January 1753, le Bon went to the soldiers' barracks in the King's Bastion to pick up a book on arithmetic he had earlier left in one of the soldiers' rooms. Intoxicated and unable to open the door leading to the barracks rooms, Le Bon noticed that a nearby door to the Chapelle de Saint-Louis was open. Entering, he climbed the stairs to the balcony and then down into the body of the church by slipping over a partition wall on the ground floor level. Intent on praying, or so he claimed later, he was approaching the altar when he noticed the flower arrangement was not the same as he was familiar with in France (the bouquets were to one side rather than between the candlesticks). Climbing on the altar to shift the flowers Le Bon accidentally cut himself, leaving blood-stains on the purificator, tabernacle, and picture frame. The intruder also dropped some bread and onions in the general area of the altar when he withdrew a handkerchief to wipe the blood off his face. Then, tired of stumbling around in the chapel, Le Bon took two small candles, climbed back out the way he had entered, and left the chapel.

Le Bon's nocturnal visit to the parish church was not discovered until the following morning when the verger arrived at the chapel around 8:30. The scene that greeted him was one that indicated a serious profanation of a holy place. There was mud and blood splattered all around, evidence that someone had walked on the altar, a niche was broken off the tabernacle, two candles had been stolen, and food (bread and onions) had apparently been consumed in the altar area. The desecration was reported immediately to the parish priest, Isidore Caulet, who in turn notified the royal officials. An investigation was begun which quickly led to the arrest of Yacinthe Gabriel Le Bon, for the night before he had stopped at the King's Bastion guardhouse to obtain a light for the chapel candles he had taken. The case dragged on for twenty-one months with witnesses being called and several interrogations of Le Bon taking place. The prosecutor, arguing that "it is important to make an example" of the accused to protect God's temple and religion, urged that Le Bon be punished with the full rigour of the ordinances. He advocated that the young man be hanged and strangled until dead with his corpse being left at the town square for twenty-four hours, and then transferred to the fork in the roads of the fauxbourg for a further period of public display. The court's decision, however, was more lenient, as it obviously took into account Le Bon's drunkenness and the fact that he had not tried to force the tabernacle. Le Bon's punishment was to be led to the main door of the Chapelle de Saint-Louis, dressed only in a *chemise* and with a rope around his neck and a candle in his hands, to make an *amende honorable*, asking on his knees for the forgiveness of God and king. On his front and on his back were to be signs that read "profaner of Sacred Places." Following that act of atonement he was to be fined three *livres* and banished from the colony for the rest of his life.

The way in which the royal officials handled the Le Bon case – the prompt arrest, thorough investigation, and harsh judgment – provides yet another illustration of the close ties that existed between church and state in eighteenth-century New France. A desecration of a chapel was viewed by both as a heinous crime that had to be dealt with quickly and severely. That Le Bon got off as lightly as he did was fortunate for him, as he could have easily been executed for his drunken misadventure. That possibility, or lesson, would not have been lost on most of the inhabitants of the town.

The Le Bon case provided a temporary diversion for the people of Louisbourg, undoubtedly scandalizing some, intriguing others. Whatever the reaction, at least the incident could not be blamed in any way on the Récollets. For that the friars must have been thankful, since there was much criticism of them on other grounds at the time. The harshest judgments were as usual issuing from Abbé de l'Isle-Dieu, who wrote a report in 1753 detailing the religious situation on the island.[145] The information in his report must have come from Abbé Pierre Maillard. According to the report, although five friars were required at Louisbourg there were only three, two of whom, Paulin Lozach and Patrice Lagrée, deserved to be recalled to France for their "bad conduct." Isidore Caulet was the only one considered worth keeping, but solely as military chaplain. Therefore four new Récollets were needed: chaplains for the Royal Battery and hospital, a curé, and a vicar to assist him. The last position was a new one deemed necessary because of the increase in the town's population since 1749.

Outside the capital the situation was just as serious. The Récollets at Port Dauphin, Port Toulouse, and the combined mission of Laurembec and La Baleine were "very poor subjects" who said mass but did little else. Worse yet, there were populous areas which were without any regular spiritual assistance. Niganiche and St Esprit needed parish priests of their own while L'Indienne, Baye des Espagnols, and Labrador were sizeable enough to share one among them. A fourth area where a resident priest might soon be needed was along the Mira River where the Comte de Raymond was establishing new settlements. In summary, the Récollets of Brittany ought to send ten or possibly eleven new friars to the colony. Isle-Dieu's report concluded that if the provincial could not supply that many Récollets, then the parishes and missions of Ile Royale should be handed over to an institution that could, such as the Séminaire du St Esprit in Paris, which incidentally was the seminary Abbés Maillard and Le Loutre had both attended.

The provincial of the Récollets of Brittany (once again it was the former Louisbourg curé Etienne Le Goff) did not appreciate Isle-Dieu's interest in the Ile Royale situation. Le Goff replied sarcastically that it surprised him that Isle-Dieu could know the colonial situation better than he did, when the abbé had never been outside Paris.

By the spring of 1753 the minister of marine appears to have begun to have doubts about the Récollets. When Rouillé learned that only three new friars would be sent out that year he reminded the Brittany provincial that if the Récollets were unable to dispatch enough good subjects to Ile Royale they had only to ask to be relieved of that responsibility.[146] Le Goff did not act on the offer. Instead, he designated Clément Rosselin to be the new commissaire of the Ile Royale Récollets.[147]

Rosselin and two other friars reached the colony in early summer, whereupon he became the new curé. In November 1753 Rosselin signed a parish record entry as a vicar-general of Bishop Pontbriand, but that appears to have been the only occasion when he used the title.[148] Throughout his two years on the island Rosselin remained subject to the supervision of Pontbriand's trusted representative Abbé Maillard. The subordinate position irritated Rosselin and his fellow Récollets yet there was nothing they could do about it except complain, which they appear to have done quite frequently.[149]

According to Abbé de l'Isle-Dieu, Pierre Maillard never lacked opportunities to criticize the shortcomings of the Brittany Récollets. In early 1754 Maillard was confronted with a particularly glaring error by one of the friars. The Récollet in question was Hyacinthe Lefebvre, the chaplain at Port Dauphin. In February Lefebvre travelled to Baye des Espagnols following a request from the commandant there, Ensign Jules Caesar Felix Bogard de La Noue, to provide spiritual comfort to people who were critically ill. When Lefebvre reached the settlement de la Noue asked him instead to sanctify a marriage between himself and Marguerite Guedry, daughter of a local family. De la Noue lied to the Récollet by telling him that he had obtained his commander's permission to marry. Lefebvre agreed to the request and the marriage was celebrated shortly after, on 11 February, in the bride's house, with only one bann having been read the previous day.

A few hours after the wedding a detachment of soldiers from Louisbourg arrived to arrest de la Noue and take him back to the capital for defying his commander's order not to marry the girl. The marriage was subsequently annulled because permission had not been given and because

Hyacinthe Lefebvre did not have the authority to perform the service, being from the parish at Port Dauphin. Baye de Espagnols was considered part of the parish of Louisbourg and therefore only the Louisbourg curé or his designate could celebrate marriages there. Moreover, wedding banns could only be dispensed with by someone so empowered by the bishop. Lefebvre did not have that authority so the marriage was invalid on that count as well.

Innocent or kind-hearted as Lefebvre's participation in the de la Noue wedding may have been, it was an extremely unwise act. By giving his blessing to a marriage that broke important rules of both church and state he gave further evidence to the Récollets' detractors of the general ignorance and laxity of the Brittany friars. In fact, one contemporary observed that Abbé Maillard was not at all unhappy with the incident as it gave him additional justification "to get rid of the monks."[150] Hyacinthe Lefebvre was recalled from Ile Royale for his role in the de la Noue marriage, but whatever hopes there were that the minister of marine would agree to oust all the Récollets in the colony were not realized. As a result, complaints about the Récollets' failings continued. For their part the friars' superiors promised improvements in the future.[151]

In 1754 Clément Rosselin continued as Récollet superior and curé at Louisbourg. But there were changes of significance. In June, Isidore Caulet, the longest serving religieux in the history of the colony, died at Louisbourg, aged sixty-three.[152] During the summer, Gratien Raoul, the first Récollet of Brittany to have served on the island, returned to Louisbourg after an absence of nearly forty years. He subsequently passed to Ile Saint-Jean where he became the superior of the Récollets there.[153]

The following year, 1755, was the first in which Abbé de l'Isle-Dieu expressed optimism about a development concerning the Récollets. The cause of the vicar-general's enthusiasm was the appointment of Ambroise Aubré as the latest commissaire of the Brittany friars. Chaplain and curé at Port Lajoie (Charlottetown) intermittently since 1739, Aubré was regarded by Isle-Dieu as "a very good subject, a very good religious, and with a mild and conciliatory character." The reputation was based both on Isle-Dieu's personal recollections of Aubré from time spent together in Paris and on reports of the friar's excellent work on Ile Saint-Jean. Isle-Dieu expected Aubré to get along well with Abbé Maillard, since the Récollet fully recognized the latter's jurisdiction over him. Aubré raised the vicar-general's expectations with a promise to put the Récollet mission "in the order that it should be." Hopeful of great improvements in the spiritual care of Ile Royale, Abbé de l'Isle-Dieu worried only that Ambroise Aubré, "whose health is very delicate," might become ill at Louisbourg and be forced to make an early departure from the colony.[154]

Aubré sailed from Rochefort in July 1755 and arrived off Louisbourg in mid-August. Hostilities having begun again with the British, though war would not be declared officially until 1756, the harbour was blockaded at the time. But with good fortune Aubré's ship was able to slip past the enemy vessels and into port.[155] The Récollet quickly took steps guaranteed to please his ecclesiastical superiors. Soon after his arrival he instituted one of the changes recommended by Maillard and Isle-Dieu when he assigned a friar as a vicar to assist the curé in his many parish duties. He left Clément Rosselin as the curé until the latter's departure in the fall, at which time Aubré himself became the new parish priest of Louisbourg.[156]

The war with Great Britain came to dominate life in Louisbourg from 1755 onward. Within the colony there were blockades off the coast, renewed planning for improvements to the fortifications, and the arrival of additional troops: over 1,000 regular army soldiers in 1755 and almost 1,400 more in 1758. Within the region there were the deportations of the Acadians of Nova Scotia and Ile Saint-Jean. On the Canadian frontier there were major battles with British troops throughout the late 1750s. Louisbourg, having been captured during the last war, must have been especially sensitive to these developments. Experience had shown that the inhabitants' houses, investments, and lives were all in possible jeopardy once war began.

War, the anxieties it fostered, and the behaviour it affected were spiritual as well as secular concerns. In recognition of that fact, combined with the particular vulnerability of Louisbourg, Bishop Pontbriand issued in February 1756 a pastoral letter on the war to his clergy and parishioners on Ile Royale. The twin objectives of the *mandement* were to remind the inhabitants that "earthly powers are nothing before God" and that they must lead righteous lives if they hope to avoid disaster; because "if the sinners persevere in their disorders, we dare to say it, everything is to be feared for the Colony. And we will perhaps soon see Louisbourg ... fall a second time into the hands of the Enemy." The people were urged to show a prompt and sincere rejection of their public and private sins, or else suffer the consequences. In particular, Pontbriand directed the clergy and people of Ile Royale to carry out four measures. First, to add the prayer *Deus refugium* to the others said during religious services; second, to have a procession (carrying a statue of the Blessed Virgin) on the first Sunday of each month; third, to sing antiphons to St Joseph and St Louis for the protection of the king and the royal family; fourth, to expose the

Blessed Sacrament in every parish church on the island on the fourth Sunday of each month and before the benediction sing *le miserere* and recite the prayer *Deus qui culpâ offenderis*. The various prayers were to be continued for roughly seven months, until 1 October 1756.[157]

The Récollet commissaire Ambroise Aubré undoubtedly saw to it that the directions contained in the bishop's pastoral letter were carried out accordingly. Abbé de l'Isle-Dieu's assessment of his leadership of the Louisbourg parish and of the other Récollets on the island indicate that he was conscientious in performing his various duties. By the spring of 1756, however, Aubré was asking to return to France, citing poor health as the reason. Isle-Dieu resisted the idea and asked Bishop Pontbriand to try to convince the superior to remain in Louisbourg where he was so desperately needed.[158] The appeal seems to have worked because Aubré stayed on in the town, albeit with a reduced parish workload,[159] well into the next year. At last, in the fall of 1757, his duties as curé, superior, and commissaire were taken over by the former Récollet chaplain of the Hôpital du Roi, Constantin Souben.[160] For reasons unknown Aubré did not return to France at the time. He was in Louisbourg in March 1758,[161] and may have still been there three months later when the town was besieged by the British.

The second attack on Louisbourg began with a successful amphibious assault in Kennington Cove (Anse de la Cormorandière) on 8 June. Eleven days later the first enemy battery opened fire. In spite of the siege the Récollets attempted to carry on parish activities more or less as usual. From 13 June to 19 July 1758 there were numerous baptisms and burials in the town.[162] On 9 July a house belonging to the "monks" was hit by a cannon shot but no one seems to have been injured.[163] The bombardment of the town escalated in the days that followed, presumably making it increasingly difficult for the friars to minister to their parishioners. After 19 July the entries in the parish records stopped. Three days later the Chapelle de Saint-Louis, Louisbourg's parish church, was destroyed in a fire that consumed the entire barracks building except the governor's apartment.[164] The end of the siege was fast approaching. On 26 July the French capitulated and the next day the British took possession of the town for the second and final time. The night before the occupying army entered Louisbourg, according to Thomas Pichon, "the priests spent the whole night marrying all the girls of the place to the first that would have them for fear that they should fall into the hands of heretics."[165] Although Pichon perhaps exaggerated the numbers involved, it is not at all unlikely that there were many marriages on the eve of the occupation. Conquering armies were known for their raping and pillaging so that any step taken to minimize the possible damage and disruption, such as by reducing the number of single women, deserved consideration.

It was only a matter of days between the capitulation and the departure of the first refugee ships for France. For most inhabitants it must have been a hectic and traumatic time,[166] a period in which they looked to the Récollets for comfort and consolation. In France, the Récollet curés and chaplains initially remained attached to the civilians and soldiers of Ile Royale.[167] By July 1759, however, most had returned to convents in Brittany. Only the military chaplain, Pierre d'Alcantara Cabaret, was kept on the royal payroll, to serve the troops from the colony.[168] When those troops were either discharged or assigned duty elsewhere Cabaret likely also returned to one of the Brittany convents. At that point the long involvement of the Récollets of Brittany in the history of Ile Royale was over.

During their four decades in the colony the Récollets had provided spiritual advice and direction to thousands of colonists, soldiers, and visiting fishermen in roughly a dozen settlements on Ile Royale and Ile Saint-Jean. In Louisbourg alone there were in excess of 550 marriages, 2,200 baptisms, and 1,100 burials performed by the more than forty different friars who served there over the years. The workload was heavy and conditions were often far from ideal. Not only was there no real parish church in the capital nor enough Récollets to meet the needs of all the settlements on the island, which therefore made periodic visits to isolated outports essential, but the friars often found themselves roundly criticized for their shortcomings by various bishops of Québec and their vicars-general.

The main complaints were of the Récollets' lack of education and their failure to perform basic parish duties. In the bishops' eyes, the friars lacked the formal training and dedication which was normally found in secular priests. For that reason, and also because they would have had greater control over seculars, the bishops and vicars-general always favoured replacing the Louisbourg Récollets with secular priests. That the bishops' recommendations on that point were never acted upon reveals their relative lack of influence with the minister of marine concerning matters on Ile Royale.

Only in the late 1750s, when it became obvious that the Récollets of Brittany were unable to meet the needs of all the parishes on the island, did the minister seem to give serious consideration to replacing the friars. Before then he simply dismissed the subject by pointing first to the royal letters patent which had been issued to the Brittany Récollets and second to the apparent popular support for the friars. That popular support, as revealed in petitions and letters in defence of the Récollets, provides perhaps the best insight into how well the friars actually served their parishioners. Beloved for their simple piety and down-to-earth ways, the Récollets of Brittany were probably regarded by most colonists as being well suited to the demanding and tiring work of serving as the curés and chaplains of Ile Royale.[169]

3 Serving the King's Hospital: The Brothers of Charity of Saint John of God

> ... a religious order ... which devotes itself solely to the service of the indigent and sick. The religious ... are without contradiction the most respectable of all ... as they are valuable both to society for their work and to religion by their example.
>
> *Encyclopédie, ou Dictionnaire raisonné* (1757)[1]

French colonial policy in the sphere of religion was firmly rooted in the belief that no religious communities should be established overseas except those which were demonstrably useful to society. Contemplative orders were considered an extravagance which both the colonies and the king's treasury could live without. Colbert's remark that "the religious of both sexes ... produce only useless people in this world, and very often devils in the next world" is the best illustration of that utilitarian attitude. Where *religieux* definitely were welcomed was in the broad field of public welfare. Charity for the poor, education of the young, and health care for the sick and disabled were some of the areas generally left to the church. To religious communities who met such needs the secular authorities offered "protection ... assistance in the way of open passages, freight allowance, exemptions, special concessions and subsidies."[2]

Louisbourg, as a populous fishing base, commercial entrepôt, and garrison town, had obvious requirements in the area of public welfare. Among the most important was the need for suitable hospital care for its resident and transient population. When officials within the Ministry of Marine addressed themselves to that question during the early years of settlement of Ile Royale they turned to a well-known hospital order, the Brothers of Charity of the Order of Saint John of God.

The Brothers of Charity were mendicants dedicated to the care of the sick and infirm. Founded in Spain in the mid-sixteenth century by Saint John of God, the order spread through France and Italy in the seventeenth and eighteenth centuries. By 1789 there were 355 brothers serving in thirty-nine hospitals in France and its colonies, with a total of about 5,000 beds under their care.[3] Each brother took four vows, those of poverty, chastity, obedience, and hospitality. Collectively, they were regarded by their contemporaries as conscientious and skilled.[4] On the basis of that reputation the medical order was asked in 1716 to go to Ile Royale to operate the nascent colony's hospitals. The order accepted the responsibility and four brothers, accompanied by four servants, sailed for the island that summer.[5] For several years they were dispersed in different settlements. Then, with the decision in 1719 to make Louisbourg the principal town and stronghold of the colony, the brothers were all brought together in the capital.

At Louisbourg, the Brothers of Charity were initially in charge of a rudimentary hospital on the north shore of the harbour. When a larger and more sophisticated Hôpital du Roi with 100 beds and its own apothecary, bakery, chapel, kitchen, laundry, and morgue was completed in 1730 on a centrally located town block, the brothers moved in and began to run it.

Day-to-day tasks in the Louisbourg hospital were in the hands of several brothers and their servants, all of whom worked under the direction of the resident superior. Overall administrative responsibility, however, did not lie with the brothers. Since the substantial capital and operating costs of hospitals like the Hôpital du Roi in Louisbourg were paid for out of the royal treasury, the king required that royal officials oversee the facilities to ensure that the state and the patients got the best possible return for the money spent. To achieve that end hospital facilities and records were scrutinized by various officials. The particular duties with which the royal officials were charged were outlined in a 1689 ordinance of Louis XIV.[6]

At Louisbourg, principal responsibility for the hospital fell to the commissaire-ordonnateur. Each new appointee to that position received general instructions from the minister of marine directing him to keep the cost and quality of health care at acceptable levels.[7] The single most important thing the commissaire-ordonnateur did to meet that goal was to assign a clerk to the Hôpital du Roi whose duties included verifying the admission and departure of patients and the quality and quantity of medicine used. That position appears to have been filled first in 1731 when Philippe Carrerot was named to the post.[8]

Uncertain as to how well the commissaire-ordonnateur and his staff would carry out their responsibilities, the minister of marine notified the colonial governor that he too must ensure that the hospital was well run. Specifically, he was to conduct periodic inspections of the facility.[9] The Brothers of Charity did not always share the royal officials' perspectives on what constituted adequate health care, so it was probably inevitable that conflicts would develop. The most contentious issues were those which related either to the attitudes and behaviour of the brothers or to the cost of the health care they provided.

Royal control over the Louisbourg Hôpital du Roi made it less of an "ecclesiastical institution" than many of the other hospitals in France and New France. Nonetheless, it would have retained a definitely religious atmosphere. Military regulations and king's ordinances specified that patients were to be confessed soon after admission, mass said daily at a set hour, and prayers said each evening. The brothers themselves, according to the rules and customs of the Order of Saint John of God, were to say their prayers morning and evening, speak only when necessary, observe the required feasts, and renew their vows frequently. As for health care, they were supposed not only to look after their patients' illnesses, but also to inform them of the need to purify their souls while the body mended.[10]

On Ile Royale the early years of the Brothers of Charity were characterized by relatively peaceful relations with royal officials. The few quarrels that arose appear to have been brief and not very serious. In 1716 the *religieux* complained about their poor accommodation at Port Dauphin; three years later there was an internal dispute among the brothers; in 1720 they expressed reluctance about relocating from their north shore property to be nearer to the Louisbourg soldiers' barracks.[11] No major controversy or criticism arose concerning the brothers until 1726, when they had been in the colony for a decade.

In 1726 Governor Saint-Ovide complained that for some time the sick in the north shore hospital had been poorly looked after by the brothers. He claimed that the *religieux* were so preoccupied with treating civilians in town, including giving shaves, that they were neglecting the soldiers, sailors, and others in the hospital. Particularly scandalous was the fact that there was frequently no surgeon in the facility. The governor's outrage was brought to a head when a soldier with a broken arm was taken to the hospital and given no care whatsoever. Seventeen hours after the man was admitted his arm had swollen to a size larger than his thigh. The soldier's agony did not end until Governor Saint-Ovide sent one of his staff officers to find a surgeon to treat the man's injury. The governor relayed the incident to the minister of marine as an illustration of how the brothers were ignoring their responsibilities. The comte de Maurepas appears to have been persuaded by the story. He passed on Saint-Ovide's remarks to the provincial of the order, adding that he expected such neglect to end.[12]

The brothers seem to have taken the minister's advice to heart. Over the next few years there were no further comments about their lack of attention to hospital patients. In 1730 new complaints began, but they related more to the recently finished Hôpital du Roi than to the *reli-*

gieux. The strongest criticism came from the acting commandant of Ile Royale, François le Coutre de Bourville. On the basis of reports from military officers who made daily visits to the hospital, Bourville asserted that the facility was barely adequate. Vermin in the building, rotten mattresses, a shortage of sheets, shirts, and bed surrounds, wards that were cold due to a lack of firewood, and food worse than in the barracks were the most serious problems. Those shortcomings required royal expenditure if they were to be corrected. The only failing for which the brothers were directly responsible was the absence of a competent surgeon in the hospital. The brother who occupied that position was described as "not very capable." Bourville had attempted to have the surgeon-major of the garrison, Jean-Baptiste La Grange, assigned to the hospital but the superior of the brothers refused to allow it. Consequently, the acting commandant asked the minister of marine to order the brothers to send out a trained surgeon the following year. As requested, a *religieux* (probably Boniface Vimeux) who was a "very good Surgeon" arrived in 1731.[13]

The furnishing and supply situation at the hospital improved during 1731 and 1732. Nonetheless, the brothers were still without hundreds of essential articles. On their behalf the commissaire-ordonnateur submitted a long list of the bedclothes, instruments, tools, utensils, and other things which the facility was still without.[14] Gradually, the orders were filled. As the needed supplies came in the tasks of the Brothers of Charity were made that much easier. Concomitantly, the assessment of their abilities became increasingly favourable.[15]

In 1732 hospital care must have suffered a setback when three of the *religieux* at Louisbourg died,[16] quite likely victims of the smallpox epidemic which struck the town that year. Replacements were sent out the following year. As of October 1734 there were five brothers and six servants in the hospital, the superior being Félix Camax and the surgeon Boniface Vimeux.[17]

The only complaint about the Brothers of Charity during the early 1730s was of their tendency to show disrespect and a degree of insubordination towards royal officials in the colony. Such an attitude was considered unacceptable and the minister hoped that the new brothers sent out in 1733 would be "more tranquil and more manageable." Moreover, he encouraged the commissaire-ordonnateur to exercise, albeit carefully, his authority over the hospital.[18] The combination of more amenable brothers and a more assertive commissaire-ordonnateur seems to have ended, at least temporarily, their obstreperous attitude toward the civil authorities.

After a few years of harmonious relations the Brothers of Charity petitioned the minister of marine for numerous improvements to the Hôpital du Roi. Among the things asked for and granted were rooms for sick officers, additional servants from the pool of salt smugglers (fauxsauniers) sent to the colony each year, another grant of meadow land for grazing animals, and a new hospital kitchen. The last item was particularly needed since the existing kitchen was below ground level and there were often problems with water leakage and with the fireplace smoking too much.[19] Although some other requests of the brothers were turned down, the relative speed with which royal officials agreed to the above petitions indicated a shared concern for the amelioration of hospital care in Louisbourg. Excluding the wrangles over patient costs during the period (which are discussed below), the late 1730s was a time of generally good relations between the civil authorities and the medical order.[20]

The apparent harmony became somewhat strained after François Bigot arrived in 1739 as the new commissaire-ordonnateur. There were several factors at play. To begin with, twice during the 1740s the commissaire-ordonnateur clashed with the superior of the Brothers of Charity over who, or rather what kind of case, should be admitted to the Hôpital du Roi. The first incident occurred in 1740 when Bigot thought that a prisoner who had begun to manifest "marques de la folie" should be placed in the hospital. The superior, Boniface Vimeux, disagreed strongly. The commissaire-ordonnateur ultimately broke the impasse by using his full authority over the facility and forcing admission of the man. The fact that the man suffering from folie would be placed in a room with bars on the windows seems to have helped relieve the brothers' fears about accepting him as a patient.[21]

Although Vimeux bowed to Bigot's wishes in that particular case he was unwilling to agree that a principle was established whereby he was forced to admit people suffering from mental illnesses. The superior indicated that he would seek a different decision from the authorities in France. François Bigot's opinion was that the brothers should be obliged to accept such cases. He felt that if a mentally ill patient was "violent," as the man in 1740 was not, he could be left alone in a room with hands and feet tied. Indeed, the commissaire-ordonnateur recommended that two small stone cells be constructed in the tower of the hospital and specifically reserved for the mentally ill. The individuals detained in those cells were eventually to be returned to their home parishes.[22] If the minister of marine took a stand on the issue, his views have not been found. Certainly, the stone cells suggested by Bigot were never constructed.

A separate dispute which arose between François Bigot and Boniface Vimeux in the 1740s concerned the admission of patients with venereal diseases. During the early 1730s soldiers in the garrison who had a venereal disease were routinely sent back to France to receive mercury treatments for their afflictions.[23] The Louisbourg brothers maintained that they had not been trained to treat such maladies and that they would not accept any cases in the Hôpital du Roi. Undoubtedly they feared that the diseases would spread to other patients and possibly to themselves. Such fears were so commonplace at the time that the practice was to keep people with venereal diseases carefully segregated from other patients. An observer in France commented that it was impossible for a human being to be attacked "in a more hideous or cruel fashion" than to suffer from venereal afflictions.[24] Evidently the Brothers of Charity did not think they could ensure a satisfactory degree of isolation for those cases and hence did not want to admit them. The governor and commissaire-ordonnateur, on the other hand, argued that it would be more convenient as well as cheaper if the brothers would treat the diseases in the Louisbourg hospital. In 1736 the colonial officials apparently reached an agreement with the order so that the latter would receive 200 *livres* for each soldier they treated afflicted with venereal disease.[25]

By 1741 the agreement had fallen through and the brothers were protesting that they did not wish to accept people with these afflictions. However, as was the case with the man with *folie*, François Bigot simply overruled the objections and had soldiers suffering from venereal diseases admitted to the hospital.[26] It took almost two years but at last, in 1743, the Brothers of Charity had become accustomed to the idea of treating such patients and did so without protest.[27] During the 1750s the approach to the treatment of venereal diseases changed slightly, with the Louisbourg brothers looking after only minor and intermediate cases, while the worst ones were sent back to France.[28]

The admittance of unwanted patients to the hospital was only one of the issues straining relations in the 1740s between the brothers and royal officials like François Bigot. Of at least equal importance were the concerted efforts made by the commissaire-ordonnateur during the same period to reduce hospital expenditures on patient care. To understand that issue it is necessary to look at the background to the financing of the hospital.

Before the Brothers of Charity came to Ile Royale it was the expressed hope of the minister of marine that most of the operating expenses of a major hospital in the colony would be met through the collection of a tax on the cod fishery. The custom at Plaisance had been for the fishermen and merchants to contribute to the hospital there on the basis of their involvement in the fishery. Their contributions paid for food, supplies, laundry, and some staff salaries. The minister assumed that a similar arrangement could be instituted at Louisbourg.[29] In 1715 a tax of a *quintal* (48.95 kilograms) of cod per shallop was imposed on Ile Royale which generated an income of 4,524 *livres*.[30] The sum was considerable but it was obtained in the face of strong opposition from those taxed. Ship captains and fishing proprietors complained that since there was no major hospital near their fishing base at Louisbourg neither they nor their crews were receiving the hospital care for which they were paying. The officials within the Ministry of Marine agreed and in 1716 the tax was lifted.[31]

Five years later, with construction under way on the major hospital on Block 13, the governor and commissaire-ordonnateur of Ile Royale suggested that the tax could be reimposed without opposition. They believed that the fishing proprietors and ship captains would see the obvious benefits such a facility would confer on the community and willingly contribute. They estimated the tax would bring in about 5,000 livres annually. The imperial authorities in France were more than pleased to hear of the apparent change in attitude among the colonists. Accordingly, in 1722 they issued an ordinance reestablishing a tax of a quintal of cod per shallop. Initially the proceeds were to help offset the cost of hospital construction; thereafter they were to pay for the building of a parish church and presbytery.[32] Contrary to expectations, the tax was not well received by those active in the fishing industry. By November 1723 only about 1,500 livres had been contributed. As a result the tax was withdrawn for the second and final time.[33]

The failure to impose any kind of hospital support tax meant that virtually every cost associated with the treatment of the sick and injured had to be met with funds from the royal treasury. The dependence on royal grants was in sharp contrast to the situation at a hospital like the Hôtel-Dieu in Montréal, where only 9 per cent of its revenue came from the king.[34] At the Louisbourg Hôpital du Roi, the king paid for the construction of the massive building as well as for firewood, furnishings, medical supplies, and provisions. As for patients, the groups whose care was entirely paid for out of royal funds were soldiers from the garrison, sailors off king's ships, discharged soldiers, poor inhabitants, and prisoners of war. During the 1750s military officers were also treated in the hospital at royal expense.

In almost every year the vast majority of patients came from the ranks of the ordinary soldiers of the Louisbourg garrison, who formed one-fifth to one-quarter of the total population of the town. Generally soldiers outnumbered all other groups of hospital patients combined by a ratio of eight or nine to one (see Table 4). The only time when another category was close to that ratio was when large ships arrived in port and disembarked dozens of sick sailors or soldiers, the latter often being destined for Canada. In 1744, for instance, more than two-thirds of the crew (84 of 120) of a Compagnie des Indes ship were so ill that they were admitted to the hospital shortly after anchoring.[35] A much worse situation had occurred a

TABLE 4
Time Spent by Patients at the Hôpital du Roi, Louisbourg, 1731–57 (in days)

Year	Soldiers	Sailors, Officers, Poor Inhabitants, Prisoners, etc.	Total	1 as % of 3
1731a	1,043	119	1,162	89.8
1732	5,811	1,048	6,859	84.7
1733	8,333	421	8,754	95.2
1734	8,746	1,375	10,121	86.4
1735	8,760	1,023	9,789	89.5
1736	8,540	1,506	10,046	85.0
1737	8,268	777	9,045	91.4
1738	6,480	1,602	8,082	80.2
1739	5,758	1,651	7,409	77.7
1740	5,393	495	5,888	91.6
1741	6,985	55b	7,040	99.2
1742	6,728	347	7,075	95.1
1743	7,931	231	8,162	97.2
1744	7,093b	1,952	9,045	78.4
1749d	7,545	377	7,922	95.2
1750b	17,043	2,356	19,399	87.9
1751	10,074	2,778e	12,852	78.4
1752	13,755	9,141	22,896	60.1
1753	10,120	3,021	13,141	77.0
1754b	8,196	2,134	10,330	79.3
1756a	1,535	2,070	3,605	42.6
1757b	7,603	7,853	15,456	49.2

SOURCE: Table 5. By dividing the expense figure in each column by the per diem rate paid to the Brothers of Charity (16 sols per day for soldiers, 25 sols per day for those in the other category), it was possible to ascertain the number of days spent in the Hôpital du Roi.

a Last three months of the year
b First nine months of the year
d Mid-August to 31 December
e Precise period unclear

dozen years earlier when three king's ships sailed into port with a total of about 300 sick aboard.[36] Obviously, not all of them would be cared for in the Hôpital du Roi with its 100-bed capacity.

Such experiences prompted the local officials to recommend that a separate health care facility be constructed on the far shore of the harbour capable of accommodating 120 to 160 patients from ships.[37] The proposal was not adopted during the first French occupation but it seems to have been acted upon during the 1750s. At least there is a 1754 plan which identifies two small hospitals on the north shore which are for the "use of King's vessels."[38] Even with the addition of those hospitals it was still not always possible to accommodate all the sick in the town. In 1755, for instance, the sick crew members off *La Valeur* had to be cared for on two ships moored in the harbour while their officers were housed in town.[39] Except in unusual circumstances the Brothers of Charity had little to do with these special hospitals for visiting ship crews. Their concern was the Hôpital du Roi.

At the King's Hospital there was one category of patients whose hospitalization costs were not paid for out of royal funds: civilians who could afford to pay for their own care. As it was, not many of that group seem to have gone to the hospital. They preferred instead to be treated and, if it came to it, to die in their own beds. Their reluctance to enter the hospital stemmed from a variety of causes. "Everyone who could possibly afford it was nursed at home, as a matter not just of prestige, or of privacy, comfort or quiet, but of safety from vermin and from cross-infections."[40] In short, hospitals in the seventeenth and eighteenth centuries were "associated more with death than healing."[41]

By the 1730s, at which time the Hôpital du Roi was completed and there were normally five or six Brothers of Charity serving there, the annual allocation for hospital expenses stood at 13,600 *livres*. The breakdown was as follows: 500 *livres* for each of six brothers, 3,000 *livres* for the upkeep and replacement of furnishings and instruments, 600 *livres* for medical supplies, 1,000 *livres* for the brothers' living expenses in the colony, and 6,000 *livres* for patient expenses.[42] In terms of total royal expenditures on Ile Royale the allotment for health care was relatively small, generally from two to four per cent. As long as hospital expenses remained within their allocated ceilings there was no complaint from officials within the Ministry of Marine. Commencing in 1733, however, the cost of patient care consistently exceeded the 6,000 *livres* appropriation. In both 1734 and 1736 expenditures on that item reached over 8,700 *livres* (see Table 5).

The minister of marine, the comte de Maurepas, was understandably distressed. In his view, the Brothers of Charity were well provided for in the colony and there should be no need for expenditures beyond the allotment. In addition to the pieces of land they had been granted on the north shore of Louisbourg harbour and on the Mira River, where the brothers were to raise crops and animals to help feed their patients, they received per patient payments far in excess of those paid elsewhere in New France. For example, at Québec, the hospital order there was paid 6 *sols* per day for each hospitalized soldier; at the Hôtel-Dieu in Montréal, the figure

TABLE 5
Annual Expenditure on Patient Care at the Hôpital du Roi, Louisbourg, 1731–58
(to nearest livre tournois)

Year	Soldiers	Officers	Sailors, Poor Inhabitants, Prisoners, etc.	Total
1731a	834		149	983
1732	4,649		1,310	5,959
1733	6,666		526	7,193
1734	6,997		1,719	8,716
1735	7,008		1,279	8,287
1736	6,832		1,882	8,714
1737	6,614		971	7,586
1738	5,184		2,002	7,186
1739	4,606		2,064	6,070
1740	4,314		619	4,933
1741	5,588		69b	5,657
1742	5,382		434	5,816
1743	6,345		289	6,634
1744	5,674b		2,440	8,114
1745				19,490c
1749d	6,036		471	6,507
1750b	13,634		2,945	16,579
1751	8,059		3,472e	11,532
1752	11,004		11,426	22,430
1753	8,096	549	3,227	11,872
1754b	6,557	398	2,270	9,225
1756a	1,228	107	2,480	3,815
1757b	6,082	705	9,111	15,899
1758				22,329f

SOURCES: The bordereaux for the years indicated, as follows: AN, Colonies, C11C, vol. 11, fol. 79v.; ibid., fol. 86v.; ibid., fol. 95; ibid., fols. 102v.–3; ibid., fols. 121v.–2; ibid., fol. 130; ibid., fol. 179; ibid., vol. 12, fols. 12–12v.; ibid., fol. 53; ibid., fol. 79v.; ibid., fol. 96; ibid., fols. 110v.–11; ibid., fol. 144; ibid., fols. 183–83v.; ibid., fols. 191v.–2; ibid., vol. 13, fol. 78v.; ibid., fols. 114–14v.; ibid., fol. 136v.; ibid., fol. 178; ibid., vol. 14, fols. 19v.–20; ibid., fols. 52–52v.; ibid., fols. 75–75v.; AN, Colonies, B, vol. 112, fol. 468, Ministre à de Ruis, 2 mai 1760; ibid., fol. 215, Ministre au Procureur Syndic de l'ordre des frères de la charité à Paris, 30 mai 1760.

a Last three months of the year
b First nine months of the year
c 1 October 1744 to 31 July 1945
d Mid-August to 31 December
e Precise period unclear
f Final payment for expenditures during 1758 siege

was 11 *sols* 3 *deniers*.[43] In Louisbourg, by the 1730s, the Brothers of Charity were receiving 16 *sols* for each day a soldier spent in the hospital, as well as that soldier's ration. For all the other categories of patients (sailors, poor inhabitants, prisoners, etc.) the brothers were compensated at the rate of 25 *sols* per person per day.[44]

Commissaire-ordonnateur Le Normant responded to the minister's criticism of rising hospital costs with the explanation that there were two factors causing the increase. The first was the deplorable lifestyle of the soldiers, who comprised the largest single category of patients. According to Le Normant, the soldiers' leisure time was often devoted to an excessive consumption of alcohol, with the result that they were particularly susceptible to illnesses and accidents. The second factor was that the brothers themselves were not prompt about discharging patients whose health had been restored. As a result, the expense mounted needlessly. Le Normant was not optimistic of improving either situation. He claimed he could do nothing about the soldiers' recreational pursuits and he was not hopeful of changing hospital procedures. While he supported Governor Saint-Ovide's proposal to have a military surgeon make weekly inspections looking for healthy patients, he worried that the brothers would object strenuously.[45] The minister of marine refused to accept that either situation could not be rectified. Anxious to see a reduction in hospital expenses, he instructed Saint-Ovide to curb drunkenness in the garrison and informed Le Normant that regular inspections of the hospital by the surgeon-major should be introduced.[46]

The minister's directions reached Ile Royale in the spring of 1737. The more difficult instruction to implement would seem to have been the one to diminish drunkenness among the soldiers. What action, if any, Governor Saint-Ovide took on the question is not known. The second instruction, the one concerning hospital inspections, should have been relatively easy to carry out. Yet Le Normant moved very slowly on the matter. Given Maurepas' clear direction on the issue his tardiness is difficult to understand. A possible explanation lies in the commissaire-ordonnateur's handling of another hospital matter at about the same time.

On that occasion the Brothers of Charity placed a sign with the order's motto, *Charitas*, above the main door to the Hôpital du Roi. Le Normant had the sign removed because it erroneously implied, at least to him, that the hospital belonged to the order rather than to the king.[47] Having drawn the lines of jurisdiction so precisely in that issue, the commissaire-ordonnateur may well have been reluctant to introduce inspections out of a fear that the brothers would protest they were an encroachment upon their specific area of concern. Although it is not known whether or not the incident over the sign contributed to Le Normant's attitude on the subject, the fact remains that he failed to initiate regular visits to the hospital by a military surgeon. Admittedly in 1737 and 1738 the cost of patient care declined to between 7,100 and 7,500 *livres*, but those figures were still well above the 6,000 *livres* appropriation. The difference that inspections would make was not to be seen until 1739 when a new commissaire-ordonnateur, François Bigot, arrived in the colony.

Unlike Le Normant, Bigot did not hesitate to initiate regular hospital visits by military surgeons. The brothers soon became accustomed to the measure and the desired reduction in expenditures was achieved. The contrast between hospital costs during Le Normant's period as commissaire-ordonnateur and Bigot's is striking. In Bigot's first year in the colony the cost of patient care was only slightly above 6,000 *livres*; during the next three years the figures were below the appropriation, even dipping to below 5,000 *livres* one year. In 1744 expenditures did climb to over 8,000 *livres* again, but that was due to extraordinary circumstances. With the declaration of war that spring and the incarceration of hundreds of English prisoners in the town during the summer months it was inevitable and acceptable that patient costs would exceed the appropriation. Thus, in general, during François Bigot's term as commissaire-ordonnateur, hospital costs were kept within the financial bounds set by the minister of marine (see Table 5).

Notwithstanding Bigot's success in bringing down expenses from the high levels of the 1730s, the commissaire-ordonnateur hoped for greater savings and increased efficiency at the Hôpital du Roi. In 1742 he recommended to the minister of marine that the brothers be withdrawn from Ile Royale and the hospital operation handed over to a women's medical order, the Grey sisters (*Sœurs Grises*), whom Bigot stated would be more economical. Perhaps Bigot's jaundiced view of the brothers was coloured by the disputes he had had over the admittance of the man with *folie* and of soldiers with veneral diseases, but perhaps not. Women's nursing orders were held in extremely high regard during the era, for their compassion, "spirit of sacrifice and self-abnegation."[48] So Bigot's proposal may have been based purely on a heartfelt conviction that the colony would be better served with the Grey Sisters running the hospital. The commissaire-ordonnateur claimed that the sisters were not only more economical than the brothers but also more charitable, and would keep the hospital cleaner and the patients better fed. The minister acknowledged that Bigot's suggestion had merit, yet not enough to cancel the patent letters that had been issued to the brothers of Saint John of God.[49] Consequently the brothers continued to serve in Louisbourg until the events of 1745 forced them to leave.

The besieging of Louisbourg in the spring of 1745 must have had a profound impact on the Brothers of Charity. The opening of hostilities meant that they were faced with far more and graver injuries than was normal, injuries that often called for immediate attention. Midway through the siege the hospital itself came under fire when an enemy cannon shot smashed through a wall of its chapel. During the latter half of the attack the Hôpital du Roi was undoubtedly among the busiest places in Louisbourg. As the bombardment of the town grew steadily heavier, injuries to soldiers and civilians alike probably kept the brothers and their servants active around the clock. The best indication of the immense workload they faced during the siege and its aftermath are the costs incurred by the brothers on behalf of their patients. The total for 1745 reached over 19,000 *livres*, more than three times the average figure from the 1740s (see Table 5). The siege ended in late July but the medical work did not end then. Thereafter the sick and injured had to be made ready for the transatlantic crossing. When the soldiers and inhabitants departed in July so did the Brothers of Charity. The last brother to leave, having stayed behind to sail on the final ship, was Grégoire Chomey.[50]

A written description of the Louisbourg hospital in 1745 is provided by an anonymous soldier in the army of New Englanders who conquered and occupied the town. The diarist first noted the great length of the building: 20 rods (330 feet or 100.6 meters). Its walls, "Built of Stone and Lime," were two feet thick and rose two storeys, with "a Great many Large Sash Windows with Iron Grates to Each of'em." On the ground floor the soldier found two large wards that were "Well furnished with Beds and Curtains." Two more wards were located on the floor above, all of which were supplied with a "Great Deal" of linen and a "Great many" pewter vessels. Rising above the hospital was a "Steeple and a good Bell hanging in the Same." Residential quarters were located at either end of the main building while the outbuildings at the corners of the property contained kitchen, wells, and large copper pots for cooking, brewing, and so on. The entire property (Block 13) was enclosed by a wall measuring twelve feet high and four feet thick. The arched gate entrance to the interior yard, which was cultivated as a garden, and apparently contained two sun dials, was topped, appropriately enough, by a cross.[51]

Shortly after the Brothers of Charity disembarked at Rochefort the bishop of Québec recommended to the minister of marine that if Ile Royale was returned to France the brothers should not be sent back to Louisbourg. Bishop Pontbriand did not mention at the time which order he had in mind to replace them, but three years later he made the surprising suggestion that the Hôpital du Roi be handed over to the Sisters of the

Congregation of Notre Dame, a community of teachers not concerned with medical care. A women's order, Pontbriand asserted, would be less expensive and they could tend female patients as well as male, unlike the brothers. As before, the minister chose not to act on the suggestion. His view was that if the colony was handed back the Order of Saint John of God remained the order chosen to serve the Louisbourg hospital. Interestingly enough, when Ile Royale was actually returned to France by the Treaty of Aix-la-Chapelle (1748), François Bigot, formerly a detractor, was among those advocating that the brothers again be put in charge of the Hôpital du Roi. He even specified that Boniface Vimeux should be sent out again as the local superior. Bigot's wish was fulfilled in the summer of 1749. Accompanied by four brothers and numerous servants, Vimeux once more took charge of the hospital.[52]

In the four years since the French had been in Louisbourg the hospital had undergone drastic changes. One estimate of necessary repairs placed the cost of renovating the building at 21,735 livres.[53] An initial lack of beds[54] might be overcome rather easily, but the same was not true of other shortcomings. For instance, there was a serious problem of stench. Used as a barracks for four years by the British, the large wards had acquired a strong disagreeable odour which no amount of cleaning could eliminate. The only solution was to replace the floors and whitewash the walls.

The renovations in the hospital continued into 1751. In an effort to increase illumination two new casement windows were constructed in each of the ground floor wards. For security those new windows and all existing ones on the ground level were barred. There was a minor disappointment that year when a supply of beds arrived from France. The quality of the beds was satisfactory but they were judged to be too narrow for two patients and too wide for just one. As a result, the beds were made smaller. Other work was done on the hospital chapel, sacristy, kitchen, and lodgings of the brothers.[55]

The operation of the Hôpital du Roi after 1749 was characterized by the same problem which had occurred frequently in the first period; namely that the expenditures on patient care were excessive. However, in contrast to the practice before 1745, the Brothers of Charity were not blamed during the 1750s when costs consistently outstripped the allocation. The annual appropriation was raised from 6,000 to 10,000 livres during the second period on the basis of an initial 500-man augmentation to the Louisbourg garrison. Initially, the increases in livres and manpower were roughly proportional. After 1755, in which year 1,000 more troops arrived in town, the attempt to keep the allocation proportional to the size of the garrison was given up entirely.

The commissaire-ordonnateur, Jacques Prévost, always claimed that the overexpenditures on patient care were understandable, the result of exceptional circumstances. The worst year was 1752 when costs exceed the appropriation by over 100 per cent (see Table 5). Prévost explained that the expenses mounted because of the unexpected stay in port over the winter of La Fidèle.[56] To have driven hospital costs up to that level many of the crew off the king's ship must have recuperated for several months in the hospital. In another very expensive year, 1757, the commissaire-ordonnateur attributed the excessive patient costs to other causes: the large number of English prisoners detained in the town and the extreme fatigue of French soldiers encamped along the coastline during August and September.[57]

A glimpse into the kind of treatment certain types of illnesses received from the Brothers of Charity during the 1750s is provided by one of their patients, Michel Le Courtois Des Bourbes. An officer in the Louisbourg garrison, Des Bourbes went to the brothers for medical treatment in early 1756, after having suffered through eight months of nightmares, heartburn, indigestion, and migraine headaches. In the opinion of the brother who treated Des Bourbes, the officer's problem was that his blood was too thick and that he had "bad agents" (mauvais levains) in his stomach. The cure was thought to lie in bleedings and in the taking of appropriate potions or infusions (ptissannes) to purge the sickness from his body. Unfortunately the effect of the treatment, which lasted for a month, was the opposite of that which was intended and Des Bourbes became even more ill. As a result the brother recommended that he enter the Hôpital du Roi where it would be easier to look after him. Des Bourbes agreed and was admitted to the officers' ward. In the course of the next three weeks he was bled six more times and given four different medicines. He was then released, feeling considerably weaker.[58]

Ineffectual as it was, the treatment which Des Bourbes received from the Louisbourg Brothers of Charity was basically the same as that which he would have received anywhere else in that era. Bleedings, enemas, infusions, sweating, and starving were the common remedies for a wide range of afflictions. Sometimes they worked, but more often they did not. One simply submitted to them and hoped for the best.[59]

Des Bourbes' medical complaints seem to have been real enough, but the same does not appear to have been true of some other patients during the 1750s. In 1756 the commissaire-ordonnateur alleged that officers in the Artois and Bourgogne regiments were sending soldiers to the Hôpital du Roi for the sole reason that their men could obtain fresh meat there. When some apparently healthy men were turned away the brothers received much abuse from the officers.[60] The following year Prévost asserted that there were Marine officers who, whenever they were sick, had their servants admitted to the hospital with them. Prévost asked the minister to put a stop to the unjustifiable practice, which cost the royal treasury 25 *sols* per day per servant.[61]

While they were not held responsible for the high costs of patient care in the 1750s, the Brothers of Charity did not go through these years without criticism. In 1753 Jacques Prévost complained to the minister of marine that the brothers' latest superior, Alexis de la Rue, was openly flouting the commissaire-ordonnateur's authority over the Hôpital du Roi; Prévost cited two incidents to support his contention. The first concerned the butchering of meat for the hospital. Prévost explained that until recently the required supply of fresh meat had been prepared by the butchers of Louisbourg. Following Alexis de la Rue's appointment as superior in 1752[62] the practice had changed. De la Rue had begun having cattle slaughtered on the hospital property, presumably in an effort to save money. When the town butchers protested the innovation and the corresponding loss of income Prévost requested Father Alexis to stop butchering until the minister gave his opinion on the subject. De la Rue chose to ignore the commissaire-ordonnateur's request, claiming that the hospital was the convent house of the Brothers of Charity and therefore exempt from normal regulations over matters like butcheries. Prévost did not share that interpretation and turned to the minister for a ruling.

The second incident revolved around a drummer who was injured in a duel and admitted to the hospital. Much to the irritation of the commissaire-ordonnateur, who held principal responsibility for justice in the colony, Governor Raymond tried to take the lead in the investigation of the duel. As the royal officials disputed the case, Alexis de la Rue did what he could to increase his own power and authority within the hospital. According to Prévost, the superior was claiming rights and privileges which were totally unwarranted in a building belonging to the king. As with the butchery issue, the commissaire-ordonnateur asked the minister to put a stop to the superior's pretentions.[63] The minister's response to the above issues has not been found but it is likely that in both cases he gave his support to Prévost.

The 1750s also witnessed charges concerning improper behaviour by the Brothers of Charity. One allegation was that they may not have strictly observed their vows of chastity. In January 1752 Governor Raymond reported to the minister of marine that he had been forced to speak to the brothers, and even send one back to France, because of the irregular lives some of them were leading, especially with regard to women. Raymond blamed the irregularities on the brothers' superior, Boniface Vimeux, who he said was an "honest man" who might have the ability to head a religious community back in France, but was too obliging to do so in the colony. The governor hoped for closer supervision from Vimeux's replacement, Alexis de la Rue.[64] Another critic hinted at sexual irregularities when he claimed that the brothers often went separately to visit their Mira River and Barachois properties where they kept, respectively, a pretty young servant and a young woman.[65] The third person to suggest that some of the brothers were less than chaste was Thomas Pichon. In a work published after his defection to the British, and obviously catering to the anti-Catholic prejudices of his new countrymen, Pichon recalled that during his years in Louisbourg as Governor Raymond's secretary the Brothers of Charity frequently treated civilians in their own homes, a practice which he thought enabled them to do great "mischief." "I believe that if there are some married women who do not complain of them, there may be several husbands who have a great deal to lay to their charge. Indeed in the chirurgical business, the branch which pleases them the most is man-midwifery, and probably they have more reason than one to be fond of it. In short, indecent as these things may appear in the recital, they are far from being exaggerated ... I am for absolutely expelling them all." Other complaints Pichon had of the brothers was that they "generally consult their own profit, and not the preservation of the patient" and that were it not for the governor keeping "a careful eye over their conduct, the poor people that are sent to this hospital, would be sure of being sent to their grave."[66] Largely because of the brothers' improper behaviour, Pichon, like Raymond and several others, thought that Louisbourg and the Hôpital du Roi would be better served if the Order of Saint John of God was replaced by the Grey Sisters.[67]

Yet another complaint during the 1750s was that there were not enough brothers to serve the hospital adequately. The blame for that shortcoming of course did not lie with the brothers in Louisbourg, but with their provincial in France who was responsible for deciding how many religieux were sent to the colony. The problem was first identified in 1749 when colonial officials stated that seven not five brothers would be required.[68] The accuracy of that prediction was soon borne out. In 1750 the commissaire-ordonnateur maintained that with the larger garrison not only were additional brothers required but also more nurses and servants.[69] By the end of 1751 the number of brothers had increased to six, still one short of the desired number. The situation remained the same for several years because the arrival of new religieux appears always to have been balanced by the departure of an equal number of others.

In 1754 a new problem was identified which prompted Jacques Prévost to call for yet another Brother of Charity. Prévost claimed that the Récollet friar assigned to the hospital chapel was often being forced by his superior to neglect his duties to the patients. A shortage of Récollets to meet all the needs of the parish lay behind the problem, but Prévost was not hopeful of more friars coming to the colony. A better solution, he thought, would be to have one of the Brothers of Charity who was ordained as a priest sent out to assume the duties of the hospital chaplain.[70] The idea seems to have been accepted but it is not known when the first priest of the order arrived in the colony. In 1758 a forty-eight-year-old priest named Odilon Bonet was serving in the Louisbourg hospital.[71]

The staff shortage at the Hôpital du Roi at last came to an end in mid-1756. Four Brothers of Charity were dispatched to the colony in the spring, bringing the number of brothers in Louisbourg to seven.[72] Unfortunately, the situation was short-lived. In March 1757 two of them died, in October another passed away, and in November two more expired, among them hospital superior Alexis de la Rue. The impact on the Hôpital du Roi of the five deaths is easily imagined. As of late November 1757 there were but two young, inexperienced brothers left to run the demanding hospital operation. Those two were "rather good fellows, but without experience in medicine or surgery." The commissaire-ordonnateur beseeched both the provincial of the Brothers of Charity and the minister of marine to do everything they could to send out six brothers, at least two of whom were trained surgeons, and four servant nurses at the earliest opportunity in 1758. On the latter point Prévost explained that the hospital had lacked qualified nurses for years. More out of desperation than choice the practice had been to use soldiers in that capacity. But by 1757 the soldiers did not want such jobs anymore, the chances of illness or infection being too great.[73]

The plight of the Louisbourg hospital was quickly and fully appreciated. By January 1758 it was decided that the first ships to sail to Ile Royale in the spring would carry six Brothers of Charity and six garçon infirmiers (apprentice or servant nurses). One of these brothers, Potentin Bernard, was named to be the new, and as it turned out the last, superior of the Hôpital du Roi.[74]

A short time after the contingent reached Louisbourg the town was blockaded and besieged by British sea and land forces. The first troops came ashore at Kennington Cove on 8 June. The very next day Odilon Bonet, the priest sent out by the order to serve the hospital, passed away. His death was apparently unconnected with the assult because the first enemy battery did not commence firing until 19 June. Thereafter, until the French capitulated on 26 July, the firing was often heavy, with numerous casualties and great damage done to the town. On 20 June a Brother of Charity named Pasteur Harreault was killed after being hit by a cannon shot.[75] During the night of 6 July mortar bombs rained down on the town. One struck the Hôpital du Roi, killing the surgeon-major of one of the regiments and mortally wounding two of the brothers. The hospital was evidently seriously damaged for on the following day Governor Drucour requested Admiral Boscawen to provide a location where the French sick and wounded could be treated. Boscawen offered Drucours the choice of either the island where the Island Battery was or a vessel anchored in the harbour.[76] Drucour's answer is not known. Less than three weeks later the siege was over, with about 100 French dead and over 200 injured.[77]

The workload of the four remaining Brothers of Charity in the last weeks of the siege and then afterward must have been tremendous. Certainly the costs they incurred were extremely high. The value of food, drugs, supplies, and care they provided during the 1758 ordeal was placed at over 22,000 *livres*, a debt which was finally settled in May 1760.[78] The year before, the four brothers who had accompanied the soldiers and inhabitants of Louisbourg to France had been given other assignments within their order.[79]

The years the Brothers of Charity spent on Ile Royale were not easy years. The hospitals in which they served, even the impressive Hôpital du Roi, had definite limitations and drawbacks in terms of furnishings and supplies. Moreover, relations with local royal officials were often stormy, with disputes over the cost and quality of health care as well as over other issues such as the kinds of cases that could be admitted for treatment. A few of the brothers were judged to be incompetent and there were calls to have the hospital run by a rival medical order, the Grey Sisters. But perhaps the most serious problem to face the brothers, particularly during the 1750s, seems to have been a simple lack of trained staff in the hospital. Working in a hospital in the eighteenth century had its risks at the best of times, so little protected was the medical staff from infection and disease. With the shortage of qualified personnel which sometimes existed at the Hôpital du Roi, the risks must have been higher and the work that much more arduous. Compounding the situation at Louisbourg were the sudden arrival in port of ships carrying sick and diseased crewmen and the two sieges, with their terrible impact on the town. The demands and difficulties of the work at Louisbourg apparently took its toll on the Brothers of Charity. In the course of the thirty-eight years the order served there, thirteen brothers passed away in the town and another died at sea.[80]

The years of sacrifice and service on Ile Royale were finally commemorated in 1938, 180 years after the last brother had sailed from the colony. In that year a monument to the Brothers of Charity who had served at Louisbourg was raised on Rochefort point, just beyond the ruins of the historic town.[81]

4 The Sisters of the Congregation of Notre-Dame and Female Education

... a kind of religious women, different from nuns. They do not live in a convent, but have houses both in the town and country ... Their business is to instruct young girls in the Christian religion, to teach them reading, writing, needle-work, and other female accomplishments.
Peter Kalm, *Travels into North America* (1749)[1]

In modern English usage the term "education" generally refers to the teaching and learning process which occurs within a formal setting or institution, such as a school or university. Older meanings of the word, relating to a person's background and breeding, are seldom used any more. In French, however, *éducation* has retained the denotations referring to behaviour and moral development. Two centuries ago those two broader meanings of the word predominated. Eighteenth-century definitions mentioned not only the cultivation of intelligence but also the inculcation of proper manners, morals, and physical health. Charles Pinot DuClos, novelist, historiographer, and moralist in eighteenth-century France, was typical in that he distinguished clearly between *instruction* and *éducation*. In his opinion there was an ample amount of the former but far too little of the latter in French society.[2]

When one spoke of someone else's education it was understood that he was referring to nearly every aspect of how that person was raised. Antisocial or crude behaviour, for instance, was thought to reveal a want of education. One dictionary expressed the relationship in this way: "It is said that a crude and uncivil person is one that has no education."[3] Similarly, one's religion and morality were thought to reflect his or her education. Bishop Saint-Vallier had that idea in his mind when he wrote in the *Rituel* for the Diocese of Québec that the purpose of marriage was to have children and to educate, or raise, them with their salvation in mind. This was made clear to each couple near the end of the wedding ceremony when the priest informed them that they were to bring up their children "with a holy and Christian education."[4]

The behavioural aspects of the eighteenth-century concept of education naturally carried over into formal or institutional education. The development of religious and moral principles in young people was viewed as an essential element in the learning process. According to DuClos, virtues and vices were both inherent in the human heart. It was only after the former had been cultivated and the latter suppressed, through education, that instruction on particular subjects could begin. Given such a perspective, it was not surprising that formal education in *ancien régime* France was left principally to the Roman Catholic church. In each diocese the bishop represented "the virtual minister of public instruction."[5]

The situation was slightly different in New France because there the state often provided the financial support without which many of the schools might not have existed. Beyond the question of funding, however, royal officials were interested in little more than the end result a sound education could provide, namely a moral and loyal populace. The learning process itself was considered principally a religious concern. The subject matter reflected that perspective, filled as it was with devotional reading material.

Many if not most of the people who taught in New France belonged to the clergy. What lay teachers there were came under a substantial degree of clerical control. An ordinance issued in Canada in 1727 stipulated that all lay instructors in the colony had to obtain the approval of both the intendant and the bishop of Québec before being allowed to teach. Thereafter, parish priests were to keep a close eye on them. To help ensure that nothing untoward developed in their classes, unmarried teachers were forbidden to instruct children of the opposite sex. The nature of the ordinance and the fact that it seems to have been "the only legislation on schools passed during the French regime"[6] demonstrate clearly the pre-eminent role which the church played in colonial educational matters.

With regard to Ile Royale, the attitude of officials in France toward formal education is probably best described as uninterested. The need to set up or supervise schools in the new settlements was never once discussed by the minister of marine during the detailed preparations for the founding of the colony in 1713. Possibly the minister, the comte de Pontchartrain, assumed that the Récollet missionaries being sent to the island would open parish schools for the colonists' children. Just as likely, however, the minister never gave a thought as to how the young people of Ile Royale would be educated. As it was a moral and religious matter, he probably assumed that the bishop and the *religieux* would do whatever was necessary.

The colonial administration's lack of concern about education on Ile Royale continued well after the initial settlement period, when it could be argued that the relatively small number of children did not warrant the establishment of any schools.[7] By the mid-1720s that was hardly the case, as there were then over 300 children in Louisbourg.[8] Yet the attitude of the imperial authorities remained the same. The minister still did not believe that any special effort was required to bring teachers into the community.[9]

The minister's view was not shared by royal officials at the local level, who knew the situation first-hand. As a rule, the governors and commissaires-ordonnateurs of Ile Royale generally demonstrated considerable interest in educational matters in Louisbourg. In fact, the first recorded proposal for a school in the town came from Commissaire-ordonnateur Mézy in late 1720. Mézy recommended to the Conseil de Marine that it undertake the construction of a school building at Louisbourg out of royal funds, as one of several ways to foster in the colonists a feeling of attachment to the new settlement. The other edifices which he thought would contribute to the growth of a community spirit were a parish church, hôtel de ville, and hospital. The commissaire-ordonnateur described the public school he envisioned as a place where the children of the town "could attend daily to receive religious instruction and learn how to read and write."[10] The fact that Mézy placed the inculcation of religious faith and values before instruction in reading and writing was not accidental. Rather, it was consistent with the prevailing view of the time, "education" before "instruction."

Mézy's suggestion to build a school was not acted upon by the Conseil de Marine, nor by successive ministers of marine. Since the educational needs of the town were increasing with each passing year, royal officials in Louisbourg then tried a different tack. Commencing in the mid-1720s the governor and commissaire-ordonnateur forwarded proposals to France suggesting that an order of teaching sisters be sent to the colony. Not surprisingly, when that eventually did happen, in 1727, it occurred without the support of the Marine officials in France.

In later years, local officials continued to show an interest in education at Louisbourg by initiating or backing a variety of projects. One particularly noteworthy supporter of such projects was the comte de Raymond, commandant of Ile Royale from 1751 to 1754. During his few years in the colony Raymond not only established schools of mathematics and artillery for officers and cadets in the garrison, but he also gave a qualified sergeant an unconditional discharge so that he could open a school for the "young people of the town." Raymond encouraged any officer or cadet who could not already read or write to attend this school.[11] That there were young men of that rank at Louisbourg who were not literate is not really surprising. In contemporary Canada, where the educational opportunities were greater, it was the opinion of one observer, undoubtedly a visiting Frenchman contemptuous of the level of sophistication in the colony, that "even the children of the officers and gentlemen scarcely know how to read and write; they are ignorant of the first elements of geography and history."[12]

As stated above, notwithstanding the encouragement and assistance which officials on Ile Royale gave to educational projects, there was little support for such efforts from the Ministry of Marine in France. Not until 1757 did their general attitude seem to change. In that year a Sr Magellon was given the assignment to go to Ile Royale to study virtually every aspect of life. Among the subject areas he was to report on was the possibility of establishing public schools at Louisbourg where the sons of colonists could learn useful sciences. Mentioned specifically were geometry, physics, rural economy, and navigation. The traditional role of education was not overlooked for the projected public schools were described as places where the students would learn their obligations to God and king.[13] Illness prevented Magellon from sailing to Ile Royale and conducting his study, but the fall of Louisbourg in 1758 would have rendered his recommendations useless in any case.

To return to the 1720s, the period when the first major step in the field of education was taken at Louisbourg, we must look at the educational opportunities that existed in the town at the time. In general, they were quite limited. Boys or adolescents accepted as cadets in the garrison were to receive specialized education in such subjects as writing, mathematics, fortifications, hydrography, fencing, and dance; at least when there were competent instructors available. But there were relatively few cadet positions, at the time only one for each military company, and entrance was limited to the sons of officers. For boys who might have hoped for a professional career at sea Jean-René Cruchon offered instruction in navigation and hydrography, yet most parents probably could not have afforded the classes. Their best hope for giving their children, especially their sons, an education was in the area of "manual" education (that is, apprenticeship training in a craft or trade).[14] As for "formal" education, one schoolmaster was identified on the 1715 census and a few others were mentioned in 1730,[15] but there are no details about them or their schools. Since they had no subsidies from the royal treasury it is safe to conclude that their tuition fees would have been out of the reach of the vast majority of parents, had they been interested in having their children learn to read and write. As for those parents who could have afforded the tuition, the background of the teachers and the quality of the education they offered would have been the major concerns. In the event that they were less than satisfied with either aspect they were left with two options.

The first was to hire a tutor from among the group of clerks, professionals, and other educated people in the town. In that way children might learn to read, write, and do arithmetic as well as how to master such social graces as dancing.[16] The second option was to send their children to France or Canada for schooling and general edification. Probably typical of the adolescents who were sent to France was fourteen-year old Antoine Perré, a son of a well-to-do widow who was active in the Ile Royale fishery. Perré boarded for several years in the Breton town of Saint-Servant, where he received instruction from three different teachers in writing, arithmetic, dancing, violin playing, and navigation.[17]

Most parents at Louisbourg of course could not have afforded to pay local tutors or to send their children to Canada or France. The amount of formal education which their children were receiving in the 1720s was probably minimal. Occasional teaching by a relative, if there was a literate relative with the time and inclination for such things, was one possibility. Rudimentary instruction in reading and writing by the Récollet parish priests was another. The Récollets, however, were always better known for their piety and poverty than for their learning and scholarly accomplishments.[18] Catechism classes excluded, there is not a single piece of evidence suggesting that the Récollets ever ran a parish school in Louisbourg. Indeed, in 1751, the bishop of Québec's vicar-general in France complained to the minister of marine that the Récollets at Louisbourg were failing to provide the range of services usually offered by parish priests. According to Abbé de l'Isle-Dieu, the Récollets "neglect everything: instructions, confessions, administration of the sacraments, visits to the sick, catechism of the children; nothing is accomplished and everything is neglected."[19]

If one can judge by such assessments, whatever instruction the friars might have offered to the children of the town would not have been very edifying. Certainly during the 1720s the bishops of Québec did not feel that girls growing up in Louisbourg were receiving the kind of upbringing they needed. According to reports they had received, the children there were "almost completely without the necessary means for Christian education." Parents who wanted to have their children well educated had to send them to Canada, the "girls as well as the boys, to obtain a good education." Not only did children of Louisbourg possess "bad morals" but they were ignorant of the basic principles of their religion.[20] In the bishops' opinion the remedy was to send teaching sisters to Ile Royale. The group they had in mind was the Congregation of Notre-Dame.

Founded by St Marguerite Bourgeoys in the seventeenth century, the Congregation of Notre-Dame was a community of non-cloistered nuns dedicated to the education of females. In addition to vows of poverty, chastity and obedience they also took a vow to teach girls. Their motherhouse was in Montréal, but they established schools throughout New France. In 1731 there were sisters in twelve different missions.[21] By 1760 there were seventy *religieuses* belonging to the Congregation, more than twice as many as the next largest group of nuns in the colony.[22] Competent and dedicated, the Sisters of the Congregation earned the respect and admiration of their contemporaries. The only negative comment on record is by Louis Franquet, an engineer who came to New France during the 1750s. Franquet acknowledged the educational achievements of the sisters, but echoing the current of opinion in Europe on the dangers of over-education, he suggested that their very success had unfortunate social and economic ramifications. According to Franquet the Sisters of the Congregation were helping to depopulate the Canadian countryside by giving young women aspirations to better themselves in the major settlements of the colony. He believed that the girls educated by the sisters tended to turn away both from traditional roles and "from the work of their fathers." To avoid that development Franquet urged that the daughters of the colonial farmers be given no more education than that provided by parish priests in catechism classes.[23]

Bishop Saint-Vallier obviously did not share Franquet's anxieties, at least in so far as Ile Royale was concerned. For three successive years beginning in 1724 he proposed to the minister of marine that sisters from the Congregation of Notre-Dame be sent to Louisbourg to establish a school there. Each time the minister rejected the idea as premature, even though the governor and commissaire-ordonnateur supported the proposal.[24] Saint-Vallier had equal difficulty winning the backing of the superior of the Sisters of the Congregation in the motherhouse at Montréal. Marguerite Trottier (Sœur Saint-Joseph) who was later to go to Ile Royale herself, pointed out two obstacles. First, there was the question of financial support for any sisters to go to Louisbourg. Who was to provide for the nuns' subsistence? Second, the rules of the community specified that only secular priests could provide spiritual direction to the sisters. Since the Louisbourg parish was the exclusive domain of the Récollets, who were regular clergy, who would provide the spiritual guidance?

Regarding the latter concern, the bishop undoubtedly hoped that the Le Dorz controversy then raging would soon be settled by handing over the parish to secular priests. As for the financial question, it depended on obtaining royal funding, which had so far been denied. Without substantial state support he must have realized that the sisters' stay on Ile Royale would be filled with hardship. Nonetheless, by 1727 Saint-Vallier apparently felt that the educational and moral plight of the young girls of Louisbourg was so great that solutions to some problems would have to be found later. In declining health and with his dream of having "teaching houses in the farthest reaches of his immense diocese" still unfulfilled, he set out to rectify the situation at Louisbourg in unusual fashion. On his own authority and in defiance of the wishes of both the minister of marine and the superior of the Congregation of Notre-Dame, Bishop Saint-Vallier dispatched a teaching sister to the colony.[25]

The person Saint-Vallier chose to go to Ile Royale was fifty-three-year-old Marguerite Roy (Sœur de la Conception). At the time the sister was under his immediate spiritual direction because she had had a "dispute with the confessor of the community, who did not attach much importance to her visions." An excellent teacher with "high aspirations and ... [an] inclination towards the miraculous," Marguerite Roy was more than willing to participate in the bishop's plan to establish a school at Louisbourg. Later events were to demonstrate, however, that the sister's zeal was not matched by her ability to administer temporal matters. Accompanied by two lay assistants, Roy sailed to Ile Royale in the summer of 1727.[26] Her spiritual director on arrival was Father Joseph Denys, a Récollet of Paris then in Louisbourg as the bishop's vicar-general.[27] In October she opened a school which by mid-December had twenty-two boarders.[28]

Until January 1729 one of Marguerite Roy's assistants in the school was Marie-Magdelaine Nöel. Nöel, aged twenty-five, died that month with "an exemplary Devotion to the spirit of the Congregation which she has aspired to join for a long time." Her aspiration was fulfilled a few hours before her death when Zacharie Caradec, vicar-general of the bishop of Québec, accepted her religious profession. She was buried the next day in the town lot reserved for the construction of a parish church.[29]

The governor and commissaire-ordonnateur were very pleased with the beginning which Marguerite Roy and her assistants had made at Louisbourg. They were also hopeful that the minister of marine would provide financial assistance now that a sister had actually come to the colony. They proposed that a portion of the money from the sale of goods salvaged from the wreck of the *Chameau* (which had sunk in 1725) be used to establish the sisters in the town.[30] The minister was not immediately agreeable to either suggestion. But two and a half years later, in April 1730, it was agreed that an annual subsidy of 1,500 *livres* would be paid to the Congregation of Notre-Dame for a mission at Louisbourg consisting of three nuns.[31]

With a royal allowance assured, Roy decided to acquire a property where she could set up a permanent mission, accommodate boarders, and open schools for students.[32] Shortly after her arrival in the colony in 1727 the governor and commissaire-ordonnateur estimated that she could acquire a suitable house for 8,000 *livres* or less.[33] When she finally made a purchase three years later she selected the Block 20 property of military officer and engineer Josué Du Bois Berthelot de Beaucours. With a large residence, storehouse, yard, garden, and outbuildings the property certainly met the sister's needs. However, the initial cost was 15,000 *livres*, a figure subsequently reduced by the vendor to 10,000 *livres* as a favour to the religious community. By the terms of the sale the sister was obliged to pay Beaucours 1,000 *livres* a year, thereby committing two-thirds of the royal subsidy to mortgage payments and leaving little for food, firewood, and other necessities of life. To say the least, the purchase was not an astute move. By 1731 Roy was seeking additional assistance from the royal treasury to help pay for the property she had acquired. The minister of marine politely informed her that such assistance was currently unavailable.[34] The sister's financial difficulties are illustrated by the fact that in 1732 she was able to pay only 788 *livres* to Beaucours and a year later the figure was down to 500 *livres* (see Table 6).

Trying as the financial problems were, Roy was next faced with an outright attempt to have her withdrawn from Louisbourg and recalled to Montréal. The driving force behind the attempt was Pierre-Herman Dosquet, coadjutor to the absentee bishop of Québec. Maintaining that she was not suited to be the superior of the mission, Dosquet prevented three nuns from the motherhouse from sailing to Louisbourg in 1732. He explained that he considered Marguerite Roy "the most deceitful, the most scheming nun, and the one most filled with illusions that I know."[35]

The governor and commissaire-ordonnateur of Ile Royale complained to the minister of marine about Dosquet's action and offered a completely different assessment. They asserted that the sister was beloved and respected by the colonists and served as an edifying presence in the town.[36] An example of the high regard in which Roy was held, although this case was not mentioned by the royal officials, was the fact that in 1730 a woman subject to repeated beatings by her husband chose the sister's convent as a place of refuge for herself and her children.[37] Roy, on her own behalf, wrote to the minister stressing that she had gone to Ile Royale only because she was asked to by Bishop Saint-Vallier. After Saint-Vallier's death in late 1727 his successor, Bishop Mornay, had permitted her to continue her work on the island. In light of the previous bishops' approval she requested the minister to intercede with Dosquet to allow her to remain at Louisbourg and to have additional sisters sent out from Montréal. The minister discussed the subject with Dosquet, who was soon to become the fourth bishop of Québec, while the latter was in France dur-

TABLE 6
Payments on Beaucours Property by Sisters of the Congregation of Notre Dame, 1730–40
(to nearest *livre tournois*)

Year	Total Paid	Principal	Interest	Amount Outstanding
1730	1,500			
1731	1,000			
1732	788			8,045
1733	500			7,545
1734	650	273	377	7,271
1735	532	168	364	7,103
1736	922	567	355	6,536
1737	993a	666	327	5,870
1738	160	–	160	6,034b
1739	2,400	2,100	300	3,904c
1740	1,500	1,305	195	2,599d

SOURCES: *Histoire de la Congrégation de Notre-Dame de Montréal, pt. 2, XVIIIe Siècle*
4: 91–2; AN, Outre Mer, G2, vol. 190, reg. IV, fols. 11, 11v., 1733.

a   Figure in original source, apparently a miscalculation, has been changed

b   Minimum interest charges not met so balance owing increased

c   Correct figure appears to be 3,934

d   If the balance for 1739 was 3,934, the figure here should be 2,629

ing the winter of 1732–3. At the conclusion of those discussions the minister had come to agree that Marguerite Roy had to be withdrawn from Louisbourg.[38]

In the spring of 1733 the minister's decision was communicated to the royal officials on Ile Royale. The governor and commissaire-ordonnateur had no choice but to comply. It is worth noting that while they did so they felt obliged to point out that the sister's departure would constitute a serious loss to the Louisbourg community. The loss would be felt all the more acutely by the inhabitants, stated the local officials, because of the great charity Roy had shown during the recent smallpox epidemic, when she had taken more than twenty young orphaned girls into the convent house.[39]

In August 1733, while Marguerite Roy was probably preparing to leave Louisbourg, the three sisters who were to replace her were chosen at the motherhouse of the Congregation of Notre-Dame. Selected as the new superior of the Louisbourg mission was fifty-five-year-old Marguerite Trottier (Sœur Saint-Joseph), who had formerly been superior of the entire Congregation. Marie-Joseph Lefebvre-Belle-Isle (Sœur Saint-Benoît) and

Marie-Marguerite-Daniel Arnaud (Sœur Saint-Arsène), aged forty and thirty-four respectively, were named to accompany the new superior to Louisbourg.[40] Because of the great distance from the motherhouse to Ile Royale, the bishop gave them special permission to accept novices in their mission at Louisbourg. He also granted them the freedom to return to Canada whenever they felt that their establishment could be taken over by sisters recruited on the island colony. The king approved both measures.[41]

The three sisters selected in August did not sail for Ile Royale until autumn, arriving in Louisbourg fairly late in the shipping season. As a result, Roy was forced to wait until 1734 before returning to Montréal.[42] When she finally made the voyage, after seven years in the colony, it must have been with feelings of profound disappointment and bitterness. Considered a "useless burden to her community," Marguerite Roy spent her remaining years in the motherhouse "in humility, obscurity and silence." She died in December 1749, aged seventy-five.[43]

Though gone from Louisbourg, Roy left behind two legacies for the sisters who took her place. One was a legacy of admiration and good will on the part of the colonists,[44] sentiments which her successors continued to foster. Abbé Pierre Maillard, vicar-general on Ile Royale during the 1740s and 1750s, asserted in 1738 that after the arrival of the Sisters of the Congregation the whole moral tone of Louisbourg had markedly improved. Maillard stated that before the "good sisters" came to Louisbourg the inhabitants "scarcely partook of the Eucharist at Eastertime such was the state of Religion," but since their arrival, because of their good example, parishioners were taking the sacrament much more often, "nearly every Sunday and feast day."[45] Even Thomas Pichon, who generally had so little good to say about the religious of Ile Royale, admired the sisters and described the ones he knew in the 1750s as "women of true piety."[46]

The second legacy was one of debilitating financial difficulties. Those problems began with Marguerite Roy's purchase of a property far beyond her means but they certainly did not end there. Throughout their years at Louisbourg the lives of the Sisters of the Congregation of Notre-Dame were filled with hardship. Indeed, soon after Marguerite Trottier took over the mission she wrote to her superior in Montréal asking for assistance. She and the two other sisters were often ill and found it difficult to cope with teaching the boarders and day students as well as doing the many household tasks. The superior of the Congregation responded quickly to the call for help. Two sisters, Françoise Boucher de Montbrun (Saint-Placide) and Marie-Geneviève Hervieux (Sainte-Gertrude), and a novice named Catherine Paré were sent to the colony from the motherhouse in 1734. Two years later, in the second religious profession in the history of

Cape Breton, the novice took her vows and adopted the religious name of Sœur Saint-Louis-des-Anges.[47]

The additional sisters were undoubtedly of great help in operating the schools and running the house. In financial terms, however, they represented only another drain on the royal subsidy, which was fixed at 1,500 *livres* regardless of how many sisters the Congregation sent to Louisbourg. Trottier found it impossible to both live comfortably and make the full 1,000 *livres* mortgage payments. In 1734 she paid only 650 *livres* and the year after but 532 *livres*. In each case well over half of the money went to pay off interest charges (see Table 6).

The governor and commissaire-ordonnateur offered what help they could in two ways. First, they designated the sisters as the recipients of fines imposed for the violation of different police regulations.[48] Second, they purchased bedclothes and straw ticks from the sisters for use in the soldiers' barracks and in the Hôpital du Roi. Income from that source was not insignificant: 294 *livres* in 1734 and 358 *livres* in 1735.[49]

In the fall of 1735 M. Lyon de Saint-Ferréol, a vicar-general of the bishop, stopped in Louisbourg on his way to France. Pleased with the sisters' work, he observed that they were deserving of special funding to pay for their house, as well as royal letters patent officially establishing them on Ile Royale.[50] The minister of marine replied that the king was sympathetic to the sisters' needs, but not currently able to provide either financial assistance or letters patent.[51]

By the fall of 1737 the sisters' situation was such that the governor and commissaire-ordonnateur worried that they would be forced to abandon their mission at Louisbourg. The attempt to make the annual mortgage payment was leaving the six sisters without enough to live on, and forcing them to borrow money and become increasingly indebted. Fearful that Louisbourg might soon find itself without this group of exemplary teachers, the colonial officials asked the minister to consider the possibility of special help, either to pay off the current mortgage or to buy a new house.[52] The request was greeted first with surprise, then rejection. The minister relayed the king's pointed remark that the earlier call for letters patent implied the Sisters of the Congregation were well established at Louisbourg, a supposition which was apparently not correct.[53] Notwithstanding the negative response yet another appeal for aid was made in 1738.[54] The plight of the sisters was probably at its worst that year, since they fell far short of paying even the interest charges on their mortgage (see Table 6). When royal officials placed a number of orphan girls with the sisters in late 1738, food from the king's storehouse was supplied to ensure that the girls would subsist over the winter.[55] In mid-1739 the repeated pleas for aid for the Congregation were at last successful. In June the minister of marine announced that in both 1739 and 1740, 1,500 *livres* would be given to the sisters to help pay for their house.[56] The special subsidy cut the outstanding principal in half. Moreover, it probably enabled Marguerite Trottier to spend the annual grant on some neglected areas of concern in the school.

If the Sisters of the Congregation felt disappointment over the expiry in 1740 of the two-year subsidy, it was more than offset by another development that year. In May the latest governor of Ile Royale, Isaac-Louis de Forant, died after having designated the sisters as his principal beneficiaries. Forant's decision, made after having been in the colony for only eight months, testifies both to his own philanthropic nature and to the need and worthiness of the Louisbourg sisters. By the terms of the will the money from the estate was to be used to pay room, board, and tuition expenses at the sisters' school for the daughters of eight officers in the Louisbourg garrison. Should there be fewer than eight girls eligible to take advantage of the bequest, the remaining money was to be used by the Louisbourg Congregation to cover its many expenses. Forant's sister contested aspects of the will so that a final settlement was not made until 1742, when the Sisters of the Congregation were awarded 32,000 *livres*. The sum was invested in France at five per cent, thereby providing the sisters with 1,600 *livres* a year in interest payments.[57] The Louisbourg mission appeared to be on the threshold of long-term financial security.

While the sisters awaited the settlement of Governor de Forant's estate they again resorted to making straw mattresses for the barracks and even flags for the Micmacs to generate additional income.[58] When the interest on the Forant foundation began, in either 1742 or 1743, Trottier and the other sisters must have thought that with it and the 1,500 *livres* from the royal treasury their days of deprivation were over. The king, however, did not see the need to continue the royal grant now that the Congregation of Notre-Dame was receiving a substantial income from a private source. The grant was stopped in 1743[59] because royal largesse was apparently reserved for groups in greater need than the Louisbourg Congregation. As a result the sisters found themselves with almost the same income they had received since coming to Louisbourg, although the amount outstanding on their mortgage had been greatly reduced in the intervening years.

The hardships of those years took their toll of the sisters, particularly Marguerite Trottier. In the autumn of 1744, in failing health after eleven arduous years on Ile Royale, the sixty-six-year-old superior of the Louisbourg mission sailed for the motherhouse in Montréal. Accompanying and caring for her on the voyage was her cousin and fellow sister, Marie-

Joseph Belle-Isle. Trottier did not live to set foot again on Canadian soil. She died aboard the ship as it approached Québec on 6 October and two days later was buried in the cathedral.[60]

On Ile Royale Sister Marie-Marguerite Arnaud became the new superior of the mission. Roughly eight months after she assumed that position Louisbourg was blockaded, besieged, and captured by a British naval force and troops from New England. In the course of the assault the Congregation's house, probably finally paid for, was severely damaged. After the town capitulated the British are alleged to have pillaged the sisters' possessions and supplies. As for the building itself, what was left of it was converted into a guardhouse during the years of British occupation.[61] The four sisters with their boarders were transported to France as was nearly every other colonist. They reached the port of Rochefort on 24 August 1745. From there they made their way to La Rochelle where they lodged in a hospital for orphan girls, the Hôpital Saint-Etienne. On 17 September forty-four-year-old Sister Françoise Boucher de Montbrun passed away, quite likely a victim of the transatlantic crossing.[62]

The remaining sisters spent the next four years at La Rochelle, awaiting the outcome of first the War of the Austrian Succession and then the peace negotiations at Aix-la-Chapelle. Their stay there was not a happy one. They received neither the ration allowance given to most of the refugees from Ile Royale nor the full financial assistance allotted to them by the minister of marine. On the latter point the problem lay not with the minister, who authorized payments to the Louisbourg Congregation, but with lower-level officials who did not carry out his instructions. In 1746 the sisters finally received a lump sum payment of 1,040 *livres* from the royal treasury. The amount helped but it was not sufficient to cover all their room and board and other expenses at the hospital.

Fortunately, for two years the sisters continued to receive their 1,600 *livres* from the Forant foundation. Then it was stopped because they were no longer meeting the terms of the bequest. Living in misery and sickness the Sisters of the Congregation enlisted the support of the bishop of Québec's vicar-general in France, Abbé de l'Isle-Dieu. Isle-Dieu repeatedly petitioned the minister and the king on their behalf. Another who offered advice and help was Abbé Le Loutre, the missionary to the Micmacs of Nova Scotia. During a 1747 visit to La Rochelle, Le Loutre tried to persuade the sisters to sail aboard a king's ship soon to leave for Canada, where they could rejoin the motherhouse. Fearful of the voyage itself, as well as the possibility of capture by the British, the Sisters of the Congregation would not even consider it. Partly because of their refusal to accept that offer there was little sympathy in official circles for the sisters' situation at La Rochelle. When Abbé de l'Isle-Dieu sought financial aid for them he was told bluntly that their expenses would not have mounted so high had they returned to Canada in 1747.[63]

Isle-Dieu's only success in obtaining aid for the Louisbourg Congregation appears to have been with the duc d'Orléans, uncle of Louis XV. Thanks to the persuasiveness of the vicar-general the duc bequeathed an annual income of 100 livres to the Louisbourg mission in his December 1749 will.[64] With the signing of the treaty in the fall of 1748, by which the British handed Ile Royale back to France, the sisters' reluctance to sail on the high seas disappeared. In the summer of 1749, along with hundreds of former residents of the colony, sisters Arnaud, Hervieux, and Paré set sail from France. Before they left Bishop Pontbriand had suggested that the Congregation might take over the operation of the Louisbourg Hôpital du Roi,[65] but not surprisingly the idea received no support. The sisters were an educational community, not a medical order.

According to an agreement worked out before leaving France, the annual royal grant of 1,500 livres would again be paid to the Sisters of the Congregation once they reestablished schools in Louisbourg.[66] As soon as the sisters arrived in the town they discovered how difficult that would be. Their residence on Block 20, so long a cause of hardship, was no longer habitable. The sisters were forced to borrow 500 livres from a local military officer, Michel de Gannes de Falaise, to rent another house. It was so much smaller than their former residence that relatively few children could be instructed there. Of the many girls presented Arnaud decided to admit only thirty, those closest to making their first communion. Parents whose daughters were not accepted were understandably displeased by the situation.[67]

The sisters themselves were frustrated both by their inability to accept more children and by the income which was lost as a consequence. In 1749 their poor financial position forced them once again to make straw mattresses for the soldiers' barracks.[68] The governor and commissaire-ordonnateur of Ile Royale and the intendant of New France all wrote to the minister of marine asking that royal funds be provided for the construction of a large house for the use of the Congregation.[69] The minister rejected the requests, claiming that the sisters were entitled to about 12,000 livres in accumulated interest payments from the Forant foundation.[70] Unfortunately for the sisters, the minister seems to have been misinformed on that point. When the religious community stopped meeting the terms of Forant's will, by failing to provide accommodation for officers' daughters, it ceased to be entitled to the annual interest payments. Far from having a large sum of money to draw on, the Louisbourg Congregation was virtually destitute.

Compounding the financial troubles of the sisters was a personal tragedy in their midst. Soon after their return to Ile Royale, sixty-three-year-old

Sister Hervieux was struck with paralysis and became unable to utter anything other than "Fiat" ("Let it be done"). When news of the sister's condition reached the motherhouse it was decided that she must return to Montréal. In 1751 Sisters Marie Patenôtre (Sainte-Thècle) and Marie Robichaud (Saint-Vincent-de-Paul) were sent to replace both her and Catherine Paré. Remaining in Louisbourg as the superior of the mission was Marie-Marguerite Arnaud. The superior and the two new sisters were assisted in their work by two lay assistants.[71]

For the next two years the sisters struggled along as best they could with their small rented house and meagre income. In Thomas Pichon's words, they had "hardly either lodging or victuals to eat."[72] Various attempts were made to secure them additional money, including a proposal in 1752 to give them the proceeds from the sale of 2,000 livres worth of pitch and tar confiscated from a British ship.[73] That proposal and all others seem to have been rejected.

In 1753 the fortunes of the Congregation appeared to take a turn for the better. Returning from France, Abbé Le Loutre informed the sisters that royal funds would soon be forthcoming to pay for the construction of a new commodious residence on their Block 20 property. On the strength of Le Loutre's assurances Arnaud borrowed money for the project and the work began. By early October 1753 a large supply of materials had been purchased and much of the timber framing erected. A few months more and the sisters would probably have again been able to accept boarders and expand their schools for day students. But at that point fate intervened to give the Congregation yet another setback. On Sunday, 7 October 1753, a violent hurricane struck Louisbourg, driving a reported fifty vessels ashore. Among the buildings damaged in town was that of the Sisters of the Congregation. The frame of their new house was blown down and most of the materials on the property destroyed. Three days after the calamity the sisters wrote to the minister of marine beseeching him to secure the financial aid Abbé Le Loutre had said was earmarked for them. Deeply in debt and with nothing to show for their expenditures, they asked the minister to use his influence with the king to obtain the funds to build another residence.[74] The appeal was unsuccessful. The governor and commissaire-ordonnateur, as well as Abbé de l'Isle-Dieu, petitioned the minister on behalf of the sisters, but also to no avail.[75] It must have seemed to the Sisters of the Congregation that they had been forgotten in France.

In Louisbourg the sisters certainly were neither forgotten nor unappreciated. Although local officials could not allocate large sums of royal funds to the Congregation, a way was found in 1754 by which a sizeable sum of money could be given to them. In that year the commissaire-ordonnateur, Jacques Prévost, issued a regulation fixing the number of cabarets in the town at twenty-eight and compelling all owners to obtain a licence which was valid for three years' operation. The fee for the licence was set at 10 *pistoles* (about 215 *livres*), all of which was to go to the sisters.[76] If every cabaret owner had paid the full fee the Louisbourg Congregation would have received roughly 6,000 *livres*. At least some of the money appears to have made its way to the sisters for indications are that with additional sacrifices and new loans they were finally able in 1755 or early 1756 to rebuild on their property.[77]

Given the lack of financial backing from the royal treasury the erection of the new residence was a definite achievement. Yet the debts and concomitant hardship continued to take their toll of the sisters. By late 1757 the governor and commissaire-ordonnateur of Ile Royale reported that the superior, Arnaud, had asked several times for permission to return to the motherhouse in Montréal. The Congregation was simply "unable to subsist and pay its debts." Praising their conduct, zeal, and usefulness, the officials once again asked the minister of marine for special funding which would enable the sisters to stay in the colony and fulfil their teaching role.[78] The latest minister, François-Marie de Moras, was sympathetic to the plea. He replied in April 1758 that he would ask the king for a special subsidy. In the meantime supplies could be distributed to the Sisters of the Congregation "to enable them to survive."[79]

Moras' encouraging response may never have reached the sisters. Six weeks after he wrote, Louisbourg was under British naval blockade and land assault. For Marie-Marguerite Arnaud, who had already lived through one siege and lengthy exile, the events which followed the capitulation on 26 July must have been painfully familiar. Once again the inhabitants of the town were deported to France. Shortly before the sisters sailed, Marie Patenôtre developed a high fever. Her fellow *religieuses* attempted to have her departure delayed but without success. The sister's condition worsened aboard ship and ten days out of Louisbourg she died (at about the age of thirty-eight) and was buried at sea. When the remaining members of the mission, two sisters and two lay assistants, reached France they were sent to the same hospital in La Rochelle where the Congregation had lived from 1745 to 1749.[80]

In financial terms the second stay at the Hôpital Saint-Etienne was much more comfortable than the first. They received the 1,600 *livres* in interest payments from the Forant foundation every year until 1764. In addition, each member of the community, a lay assistant included, was awarded an annual royal pension of 250 *livres*. Until at least 1764 the Sisters of the Congregation continued to instruct several girls from a group of Louisbourg refugees at La Rochelle. Though they were not in great hardship both Sisters Arnaud and Robichaud longed to return to Montréal and the confines of the motherhouse. However, uncertainty, first about the outcome of the war and then about where they were most needed, kept them in France. Marie-Marguerite-Daniel Arnaud, attached to the Louisbourg Congregation since 1733 and superior since 1744, was the first to pass away. She died in 1764, aged sixty-five. Marie Robichaud died two years later.[81] The final member of the community, lay assistant Geneviève Henry, lived to see the end of the *ancien régime*. In March 1792, nine months before Louis XVI was executed, she was still residing in the Hôpital Saint-Etienne in La Rochelle.[82] It was only with Geneviève Henry's death sometime later that the story of the Louisbourg mission of the Sisters of the Congregation of Notre-Dame came to an end.

During the nearly three decades (1727–45 and 1749–58) that the Sisters of the Congregation were established in Louisbourg the kind of education they offered undoubtedly varied widely. Factors such as the number of sisters in the mission, the size and suitability of a particular residence, and their general financial situation would have determined how many girls could be accepted and what they would be doing. In the years of greatest hardship, the sisters may have been forced to cut back on the amount of firewood or on the quality of food given to boarders, and much more time was likely spent on handiwork than would otherwise have been the case, since extra income was gained through the sale of straw mattresses and other items.

The best years for the Louisbourg mission were likely those from 1742 to 1744. Compared with the hardships the sisters had known in the 1730s and would experience again in the 1750s, conditions during that brief period were close to ideal. There were six sisters in the community, their large house on Block 20 was nearly if not already paid for, and they were receiving a steady income of 1,600 *livres* a year from the Forant foundation. Under those conditions what kind of education did the Sisters of the Congregation give to their students? The curriculum was never published during the colonial period but there are two nineteenth-century texts[83] which, when looked at in conjunction with contemporary evidence, indicate the form it probably took and the methods used by the sisters in their Louisbourg school.

The educational objectives of the Sisters of the Congregation were straightforward. As one historian has observed, there was "nothing complicated or pretentious" in their approach.[84] Along with teaching reading, writing, "needlework and other female accomplishments,"[85] the sisters were to explain the fundamental articles of the Roman Catholic faith and to inculcate in their students such desirable virtues as piety and modesty. Undoubtedly, a great deal of effort went into shaping the character and demeanor of the girls. Principally that would have meant numerous sessions in which the sisters explained their interpretation of contemporary rules of etiquette and decency. Instructions on how to behave in church or at a dinner table; which games were permissible and what attitudes to adopt when playing them; how to respond to a compliment or to a young man's advances; and how to express oneself politely in every situation were some of the matters that needed attention. The simplest approach on such topics, according to a 1735 text entitled *La civilité puérile*, was to emulate the "honnêtes gens" of society, "because examples have more impact on our minds than words."[86] The Louisbourg sisters likely agreed, but would nonetheless have had much more to say about behaviour, morals, and whose examples should be followed.

The girls who attended the schools operated by the Congregation of Notre-Dame ranged in age from five or six to eighteen. There is no reason to believe that the situation was any different at Louisbourg. All of the students whose identities and ages can be determined fell within that range. Age, of course, was not the only factor influencing who was or was not to be admitted. Certain personality types, those who have "a vain and worldly temperament and who are incorrigible," were not welcomed. Similarly, girls engaged to be married were rejected because they were thought to have "a spirit and heart entirely dissipated." Students were expected to be "modest, docile and obedient." For obvious reasons children who were sick, particularly with communicable diseases, could not be accepted.[87]

The girls taught by the Sisters of the Congregation were of two basic types: boarders (*pensionnaires*) and day students (*externes*). Both groups existed at Louisbourg, apparently with the day students greatly outnumbering those who lived in the simply furnished rooms of the Block 20 residence. The only surviving indication of what the boarders' rooms contained is a 1740 list of the personal effects of two daughters of a local engineer, de Couagne. The document mentions bedclothes, a silver goblet, two silver spoons and forks, and a small armoire.[88] Given the Congregation's precarious financial situation, they could not have added many more furnishings to the girls' room. The sisters followed the same basic educational approach with both boarders and day students, alternating periods of instruction in reading and writing with times set aside for study or manual work. Whatever the activity it seems to have been nearly always characterized by religious content.

According to the nineteenth-century sources, a typical day in a Congregation of Notre-Dame school would begin with a study period, followed by a half-hour catechism lesson. Next came a two-hour class in which the students listened to pious readings and answered questions on what they had heard. Lunch was next, throughout which silence was supposed to be observed. Whether or not day students at the Louisbourg school would have stayed for this meal is not known. In the afternoon a two-hour class began in which reading, writing, and perhaps arithmetic were taught. The books read and the exercises in writing were nearly always of a religious character, and were in either French or Latin depending on the student's ability. After 1753 the catechisms, psalm-books, and books of piety used in such sessions were probably those sent to the colony by the Abbé de l'Isle-Dieu.[89] Before that date the sisters probably used the standard educational works of the period which were popular in Canada. Their titles clearly reveal the moral and religious overtones of education in the eighteenth century: *Pédagogue des familles chrétiennes, Instructions chrétiennes de la jeunesse,* and *L'Ecole paroissiale ou la manière de bien instruire les enfants des petites écoles.*[90]

Following the afternoon reading and writing period the girls would receive the Blessed Sacrament, although that practice was perhaps not followed at Louisbourg because there is no evidence that there was a chapel in the Block 20 residence. Then it was time for a light mid-afternoon lunch, after which came a study period and a reading on the life of one of the saints. The day students appear to have left at that point while the *pensionnaires* were given a half hour of free time. When that was over it was time for an hour of prayer, catechism, and rosary before dinner. After the meal the girls were given from two to two and a half hours of free time for recreation. Throughout this free time, and any other during the day, the girls were never to be left unsupervised. A period of worship followed the recreation time and then the *pensionnaires* were sent to their beds.

This routine was to be followed every weekday except the days selected for craft or handiwork instruction. On those days the religious exercises were carried out as on other days but the periods normally set aside for formal education were devoted instead "to manual work." As suggested above, more time was likely accorded to such handiwork at Louisbourg than at other schools run by the Congregation, because of the pressing need for extra income.

The girls' school week did not end on Friday. On Saturday the daily routine was again followed until mid-afternoon. There was no schooling on Sunday so the day students did not come to the convent, but for the *pensionnaires* there were numerous religious obligations to fulfil, including attendance at mass and vespers.[91]

As mentioned, the above summary of the Congregation of Notre-Dame's program of instruction is based on nineteenth-century accounts. Conceivably, a century earlier the day's activities were not scheduled quite so rigidly. Some eighteenth-century Italian schools, for example, were much more relaxed, with only five hours of classes a day.[92] On the other hand, contemporary schools could also be extremely demanding. The regulations of the Marine school established in Paris in 1669 stipulated that students attend classes in foreign languages, arms training, music, dance, mathematics, marine skills, writing, and drawing from 7 a.m. to 6:30 p.m., with meal hours (11:30 a.m. and 7:00 p.m.) given over to history lectures.[93] The standards maintained in a colony, of course, could be considerably less taxing. At the school of mathematics established at Louisbourg by the comte de Raymond in 1753 the officers and cadets did not begin their classes until 10:00 a.m. and then stayed only until their instructor "judges it time to dismiss them." The classes, held every Monday, Wednesday, Thursday, Friday, and Saturday, did not begin again until 2:00 p.m.[94] In view of the importance which the Sisters of the Congregation placed on order and supervision, it is doubtful that their approach was quite that flexible, yet it may have been slightly more so than it was to become in the next century.

Questions of scheduling aside, the other aspects of the Congregation's approach to education probably changed little from the eighteenth to the nineteenth century. Certainly, the religious and moral life of the students remained the first concern of the sisters. Nearly everything said, written, read, or done served to reinforce the Roman Catholic faith. A second aspect which was probably unchanged was the stress placed on the need for control over the students. This was particularly true for the girls who were boarding. The *Coutumier* of the Congregation states that the sisters "must employ constant surveillance, never leaving the children to themselves." Neither in the corridors nor during the recreation times or visiting periods were the girls to be left unsupervised.[95] Moreover, the girls were not allowed to write or receive letters or to have any books of their own without obtaining permission from the superior of the house. They were to eat only during the four periods set aside for meals. The order which was sought after demanded a considerable amount of imposed formality. The students were encouraged to be civil with each other but were warned not to be excessively friendly. The concern for order and formality even carried over into the arrangement followed when the girls left the house in a group. To go to mass at the parish church, for instance, the oldest girls were to go out the door first, followed in descending order by their juniors.[96]

Given these regimented lives, one wonders if the boarders were allowed any vacation time during which they could rejoin their families. According to the *Règlemens* of the Congregation of Notre-Dame there was almost no vacation during the fall, winter, and spring. The sole exception was on 1 January when the girls were permitted to go home after vespers on the understanding that they would return to the convent the following day. The only period of extended vacation for the *pensionnaires* was in late summer, from 15 August to 15 September.[97] But as with the daily study program, the Sisters of the Congregation in Louisbourg may have followed a slightly less rigid school year than that which is laid out in the nineteenth-century *Règlemens*.

Highlights of any school year at Louisbourg would have included the eight feast days, the seven principal fêtes of the Virgin Mary and the 3 June fête of the Sacred Heart of Mary, which the sisters were permitted to celebrate in special fashion (with chants and the exposition of the Blessed Sacrament in their chapel, if they had one). The mission at Louisbourg may not have had its own chapel but the fêtes were undoubtedly still treated as special days with the customary services likely taking place in the town's parish church.[98]

Though there are no figures available on how many girls attended the school at Louisbourg, during the 1740s the number may possibly have been as high as 100. In the early eighteenth century at Trois Rivières, five or six Sisters of the Congregation were able to teach over 100 students.[99] It seems reasonable to assume that the six sisters in Louisbourg during the 1740s were able to instruct about an equal number. Two factors which might have limited enrolment, available space and tuition costs, do not appear to have been deterrents at that time. On the first point, the sisters' house was large enough for a number of rooms to be utilized as classrooms, with divisions by age, ability, or by whether one was a boarder or a day student. As for the second point, in spite of their frequent financial difficulties the sisters were evidently willing to reduce tuition and room and board costs when parents could not afford the normal charge. In 1728, which is before the expensive property on Block 20 had been acquired, the fee for room and board with the sisters was approximately 12 to 13 *livres* a month.[100] After the new house was purchased the standard charge was raised to between 16 and 17 *livres* a month.[101] By 1755, at which time the sisters were in the midst of one of their worst financial crises and unable to take many boarders, the fee was almost 21 *livres* a month for a *pensionnaire*.[102] Throughout the period parents of day students would have paid less than parents of boarders, but how much less is not known.

The difficulty which some Louisbourg parents had in meeting the standard fees was fully understood by the Sisters of the Congregation. In 1739 the governor and commissaire-ordonnateur reported that one of the things which made the sisters so useful in the colony was that they were flexible in what they charged parents to send their daughters to school. The sisters "do not have a fixed charge for boarders who are unable to pay very much, they even keep them as charity cases."[103] Even during the 1750s, when the sisters' situation was desperate, they continued to instruct the "poor children of the town."[104] Such flexibility in fees, to the point of outright charity, was undoubtedly deeply appreciated by those parents with only moderate or low incomes. Of course, if money was normally a hindrance to sending a daughter to the sisters' school, it might remain a reason for not allowing her to stay there very long, even at reduced rates. Many girls probably spent only a matter of months in school, before being withdrawn because of the expense or out of a need to have her at home or a desire to have her enter domestic service in a wealthier household. For most parents the education of females was not a high priority. It might be desirable for a woman to know how to read and write and do the most basic arithmetic, but it was hardly essential.

All the available evidence suggests that the Sisters of the Congregation had a great impact on Louisbourg society. Various royal officials, clerics like Abbé Maillard, and others were of one opinion when it came to the sisters. They all praised their exemplary conduct and spoke of their edifying influence on the town. One can attempt to measure their impact quantitatively through an analysis of female literacy, but it is difficult to draw precise conclusions from such an analysis. A rudimentary way of obtaining an approximate idea of literacy in a given period is to calculate the number of individuals able to sign their names on marriage entries in the parish records. At Louisbourg, during the period 1722–45, the percentage of brides who were able to sign their marriage documents was 58 per cent (135 of 233 brides), relatively high for the era.[105] By way of comparison, that percentage was slightly higher than in contemporary Trois Rivières[106] and many times higher than in some towns in France.[107] Yet one must be extremely careful with such figures. The ability to sign one's name is not proof of a fully literate person, merely an indication that a fundamental skill has been acquired. As for attributing the high proportion of Louisbourg brides with that ability to the influence of the Sisters of the Congregation, that connection is not clear by any means. Further research on the origin and age of the brides is necessary to determine how many of them might have been educated in Louisbourg and how many in Canada or in France.

Since boys were not admitted to the Congregation's school in Louisbourg, one wonders how they fared in the town in terms of education. There were private schools and tutors available, and wealthy boys might be sent to Canada or France. But there is no evidence to indicate which or how many males learned to read and write in those days. As with the Louisbourg brides, one can determine how many grooms were able to sign their names. In mid-eighteenth century Trois Rivières slightly fewer grooms than brides were able to sign.[108] That was not the case in Louisbourg, where between 1722 and 1745 the number of "signing" grooms was significantly higher than brides. Of the 233 grooms in town during that period, 164 or 70 per cent were able to sign their marriage entries.[109] The explanation for the difference between the Louisbourg and Trois Rivières figures probably lies in the difference between the economies and societies of the two towns. Unlike the latter, the capital of Ile Royale was an important military and naval base and a trading and transshipment centre whose port ranked among the busiest on the Atlantic seaboard.[110] As a result the town contained a relatively large number of men, such as military officers, administrators, clerks, and merchants, for whom literacy was both essential and natural, given the families from which they came and the careers they had adopted. Many of the grooms who appear in the Louisbourg parish records came from these groups. By way of contrast, men much less likely to have been literate, like the hundreds of ordinary soldiers and fishermen, generally did not get married in the town. As with the brides, further research is needed to determine the area and socio-economic group from which the grooms came and how many might have been educated at Louisbourg.

In conclusion it is worth summarizing the main points of this chapter. Formal education at Louisbourg was a subject in which colonial officials in France generally showed little interest. Royal administrators on Ile Royale had a much greater concern about educational matters, but lacked the control over the treasury which would have enabled them to do much about situations they deemed unsuitable. In general, secular officials appear to have perceived the most important goals of education, at least for the masses, to be the fostering of a loyal and moral populace.

The Sisters of the Congregation drew only praise for their work at Louisbourg, though they were usually hamstrung by financial difficulties. The rules of the Congregation of Notre-Dame reveal that a disciplined approach was adopted in their schools, an approach which served above all else to inculcate the tenets and values of the French Roman Catholic Church. Finally, in an age in which males enjoyed many more rights and privileges than females it is interesting to note that the only school in continuous existence over a long period of time at Louisbourg was one exclusively for girls. Admittedly, officers, merchants, administrators, and others well up on the social and economic ladder saw to it that their sons received the kind of education considered appropriate, whether in Louisbourg or elsewhere. But for a boy whose parents could not afford to send him to Canada or France or to a local school, the chances of receiving a formal education may have been poorer than those of a daughter in the same family. Because of the sisters' willingness to reduce and at times even waive tuition costs, there were probably many girls in the town who obtained a measure of education they otherwise would not have received.

5 Faith, Morals, and Popular Customs: Religion in Life

The French, in their colonies, spend much more time in prayer and external worship; than the English, and Dutch settlers in the British colonies ... The French ... have prayers every morning and night on board their shipping, and on Sundays they pray more than commonly; they regularly say grace at their meals; and every one of them says prayers in private as soon as he gets up.

Peter Kalm, *Travels into North America* (1749)[1]

On Wednesday night, 31 May 1758, most people in Louisbourg would probably have gone to bed looking forward eagerly to the events of the next day. Thursday, until noon, was the octave of the *fête-Dieu* (Corpus Christi), the annual feast day celebrating the Blessed Sacrament. Traditionally it was a time of great festivity, with the highlight of the morning's activities being a procession of clergy and prominent lay people through the streets past kneeling parishioners. In France, in a custom which was perhaps followed in French colonial towns, people hung tapestries along the route so as to heighten the pageantry. To contemporary observers the *fête-Dieu* was "the most stately feast day of Catholicism."[2]

Thursday, 1 June 1758, however, did not dawn according to people's expectations. At seven o'clock in the morning a British fleet was observed sailing towards Louisbourg.[3] News of the enemy ships came as no surprise to the military establishment. It had contingency plans ready, the first of which was to dispatch hundreds of soldiers to fortified positions along the coast. For the civilians of Louisbourg there was little they could do about the approaching fleet except perhaps worry that there would be another summer blockade of their port (as there had been in 1755, 1756, and 1757). An assault on the town itself was obviously a possibility, though none but the most pessimistic could have foreseen that the British would shortly make a successful amphibious landing (8 June) and then capture the town seven weeks later (26 July).

What effect did the news of the enemy fleet have on the 1758 *fête-Dieu* celebrations at Louisbourg? Very little apparently. The morning's activities went ahead according to tradition with the procession of the Blessed Sacrament through the streets of the town. As it made its way along the customary route artillery salutes were fired from the batteries of the fortress and from the warships anchored in the harbour.[4] It was likely as spectacular and stately an occasion as any previous *fête-Dieu* in the town's history. Unknown to those who observed it, of course, it would be the last.

The decision to go ahead with the 1 June 1758 celebrations, in spite of the approach of the British ships, was probably not a difficult decision to make. After all, if ever there was a time to demonstrate a devotional attitude toward God and the mysteries of the faith, it was on such a day. By dutifully meeting their religious obligations the people attempted to prove to themselves and to God that they were worthy of divine consideration. Undoubtedly during the service following the procession, and on countless other occasions over the next eight weeks, there were many fervent prayers said in Louisbourg asking God to extend his protection to the town and its inhabitants.

The steadfast attachment to their faith shown by the inhabitants of Louisbourg on 1 June 1758 suggests that religious influences deeply permeated colonial society. Admittedly, the town did have a decidedly secular orientation and the devotional attitude of the populace was sometimes more conspicuous by its absence than its presence. And at times the piety of the inhabitants was greatly exceeded by their parsimony; witness the refusal either to contribute toward the construction of a major church edifice or to pay the compulsory tithe. Yet if such failings were worse or more glaring at Louisbourg than they were in France or Canada, which is arguable,[5] it was because of the weakness of the church there as an institution; it cannot be attributed to an irreligious population.

In people's everyday lives religion appears to have been as meaningful and as powerful a force at Louisbourg as in any other eighteenth-century Catholic community. From cradle to grave, in the home and in the town at large, one was surrounded by an all-encompassing popular religious faith. As in France and Canada, some aspects of that faith probably owed as much to traditional folk customs and superstitions as they did to the official teachings of the contemporary Roman Catholic Church.[6] The process of learning and living the faith in Louisbourg was an ongoing one, which commenced as soon as possible after birth.

Birth and Baptism

In most French Catholic families, concern for a person's spiritual welfare began even before his or her birth, with the selection of godparents (*par-*

rain and *marraine*). Only in Brittany was there a refusal to name god-parents before an infant was born, out of a fear that by doing so one might endanger the child's life and insult God.[7] Godparents held positions of honour and responsibility. They presented the infant for baptism, named him, and made a commitment on his behalf to accept the faith. As a result of their importance parents tended to be careful about whom they selected. The tradition in France was that the *parrain* and *marraine* of a couple's first child ought to be chosen from among the grandparents on either side of the family.[8] That custom could rarely have been followed at Louisbourg as many of the inhabitants' parents resided in France, Canada, or Acadia. In their place stood other relatives and close friends of the newborn's mother and father.

Diocesan policy, as laid down by Bishop Saint-Vallier in his *Rituel* (1703), stipulated that children (boys under fourteen, girls under twelve) were not permitted to act as godparents.[9] Largely out of necessity that rule was sometimes ignored at Louisbourg. Rather than entrust the spiritual upbringing of a child to a friend who might soon leave the colony, parents occasionally chose older brothers and sisters as godparents. Given the rationale, the church would likely have approved. In 1726 seven-year-old Jean-François Eurry de la Pérelle was named as the *parrain* to his new-born brother. Three years later he and his six-year-old sister served as godparents in the baptism of an illegitimate child in the town.[10] Children of those ages, and there are similar cases in the Louisbourg parish records,[11] could hardly have been expected to fulfil or even understand completely the functions they were performing, such as the recitation of the major prayers and articles of the Catholic faith.[12] But the fact that children would not be capable of meeting such obligations was probably not a major problem. According to Louis-Sébastien Mercier, a commentator on late eighteenth-century Paris, 98 per cent of adult *parrains* could not recite the Nicene Creed (*Credo*). Mercier added that priests tolerated such igno-rance and allowed the godfathers to mumble through the creed in a very low voice.[13]

According to Van Gennep's studies of folklore in France, parents await-ing the birth of a child had many popular ways of guessing whether they would have a boy or a girl. One simple custom was for a pregnant woman, standing upright and dressed only in a *chemise*, to allow a coin to slide between her breasts and drop to the floor. A bounce to the right was supposed to mean a boy; to the left, a girl. There were numerous other ways of forecasting, many of which involved the moon.[14] The Louisbourg records do not indicate which divining methods were popular there, but that there was an interest in such things is certain. In 1737 a pregnant Marie Catherine Auger wagered and won a pair of shoes by correctly guessing that the child she carried was a girl.[15]

When the day of birth finally came it took place in the home, not at the hospital. On occasion the Brothers of Charity or local surgeons may have helped with deliveries,[16] but not very often. Normally when a woman gave birth she was assisted by other women in the community. While there was no "official" midwife (sage-femme) in Louisbourg until 1749, there were definitely women who served in that capacity during the 1730s and 1740s, and presumably earlier. Magdelaine Beauché, wife of dancing master Simon Rondel, and a Madame LeLarge were the women identified most frequently as sages-femmes during those years.[17] The local women who acted as midwives throughout the first period of French occupation at Louisbourg apparently had no formal training in childbirth techniques. It is not known what birth complications were encountered as a result, but it is safe to assume that there were problems.[18] Complaints about their competency were relayed by the governor and commissaire-ordonnateur to the minister of marine, who it was hoped would send a trained sage-femme to the town.[19] A fully qualified midwife, a woman named Marie-Marguerite Lotman but known more commonly as "the widow Droit," was finally located in Rochefort and sent to the colony in 1749. Paid an annual salary of 400 livres, roughly equal to that of a junior military officer, Madame Droit stayed in Louisbourg until the capitulation in 1758, assisting at hundreds of births.[20]

The midwife occupied an important position in Louisbourg society, particularly during the 1750s when the specially trained "widow Droit" was in town. While her predecessors may not have possessed her skills, it is nonetheless likely that they were looked up to and relied upon by most pregnant women in the town. After all, there was really no one else to turn to for help or advice in matters of birth, where the life of a mother and infant might occasionally be at stake. In the event that the life of a newborn child was in danger, the midwife would "sprinkle" the infant so that he or she was technically baptized, and therefore a member of the Roman Catholic Church. Without such "sprinkling" (ondoiement), the child would not be able to go to heaven.

The spiritual dimension of the midwife's occupation was fully accepted by the church. Its only concern was that the women who held such positions were suitable for their weighty responsibilities. To that end Bishop Saint-Vallier stipulated in his Rituel that curés should investigate the faith, life, and morals of the sages-femmes in their parishes. Midwives were to be fully versed in the meaning of baptism and to be shown how to administer the sacrament correctly. Moreover, each midwife was to swear an oath agreeing to serve the pregnant women of the parish, to take no needless medical risks, to reveal no family secrets, and to "sprinkle" only when absolutely necessary. When the need arose to choose a new midwife

FIGURE 4
Baptisms at Louisbourg: Proximity to Birth (1722–45; 1749–58)

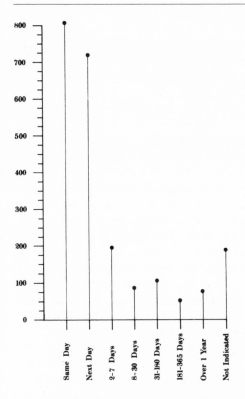

the curé was to call together the most virtuous and honest women in the parish so that they could elect the one best suited to be the *sage-femme*.[21] This practice may have been observed at Louisbourg up until 1745, but not during the second occupation (1749–58) when the town's midwife was selected in France by officials within the ministry of marine.

It was the teaching of the church in the eighteenth century that unless poor health prevented it infants should be brought to a priest for baptism within three or four days of birth. Children who had been "sprinkled" in the home were not excluded from this requirement for they had received only a provisional baptism. At Louisbourg the church's strictures on this matter were followed fairly closely (see Fig. 4). Out of slightly more than 2,200 baptisms recorded at Louisbourg between 1722 and 1758, about 70 percent were carried out within a day or two of birth and about 80 per cent within the first seven days of life. The remaining baptisms included a sizeable number in which either the date of birth was not registered or involved adult or adolescent conversions to Roman Catholicism. Roughly 14 per cent of the baptisms involved children between the ages of one month and one year. In many of those cases the delay between birth and baptism seems to have been due not to negligence on the part of parents but to the fact that the families resided in isolated settlements and had to wait until the summer before travelling to Louisbourg and the nearest priest.[22]

Births at Louisbourg may have been announced by the ringing of church bells. Whether this was the custom is not known, but it is conceivable that the Récollets of Brittany adopted the practice from their home province of tolling the bell three times to signal the arrival of a new parishioner in the community.[23] Then again, as in some French provinces, there may have been a difference in the way male and female births were announced, with the bell being rung louder, longer, or more often for the boy. In the case of illegitimate or abandoned children (enfants naturels and enfants trouvés) propriety would have dictated that the bells not be rung at all.[24]

The vast majority of baptisms at Louisbourg took place in the parish church. From the mid-1730s to 1745 and then again from 1749 to 1758 the Chapelle de Saint-Louis in the King's Bastion barracks fulfilled that role. On very rare or special occasions baptisms were also held in the chapels of the King's Hospital and Royal Battery. In a typical ceremony the infant to be baptized was anywhere from a few hours to a few days old. The newborn would have been dressed in white (one custom was to wrap the child in his mother's wedding veil) and carried to the chapel by either the godfather or godmother (depending on the sex of the child).[25]

The number of people in attendance at the baptismal ceremony appears to have been quite small. In most cases only two or three family members or friends, and sometimes the midwife, signed the parish record entries, although others may of course have attended but not signed. Large groups of signatures, a dozen or so, were usually seen only when the child to be baptized belonged to a prominent Louisbourg family, such as that of a wealthy merchant or a military officer.[26] The infant's father often attended the ceremony but his presence was not essential. Mothers on the other hand almost never attended the baptism of their children. Their absence was due not only to the proximity of baptism to the day of birth but also to an ancient popular custom which maintained that a woman was not to enter a church until she had been purified in a formal "churching" ceremony (les relevailles). The ideal practice, as described in the Old Testament and as performed by the Virgin Mary following the birth of Jesus, was to be "churched" forty days after the birth of a boy and eighty days after a girl.[27] Women in some parts of France shortened the waiting period considerably[28] and it is probable that numerous women in Louisbourg did likewise. Though not compulsory in the eyes of the church, the ceremony was definitely regarded as a worthy custom. At the end of the period, however long, the woman, with a lighted candle, went to the church for the first time to give thanks to God for having been delivered from the pain and peril of childbirth. At the church door she was greeted by the curé who blessed and purified her.[29]

The actual baptismal ceremony would presumably have been carried out at Louisbourg as set down by the bishop of Québec in the *Rituel* for the diocese.[30] In the case of a boy, the godfather named the child; in that of a girl, it was the godmother. As not every name was permissible, the *Rituel* contained a long list of saints' and other names that could be bestowed on children. The name chosen determined the person's patron saint. The ceremony ended with the registering of the baptism in the parish records, with the curé, godparents, and witnesses all signing. With that act, it was said, the child's name was written in heaven.

In the case of the baptism of adolescents and adults, categories which at Louisbourg included such people as black slaves, Catholics raised in a Protestant environment (such as New England) and Protestant soldiers in the Karrer Regiment who chose to be converted, there were departures from the standard ceremony. For instance, the individual answered for himself and the godparents occupied a more honorary role. Two requirements worthy of note were that the adult abstain from sexual relations for several days before baptism and that he or she pass those days in fasting or abstinence as preparation.[31]

The bishop of Québec did not state that illegitimate or abandoned children were to be treated differently than other infants, yet they may have been. Sometimes in France they were brought into a church by a side entrance rather than through the main door; at other times they were baptized in the sacristy.[32] At Louisbourg the illegitimacy rate was 4.5 per cent (101 of 2,233 baptisms involved illegitimate or abandoned children), which was considerably above the rate in contemporary Canada but only slightly above the rate in small towns and villages in eighteenth-century France.[33] Most of the children in Louisbourg who fell into that category received a large "B," for *bâtard*, in the margin of their parish record entry. Despite the obvious stigma of illegitimacy they had nonetheless joined the Roman Catholic Church, then probably the most important institution in French society.

Growing Up: Confession, Communion, and Confirmation
After baptism the next formal steps in a Catholic's religious life were confession, communion, and confirmation, sacraments which were administered when an individual had reached the "age of reason" and was judged

to have learned the fundamental articles of the Roman Catholic faith. Confession came first, followed several years later by communion and confirmation. The process of learning the faith in preparation for these three sacraments required a joint effort by both family and church. In the family setting parents were clearly expected to set examples for their children. Couples were instructed at the time of marriage to give their future children a thoroughly Christian upbringing.[34] In the ideal household children would grow up first observing and then participating in morning and evening prayers, grace at meals, regular attendance at mass and vespers, days of fast and abstinence, and a host of other devotional exercises. Couples were also responsible for the spiritual care of their servants.[35]

How many Louisbourg families would have approximated the ideal is of course unknown. Presumably there would have been variations from situation to situation, according to such factors as temperament and position in society. In late eighteenth-century France religious sentiment is thought to have been largely on the wane. Historians have written of the steady "secularization of religious attitudes" after 1750, with the bourgeoisie attending church and religious processions only "to be respectable." Abbé de l'Isle-Dieu himself, writing in 1752, despaired that "there is hardly any religion left in the world." Yet earlier in the century, and particularly in New France, the religious situation does not seem to have been so bleak. Admittedly, as Cornelius Jaenen has shown, the Canadiens could be "relaxed and uninhibited" at church, with men leaving during the sermon to smoke or gossip and people talking or quarrelling or racing horses around the church during mass.[36] Similarly, at Louisbourg, there was a problem with *cabaretiers* enticing customers to their establishments when they should have been at religious services. Yet notwithstanding such indications of laxness, the colonists of New France struck observers as being quite devout, at least in comparison with other areas they had seen. The Swedish botanist Peter Kalm was impressed with the people of Canada in that regard, as was the New England ship captain William Pote in his travels as a prisoner among the Acadians and Micmacs in 1745. Pote asserted that the French military officers "Never Neglected" their prayers, both "Night and morning."[37]

Details of religious upbringing at Louisbourg are rare, emerging only in a few court cases over how children should be raised. One such case came to the fore in 1755 when a father, an Irish *negoçiant* named Thomas Power, returned to town after a long absence to find that the man with whom he had left his daughter had treated her like a servant. Because of the slight done to his daughter, and to his own family name, Power took the man, Jean-Baptiste Duboé, to court. Most of the testimony dealt with the issue of the tasks the girl had been asked to perform in the household,

but there were references to religion. Duboé maintained that the "principal work" he had demanded of the girl was that she "learn the tenets of
the Roman Catholic and apostolic Religion." A witness added that on
normal working days the child had been "dressed as if it were a Sunday
and had even gone on promenades with other girls."[38]

In instances where children lost their parents, guardians (tuteurs) were
named to look after every facet of the orphans' upbringing, including their
spiritual education. Occasionally the appointed guardians disagreed over
how best to raise the children entrusted to their care. A dispute arose in
Louisbourg in 1752 between Marie-Thérèse Petit (a sixty-nine-year-old
widow) and Jean-Baptiste Guion, respectively guardian and deputy guardian of an eight-year-old girl named Catherine Koller. Guion submitted a
formal complaint to the local court in which he alleged that Petit, the
child's grandmother, was badly mistreating and neglecting the little girl.
Most of the seven witnesses backed up Guion's charges. Disciplinary
measures which Petit had been observed to use on the child included
tying her to a post in the yard, confining her in a barrel, as well as pinch-
ing, punching, and kicking her. Two of the witnesses testified that they
had seen the grandmother instructing the girl in catechism and prayer.
One reported that Petit struck the child's fingers with a fireplace shovel
when she made mistakes; the other said that the girl's errors were corrected in customary fashion, but did not give any indication as to what
that entailed. In the end the grandmother remained the child's guardian
but it was decided that the young girl should be sent to a boarding school
in Canada.[39] Marie-Thérèse Petit's use of a metal shovel to correct mistakes by her grandchild during catechism was almost certainly excessively
harsh for the era. That is not to say, however, that corporal punishment
was not a routine feature of contemporary educational programs, including
catechism classes. A tap or crack with a wooden pointer by an instructor
was a common way of making a young person aware that he or she had
made a mistake.

The church's direct involvement in religious education, as distinct from
the family's, normally began when the children were sent to formal catechism classes outside of the home. For New France Bishop Saint-Vallier
envisaged three levels of such classes and developed a program of study for
each.[40] The first he called the "petit Catéchisme," which was intended to
prepare children for their first confession and confirmation. The second
and more detailed catechism was devised for those who were preparing to
make their first communion, while the third was for those who were past
that stage and whose parents wanted them to learn more about their faith.
The bishop directed that catechism classes should be held every fifteen
days throughout most of the year and at least once a week during Lent.[41]

It is questionable whether Bishop Saint-Vallier's approach to catechism instruction was fully adopted at Louisbourg. According to Abbé de l'Isle-Dieu, the Récollet curés on Ile Royale were far from satisfactory as catechizers.[42] Their failings were never described in detail so it is impossible to say whether the friars were not holding classes often enough or were not rigorous enough in their examination of the young people, or both. The vicar-general's remarks undoubtedly echoed complaints made by Abbé Maillard, to the effect that children in Louisbourg were being confessed, confirmed, and admitted to communion without being fully knowledgeable about their faith. Given that Isle-Dieu was always hypercritical of the Récollets and that the friars themselves have not left a written record of their parish work, it is not possible to assess the accuracy of such criticisms.

Catechism classes at Louisbourg were probably held in either the Récollet convent house on Block 3 or in one of the chapels or sacristies in the town. Wherever they were held custom dictated that the group was divided into boys on one side of the room and girls on the other. If the classes were held in a chapel, then boys were seated on the gospel side (north side of the altar) and girls on the epistle side (south side of the altar).[43] The standard teaching method was a mixture of prayer, instruction by the priest, and question and answer sessions in which the priest tested the knowledge of the catechumens. The answers provided were not always what the priest was expecting. During a class at Louisbourg one Sunday in February 1758, Récollet Pierre d'Alcantara Cabaret asked a girl if she could explain the theological virtue of "L'Espérance," the proper answer being that it was the quality which enabled one to wait for eternal life with hope and assurance.[44] But to the priest she replied, "oh yes my Father, in the name of the Father, the Son and the Holy Ghost, L'Espérance is the big sergeant in the Artois Regiment who sleeps with my mother every night."[45]

Provided they had received sufficient religious instruction, children were supposed to make their first confession when they reached the "age of discretion" (the age at which one clearly knew right from wrong, which was thought to be at around seven).[46] Henceforth they were obliged to make at least one confession annually. In most cases it was made at Easter time in the parish where one resided. However, should one be in another parish at that time of year, confession was still obligatory. A certificate had to be obtained to prove to the priest in the home parish that a confession had actually been made. Another special requirement was that curés refrain from listening to confessions by females after sunset, unless the area was well lit and there were witnesses present.[47] For most children catechism classes continued for several years after their confession was made, as the young people were prepared for communion and confirmation. In special circumstances, if for instance a child was thought to be sufficiently well instructed at eight or so, the sacraments might be administered at that early age.[48] As a general rule, however, eleven or twelve was regarded as the ideal age for first communion.[49]

By the eighteenth century the act of making one's first communion had come to be regarded as a major transitional point in a person's life. In theological terms it marked "the transition to being an adult Christian";[50] in society at large it was treated as a rite of passage out of childhood and into adolescence, even though puberty might still be a few years ahead for some.[51] It was the day on which young people might be at last admitted to the family table for meals, rather than eating at a separate table or upon a large block of wood.[52] It was also a special time in every community, with a procession to the parish church of all the boys and girls who were ready to be admitted to the Holy Table. When the young people returned home after their first communion they were no longer to be treated as children. Their passage into quasi-adult status was marked not only by admission to the family table, but also by the taking on of new spiritual responsibilities. The church directed that during the next year they were to become the official readers of prayers and pious readings in the household. In some families the anniversary of one's first communion, like that of one's baptism, was an occasion to be commemorated by going to mass and then having a special meal and other festivities at home afterwards.[53] As with confession, after making the first communion it was necessary to make at least one at Easter time every year thereafter. Conditions for communion included fasting from the previous midnight, removal of all weapons by men, and the covering of head, neck, and shoulders by women.[54]

The sacrament of confirmation, through which one received the Holy Spirit and was made a "perfect" Christian, was normally administered at about the same age as the first communion. In most towns in Canada the precise date depended on when the bishop of the diocese could visit the parish and perform the ceremony. As no bishop of Québec ever visited Louisbourg it is not known exactly what was done. Most likely, young people who had grown up in Louisbourg had to make the journey to Québec to be confirmed, just as Acadians were obliged to do.[55] This would have meant, of course, that there were many adult Louisbourgeois who had never received the sacrament of confirmation.

Marriage and Maturity

With the exception of those few persons who felt either a religious calling or an inclination to remain single, marriage was the next sacrament in most people's lives. Some wed in adolescence, others quite late in life;

whatever the age, entry into holy matrimony was regarded by virtually everyone as a profoundly significant step. In religious terms it represented a sacred alliance which demanded patience and an acceptance of the spouse's imperfections,[56] understandable considerations in a culture where divorce and separation were rare. Legally, marriage was important because for those in wedlock there were strict laws governing inheritance and the transfer of property, issues of paramount importance in this as in other ages.[57] For the relatively young, the taking of a spouse had special meaning because it signified a turning point in their lives, a departure from youth into adulthood.

In strictly legal terms the age of majority in New France was twenty-five. Through marriage, however, one could assume a kind of de facto adult status in the community much earlier in life. According to civil and canon law, females could marry on reaching the age of twelve and males at fourteen, ages at which they respectively were thought to have reached puberty.[58] To marry at such early ages, or indeed anytime before a woman turned twenty-five or a man thirty, required parental consent.[59] Principally out of economic considerations parents were usually far more willing to permit the marriage of an adolescent daughter than a son. A young woman would be looked after by her spouse, or his family, but that was not the case with a young man. It was as true in New France as it was in New England that "until a son had been given the means to support a wife, or had acquired them on his own, marriage was virtually impossible."[60] In some cases, even a son who was able to support a wife might be denied permission to marry if his parents feared that they themselves would be hurt economically by his moving away from home too soon.

Most young people probably accepted without question parental control over when and whom they were to marry.[61] In a few cases, however, that control did come to be deeply resented. In seventeenth- and eighteenth-century Canada couples sometimes circumvented the normal regulations by resorting to what was known as a mariage à la gaumine (supposedly named after a man called Gaumin who introduced the practice). In those instances a couple would stand up during mass at the precise moment when the priest turned to bless the congregation, and declare themselves to be married. Church and state alike condemned the practice and in 1717 Bishop Saint-Vallier issued a specific ordinance forbidding people to marry in that manner. Thereafter, couples in Canada married à la gaumine only on rare occasions.[62]

At Louisbourg there was an attempt to wed in that fashion in 1737, a case which illustrates clearly the predicament young people could find themselves in if they attempted to step prematurely beyond parental control. The individuals involved were a twenty-six-year-old navigator named

Jean LeLarge and his twenty-one-year-old fiancée, Louise Sanson. In 1733, at which time he was twenty-two and she was seventeen, they made promises of marriage to each other; three years later LeLarge put his promise in writing, agreeing to pay Mlle Sanson 500 *livres* should he back out of his commitment. By 1737 the sole stumbling block in the lovers' path was Jean LeLarge's widowed mother who refused to give her consent to the proposed marriage. Her opposition may have been based on a fear of being left without her son's economic support, or on a simple dislike of the fiancée, or on some other unknown cause.[63] Whatever the reason the couple was faced with waiting another four years until LeLarge turned thirty and could marry without parental consent.

The prospect of having to outwait LeLarge's mother was a bleak one, so the young people sought advice on how they could best break the impasse. While at supper in the Récollet convent house one Sunday evening, LeLarge raised his dilemma with one of the friars, and suggested that he might marry à la gaumine. The Récollet informed him that one of the officers in the garrison (Michel de Gannes de Falaise) had done that very thing a few years before and that the curé had legally married him and his lover the following day. LeLarge took the conversation as an indication of clerical support for such irregular marriages and made plans to do the same with his beloved Louise Sanson the next day.

Accordingly, on Monday, 11 February 1737, toward the end of morning mass, the young couple, who had been kneeling in front of the altar rail of the Louisbourg parish church, stood up during the blessing and declared themselves to be man and wife. The parish priest was horrified by the sacrilege, picked up the chalice, and fled to the sacristy. He then submitted a formal complaint to the commissaire-ordonnateur, who held principal responsibility for justice in the colony. The colonial legal machinery quickly sprang into action. The couple was arrested that same day, LeLarge dispatched to a guardhouse, and Sanson confined in the convent of the Sisters of the Congregation. There they stayed for two months while the Conseil Supérieur investigated the case. The eventual decision by the Conseil was that the young couple be admonished, kept in confinement another fortnight, and made to pay a fine of three *livres* each (to go to the poor). They were also forbidden to live as man and wife until they were legally married. A few months after their release, in July 1737, the long wait of Jean LeLarge and Louise Sanson was finally over when they were married according to contemporary church and civil law. Precisely forty weeks after the ceremony their first child was born.[64]

Economic considerations and the need for parental consent were not the only factors to influence whom and when one could marry. For Louisbourg's military population, which ranged from one-fifth to one-quarter of the town's total population, there was the added requirement of obtaining the commanding officer's permission to marry. An ordinance of the king specified that any priest who knowingly married an officer or soldier who had not received such permission was to be considered as an accomplice in the crime of rape.[65]

Generally speaking, marriages for the ordinary enlisted men on Ile Royale were not encouraged. Under some governors a limited number of soldiers were permitted to marry and settle in the colony as farmers, to which end they were given a three-year supply of free rations and other assistance. Other governors looked on such policies with contempt. Governor Drucour, for one, was extremely critical of his predecessor's (Raymond's) liberality on the issue, claiming that the soldiers who had been allowed to marry were the "worst fellows in the garrison" and that the women were "the whores and drunkards of the Country."[66] In common with several governors, Drucour stated that he would be extremely careful before allowing any soldier to marry.[67]

The official attitude towards officers' marriages was much more liberal. Permission was usually routinely granted so long as there were no objections from their families. In 1730 an ensign in the Compagnies Franches, Georges-François de Boisberthelot, felt that he simply could not wait for official permission. With a lover, Jeanne de Goutin, who was nearing the end of her pregnancy and with no desire to father an illegitimate child, Boisberthelot apparently sought the aid of the commissaire-ordonnateur, rather than his military commander, to help him out of the predicament. The commissaire agreed to help and used his influence to have the officer and his lover married. Just in time as it turned out, for a son was born to the couple the day after the ceremony. Boisberthelot and the commissaire-ordonnateur were each censured by the minister of marine for not having waited for proper approval but there seems to have been no further disciplinary action taken, although the officer was passed over in 1744 for a promotion to which he was entitled on the basis of seniority.[68] There was considerably less understanding demonstrated two decades later when ensign Jules Caesar Felix Bogard de la Noue disobeyed a direct order of his commanding officer and proceeded to marry Marguerite Guedry, a young woman of Acadian and Micmac parentage living at Baye des Espagnols. De la Noue was arrested, the marriage annulled, and the young officer (as well as the priest who had performed the ceremony) sent back to France in disgrace.[69]

Demographic pressures were another factor which helped shape Louisbourg marriage patterns. There was a great imbalance in the town's male and female population. Both because it was a new settlement and because it was a garrison town and seasonal fishing base, men greatly outnumbered women. In 1724 the ratio was 10 to 1; in 1752 it was still 6 to 1. Even leaving aside soldiers and visiting fishermen, the ratio of civilian men to women was never less than 3 to 1.[70] One of the principal effects of such disequilibrium in the sexes was that men in Louisbourg probably tended to marry later and women earlier than would otherwise have been the case. In Canada, for instance, which by the eighteenth century had a roughly balanced population of males and females, women married for the first time about five years before men, with the mean age for brides and grooms being 22.0 and 27.7 respectively and the modal age 19 and 24. At Port Royal, the difference between the sexes was also about five years.[71] At Louisbourg the difference seems to have been closer to nine years. On the basis of those Louisbourg brides (103) and grooms (59) whose ages at the time of first marriage can be determined, the mean age for females and males was 19.9 and 29.2 respectively, with the modal age being 18 and 27 respectively.[72] To put the figures another way, 60 per cent of brides were 19 or younger (the youngest being 13 years old),[73] while only about 3 per cent of the grooms were 20 or younger. The largest group of first-time grooms, 66 per cent, were between 22 and 30 years old; the others older still (see Fig. 5).

Though in a typical marriage the husband was considerably older than his wife,[74] that was not always the case. The relative shortage of eligible women, combined with the desire to wed someone who could bring economic benefits into a marriage, occasionally led first-time grooms to marry widows older than themselves. Twenty-eight-year-old Georges Desroches' marriage to Jeanne Galbarrette, sixty-nine and twice-widowed, is the most graphic example of such a liaison but there were others.[75] In both France and Canada a vast age difference between a bride and groom was sometimes cause for a charivari, a noisy disturbance in which a crowd of pranksters chided, teased, and demanded money from the couple in question. A popular custom of the period, though denounced by the church because it derided the sacrament of marriage, an occasional charivari was likely held at Louisbourg although there is no specific evidence to confirm that.

Widows and widowers who remarried quickly after the death of a spouse could also find themselves the objects of a charivari. This was especially true in rural areas where an effigy of the dead spouse was sometimes presented to remind the surviving spouse of his or her short memory and consequent impropriety. In urban environments, by way of contrast, rapid marriages were both more common and more easily accepted, there being compelling economic, personal, and social reasons in the cities for not waiting long to remarry. That seems to have been the situation in Louisbourg where there were numerous instances of remarriage only a

FIGURE 5
Ages at Time of First Marriage, Louisbourg (1713–58)

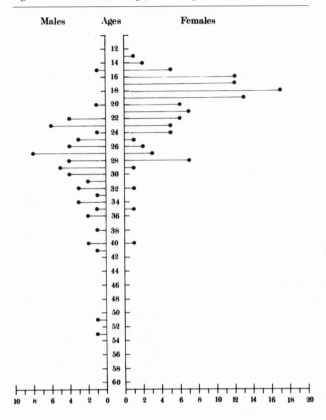

matter of weeks or months after the death of a spouse. To illustrate, in April 1725 Antoine Paris' wife (Marie-René Bauché) died. Forty-eight years old and with at least seven children to raise, four of whom were under the age of five, Paris remarried four months later, his bride being a widow named Marie Magdelaine Ferret. Three children were born of that marriage before Antoine Paris himself passed away in November 1731. As Paris had done, four months later his widow remarried (Dominique Collonques).[76]

The normal first stage in the eighteenth-century marriage process was courtship. The nature and length of courtship naturally varied with each couple, as determined by such factors as their age and social background. One standard aspect, however, appears to have been the concept of keeping company. Couples who were seen together repeatedly over a period of time, whether on Sunday promenades, at private social gatherings, or in some other context, "were assumed to have intentions of marriage." More often than not they did plan to marry, though on occasion the man's intentions differed sharply from the woman's, with the result that she might find herself abandoned and with an "unwanted pregnancy on her hands." In such a case the woman was legally entitled to use the argument that she and the man in question had regularly been seen in each other's company as proof that he should either marry her or pay child support.[77]

The women who fell victim to male deception in such affairs of the heart were usually from the ranks of the working poor, girls who saw marriage as a possible means of escape from their financial or emotional plight. Rarely were women from the higher levels of society so duped. A notable exception at Louisbourg was Marie-Anne Carrerot. Widow of a senior Marine officer (Quentin de la Salle), and daughter of a top Louisbourg *fonctionnaire* (Pierre Carrerot), Marie-Anne Carrerot was hardly the kind of woman one might expect to become an unmarried mother. Her difficulties began when she established a close friendship with Michel de Gannes de Falaise, a twenty-five-year-old lieutenant in the Compagnies Franches.[78]

For a year and a half during 1727 and 1728 de Gannes visited the widow so often that her parents, with whom she had been living since her husband's death, began to regard the young officer as a prospective son-in-law. The relationship developed into something more than friendship and in June 1728 Marie-Anne Carrerot discovered she was pregnant. Assured by de Gannes that he was a man of honour and that she had nothing to fear, Marie-Anne remained untroubled about her situation until the fifth month of pregnancy. Then, with de Gannes still doing nothing about arranging a marriage, she sought the help of the governor and the parish priest. Each offered support and consolation, but neither could prevail upon the reluctant officer to wed. Despairing of a solution to the problem, Marie-Anne Carrerot's father took her predicament to the Conseil Supérieur in late January 1729.

At court the case was made that Michel de Gannes had deceived the widow into having sexual relations with him on the basis of a false promise of marriage. With matrimony apparently out of the question the Carrerots asked that de Gannes be fined 10,000 *livres*, not only to compensate Marie-Anne for her anguish, loss of honour, and forthcoming child care expenses, but also to set an example that such deception would not be tolerated in the colony. In the end the Conseil ruled in Marie-Anne's favour but it set no specific sum as a fine; the infant was simply to carry the de Gannes name and the officer was to pay for the child's upbringing. The case probably would have ended there but there was an unfortunate epilogue. In November 1730, a year and a half after the birth of Marie-Anne Carrerot's illegitimate child, the widow attempted to block Michel de Gannes from marrying another woman, Elisabeth de Catalogne. Carrerot maintained that if de Gannes was to wed anyone it should be herself. Though her protest was undoubtedly considered with some sympathy, the Conseil Supérieur did not uphold her case and de Gannes was allowed to marry the woman of his choice.[79]

Another case of alleged male victimization of a female was brought to the Louisbourg Conseil Supérieur in November 1721. In contrast with Carrerot and de Gannes, however, the principals in this case were an adolescent, an *écrivain* named Claude Auguste de Brise, aged seventeen, and a child, eleven-year-old Marie-Louise Plantin. Marie-Louise's mother (Anthoinette Isabeau, *veuve* Plantin) claimed that her daughter had been "deflowered" by the young man during their ocean voyage to Louisbourg and she wanted the civil authorities to force the youth to marry the girl. To back up her argument she submitted a promise of marriage which she had obtained from the young man. In his defence de Brise admitted that he had been intimate with the girl, but only at her insistence and that he had refrained from "deflowering" her. As for the promise to marry, he stated that it should be considered invalid because the girl's mother had extracted it from him at knife-point. Aside from ordering a medical examination of Marie-Louise, which determined that there had not been "a complete deflowering," the Conseil was uncertain as to what to do with the case. So it passed it on to an ecclesiastical court in France, the *officialité* at La Rochelle, which specialized in cases dealing with promises of marriage. The *officialité's* final judgment in the matter is not known, but while it was considering the evidence the Marine authorities took the precaution of detaining de Brise, just in case he would have to marry young Marie-Louise.[80]

Marie-Louise Plantin's situation was quite different from that of Marie-Anne Carrerot, yet there were some striking similarities between the two cases. First and foremost was the deep parental concern shown in each instance for a daughter thought to have been exploited by a male. Though in the twentieth century there would undoubtedly be more outrage expressed over the plight of a "deflowered" child than that of a deceived and pregnant widow, the two cases appear to have been viewed with equal seriousness by the respective parents. The explanation for that similarity would seem to be that in each case the daughter's situation was such that, if left unremedied, it would not only damage or eliminate her chance of a future marriage (a serious consideration in itself), but it would also harm profoundly the reputation and social standing of her whole family. Redress through the courts was seen as the only means of avoiding either consequence.

The experiences of Marie-Anne Carrerot and Marie-Louise Plantin were not typical. In an ordinary courtship the relationship would develop to the point where a formal promise of marriage would be made or an engagement agreed upon. Depending on such factors as the couple's age, wealth, and social rank, an engagement might be verbal or written and might take place either a few days or a year or so before the wedding. Where significant amounts of property were involved, a marriage contract would be drawn up specifying precisely what the bride and groom were each bringing into the marriage. With minors the terms of the contract were settled by parents or guardians. For the poor, of course, there was no need for a formal contract since the dowries involved, if there were any at all, were too insignificant to warrant legal protection. At Louisbourg marriage contracts appear to have been drawn up for about 40 per cent of the weddings in the town, as compared with 60 per cent in eighteenth-century Paris,[81] a fact which might indicate either that there were more "poor" marriages in the colony than in the French capital or simply that there was a preference for informal agreements rather than binding legal contracts.

Marriage contracts in Louisbourg were drafted by a royal notary, usually a week or so before the wedding, but on occasion a year or more in advance and sometimes even after the ceremony. In a few instances the interval between the promise of marriage and the wedding itself afforded the parties time to reconsider their choice of a spouse. Under normal circumstances there was no difficulty in backing out of the previous agreement, provided the other person was reimbursed for any expenditures made.[82]

The first formal religious step in the marriage process was supposed to be the betrothal (fiançailles). According to the Rituel of the diocese, betrothal was a solemn act which was to take place in church in the presence of the curé and several witnesses.[83] At Louisbourg, only a single fiançailles was recorded in over thirty years of parish records,[84] a fact which suggests either that the Récollet parish priests did not force couples to go through the betrothal or simply that they did not bother to register the ceremony.

Following betrothal came the reading of banns in the church. In principle, three were required. They were to be read during high mass on successive Sundays or feast days, with at least two or three days between each publication. The repetition of the announcement was to ensure that all parishioners were aware of forthcoming weddings. If anyone knew of a

FIGURE 6
Marriages at Louisbourg: Totals by Banns and Days of the Week

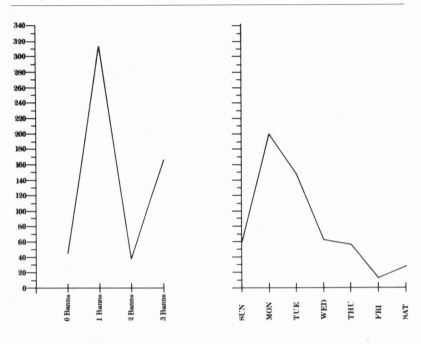

reason why a marriage should not take place, he or she was to inform the curé. The church frowned on reading fewer than three banns but dispensations were possible, for a sum of money, provided a couple could demonstrate that a hasty wedding was essential.[85] Though the bishop of Québec directed that such dispensations not be given out needlessly, the Récollet curés of Louisbourg apparently did not share the bishop's concern. Of the 565 marriages in the town's parish records, three banns were read for only 167 (29.7 per cent) of them. A clear majority of weddings (348 or 61.5 per cent) had either one or no banns published (see Fig. 6).

Though it rarely happened, people sometimes had second thoughts about a marriage partner after the banns had been read. In 1750 there was a case where the prospective bride, Acadian-born Isabelle Le Mordant, changed her mind about marrying her fiancé, Yves Glamar from Niganiche, after three wedding banns had been read in Niganiche and two in Louisbourg. Upon learning of Le Mordant's intention to marry another man (Jean Baudry), Glamar contacted the civil authorities and the parish priest to ensure that she would not be permitted to wed before returning the 500 *livres* Glamar had already given her. Glamar was apparently reimbursed to his satisfaction as two months later his former fiancée married Jean Baudry.[86]

As mentioned above, the purpose of reading the banns during mass was to ascertain whether or not anyone in the congregation was aware of impediments which could prevent a couple from marrying. Canonical impediments to marriage in the eighteenth century were of two basic types. First, there were the diriment impediments, fourteen in all, which rendered marriages null and void. These impediments forbade marriages on the basis of consanguinity and affinity (each to the fourth degree), as well as those involving cases of mistaken identity or adultery or homicide. For a sum of money dispensations could be obtained to overcome some impediments. A man who wished to marry a first cousin, a liaison which represented a violation of the strictures against consanguinity to a second degree, paid dearly for the required dispensation (in 1771 in Québec the charge was 500 *livres*). Dispensations for consanguineous relations to the third and fourth degrees were considerably less expensive (in 1766 they were 40 and 30 *livres* respectively).[87] Whatever the charge exacted in Louisbourg, a number of first cousins and more distant relatives there sought and acquired the necessary dispensations to marry.[88]

Couples who ignored the church's rules on consanguinity, and had sexual relations or married without dispensation, ran the risk of being arrested and tried for incest. In 1734 there was just such a case at Louisbourg.[89] The couple involved were Pierre Santier, a young butcher, and Servanne Bonnier, a nineteen-year-old seamstress from St Malo. Bonnier had come to Louisbourg in 1733 and begun boarding with the Santier family, to whom she was related. Over a matter of months Servanne Bonnier first became friendly and then intimate with Pierre Santier, son of the head of the household, Maurice Santier. By early 1734 Bonnier was pregnant. She concealed her condition for months, even to the point of lying to her aunt when asked directly at the beginning of Lent if she were pregnant. Once Easter passed, Bonnier revealed the truth to the Santier family, but continued to keep her pregnancy hidden from the community at large.

For reasons unknown, Bonnier's uncle, that is, her lover's father, refused to give his consent to a marriage between the two young people, even though the superior of the Louisbourg Récollets said that he would grant a dispensation. At last, on 2 September 1734, assisted by local midwife Madame LeLarge, Servanne Bonnier gave birth to a son. Word of the birth, not just illegitimate but also the product of a technically incestuous relationship, gradually spread throughout the town. When news of it reached the civil authorities, who initially believed that Pierre Santier and Servanne Bonnier were first cousins, they ordered an immediate investigation. In their eyes, not only were the young people guilty of a heinous crime, but so were the Santier parents since they had not informed the officials of an unmarried woman's pregnancy, as stipulated by royal ordinance. To the officials the Santiers seemed to condone "the debauchery of their son and the prostitution of their niece." In the course of the investigation which followed, it was discovered that the couple were second not first cousins. As a result, much of the contempt and outrage expressed by the royal officials appear to have abated. The final decision of the court on the Pierre Santier-Servanne Bonnier case has not survived, but the judgment must not have been too harsh. The couple married with dispensation soon after the incident and continued to live, and have children, in Louisbourg until 1758.

As with consanguinity, the church's restrictions on marriages between individuals of too close an affinity could also be overcome through the purchase of dispensations. The most common type of dispensation in this category was that which allowed a man to marry the sister of his deceased wife. As Louisbourg had a relatively small population, particularly in the more elite social circles, it is not surprising that there were demands for this kind of dispensation. Provided one had the money and the time to go through the proper channels there was little difficulty in obtaining the required dispensation. On at least one occasion, however, an invalid dispensation was used to allow such a marriage, with far-reaching consequences. It was rumoured that the groom, a prosperous merchant named Michel Daccarette, had given the Récollets 1,000 écus so that he could marry Catherine Gonillon, sister of his late wife. The use of an invalid dispensation, combined with the hint of a pay-off, was one of the major items cited by Bishop Saint-Vallier in his 1726–7 attempt to wrest the Louisbourg parish from Récollet hands. Because of the irregularity the curé responsible for sanctioning the wedding was recalled to France and Michel Daccarette and his wife waited twelve years before their marriage was officially legitimized.[90]

In addition to the diriment impediments, there were other impediments which rendered certain marriages illegal. The most important in this group was probably the restriction placed on when marriages could be celebrated. During two lengthy periods, Advent (from the first Sunday in Advent to Epiphany) and Lent (from Ash Wednesday to Low Sunday), priests were not to administer the sacrament of marriage. Only under exceptional circumstances were dispensations to be given at either of those two times of the year.[91] Though lax in other respects, the Louisbourg

FIGURE 7
Seasonal Fluctuations in Marriages, Baptisms,
and Burials at Louisbourg (1722–45; 1749–58)

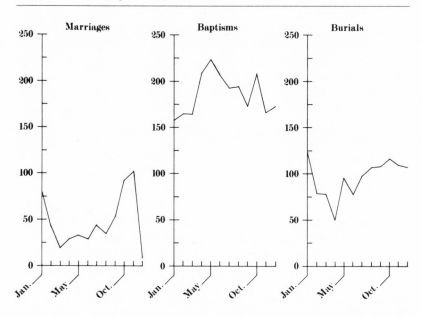

Récollets adhered strictly to church policy on this matter. There were few marriages held at Louisbourg during the prohibited periods, all of which seem to have been carried out with proper dispensations.[92]

The prohibition of weddings during Lent and Advent had a great impact on when people married in Louisbourg. The most popular months for marriages, by a wide margin, were those which immediately preceded or followed the prohibited periods (see Fig. 7). Nearly half of all weddings held in the town (269 of 565 or 47.5 per cent) took place in the three months of October, November, and January. As in most French seaside towns, the autumn months (at Louisbourg, especially October and November) were particularly popular because that was the time when the fishing and trading seasons drew to a close and the boats returned to port.[93] As for the months which fell neither near Advent nor Lent, there was little difference among them. In some French provinces marriages in May were avoided out of a fear that it was an unlucky month. Popular worries were that the offspring of a May wedding would be idiots or have red eyes or die early, or that one of the spouses would go insane.[94] Another tradition had it that May was a special time for women and that a man who wed during the month would be in his wife's "harness for the rest of his life."[95] Such fears do not appear to have been held widely among the inhabitants of Louisbourg, for there were as many weddings in May as there were in most other spring and summer months.

As with the months of the year, so with the days of the week there was a definite pattern in Louisbourg marriage habits (see Fig. 6). Close to two-thirds of the weddings (347 of 565, or 61.4 per cent) were held on Mondays and Tuesdays, with most of the remaining ones evenly distributed on Wednesdays, Thursdays, and Sundays. Far behind in popularity came Fridays (11 of 565, or 1.9 per cent) and Saturdays (27 of 565, or 4.8 per cent), presumably partly because they were days of abstinence on the church calendar and were thus not a suitable time for the customary post-wedding festivities. In the case of Friday there was also the association with the crucifixion of Jesus Christ, a fact which disinclined many people from marrying on that day. The small number of marriages on Fridays and Saturdays at Louisbourg suggests a popular concern for religious propriety since there was no formal requirement by the church that couples not be wed on those days. According to the *Rituel* for the diocese of Québec, the only days on which marriages were not to be held were Sundays or feast days.[96] The fact that a fair number of couples at Louisbourg (60 of 565, or 10.6 per cent) were married on Sunday is probably more indicative of laxity on the part of the town's Récollet curés than of the populace at large.

Regardless of the day on which a marriage took place, the *Rituel* stressed that under normal circumstances the ceremony was not to be performed before dawn, after the dinner hour, outside of the parish church or without having mass said immediately afterward. From time to time marriages were celebrated in the chapels of the Royal Battery and hospital, and on even rarer occasions in private residences,[97] but those were exceptional cases. The vast majority of marriages occurred in the chapel which served as Louisbourg's parish church. Nighttime weddings were equally uncommon. Those few that did take place (a total of nine have been identified) invariably involved people from the highest levels of Louisbourg society, usually noble officers in the garrison.[98] In this custom as in so many others Louisbourg seems to have followed the practice in France, where nighttime weddings were associated with the nobility or their bourgeois imitators.[99]

Before the marriage ceremony took place it was the responsibility of the curé to make sure that both the man and the woman were well instructed in the Catholic faith. Usually the priest's questions were taken very seriously by the prospective bride and groom, though not always. Louise Denys de la Ronde, fiancée of a Louisbourg military officer named

Claude Elizabeth Denys de Bonnaventure, used the occasion to make a ribald joke at the expense of a zealous young priest at Québec. Questioned by the curé as to whether or not she knew what the sacrament of marriage was, Mlle Denys de la Ronde replied that she knew nothing about it yet but if he was curious she would tell him the news in a few days. Everyone present laughed except the priest, who lowered his head in embarrassment.[100]

The eighteenth-century marriage ceremony itself was basically the same as the modern service, though there were differences in phraseology and in some of the ideas expressed (in 1767 Bishop Briand significantly altered the words spoken by the bride and groom).[101] In a lengthy discourse the priest explained that it was Christ himself who had made marriage a sacrament and that it must first and foremost be regarded as a profound spiritual union between a man and a woman. The groom and his bride were respectively to take as their models Christ and his Church, with the bride demonstrating the same submission and tenderness towards her husband as the Church showed toward Christ. If God blessed the marriage with children, the priest continued, the couple was to make sure that they were baptized and given "a completely holy and Christian education." The curé concluded with a warning to the bride and groom that they must show patience, understanding, and support for each other and that they must never allow themselves to give in to sentiments and actions "contrary to decency and Christian modesty." At Louisbourg six to ten people generally signed the marriage entry in the parish records, though sometimes as few as three or four or as many as twenty to twenty-five signed the document. How many were in attendance at any given wedding is of course unknown, though the marriages that involved socially prominent families tended to be the ones with the greatest number of witnesses on the marriage entry.[102]

There was a wide range of popular customs surrounding marriage in the eighteenth century, most of which were thought to bring either good luck or fertility to the bride and groom.[103] Which practices were observed in any given marriage would have depended on factors like the place of origin and social rank of the families involved. Particularly noisy customs such as the firing of shots in the early morning of a wedding day probably did not enjoy the same popularity in the urban setting of Louisbourg that it had in some rural areas. The only known instance of that custom being followed on Ile Royale occurred in 1754 in the settlement of relocated Acadians at Baye des Espagnols (Sydney).[104]

Discussion of marriage practices leads inevitably to the subject of sexual relations. There were a fair number of couples at Louisbourg who at the time of marriage either already had children (who were then legitimized

TABLE 7
Interval between Marriage and Birth of First Child

Period	Number of Marriages	Number with 1st child in less than 8 months	Percentage with 1st child in less than 8 months
1722 to mid-1744	218	29	13.3
1749 to mid-1757	307	30	9.8
Both periods	525	59	11.2

SOURCE: The Louisbourg marriage and baptismal records from which the intervals were calculated are in AN, Outre Mer, G1, vols. 406, 407, 408, and 409.

as part of the service in the church)[105] or were obviously soon to have one. Though it is not possible to know precisely how many brides and grooms may have been sexually intimate before marriage, it is possible to calculate the minimum number by measuring the interval between the wedding day and the date of birth of the first child. As Table 7 shows, the number of brides at Louisbourg who were pregnant on their wedding day ranged from 9.8 to 13.3 per cent, depending on the period in question.[106] How many more had had sexual relations but had not become pregnant is of course unknown.

The figures suggest that there was a slight decrease in premarital sexual activity during the 1750s, as compared with the period from 1722 to 1744. That, however, is not necessarily true. Many of the couples marrying at Louisbourg in the 1750s were from smaller settlements on Ile Royale, which were often not served by a resident Récollet priest. After being wed in the colonial capital they likely returned to their home communities, where some of them may have had children eight months or less after the ceremony. If so, the baptism of their children would not normally have been contained in the Louisbourg parish records. Consequently it is conceivable that there were more pregnant brides marrying at Louisbourg during the 1750s than are shown in Table 7.

Some of the brides known to have been pregnant at the time of marriage were well into their pregnancy. A total of twenty-four women gave birth twenty weeks or less after the wedding ceremony, and nine of these had a baby four weeks or less after the service. Among the latter group were three brides who gave birth on the very next day after the ceremony in church. The fact that some couples could wait so long before marrying suggests that there was no commonly felt need to hide a pregnancy or to hurry into matrimony. Strictly speaking, there should never have been hidden pregnancies. A sixteenth-century ordinance aimed at preventing infanticide required all unmarried women to declare their pregnancies, and parish priests were to read out this law before mass every three months. It is possible that in some Louisbourg families premarital sex was fully accepted once a couple was betrothed. Such sexual permissiveness had been common in France until the mid-seventeenth century and the attitude may have survived in certain regions and among some social groups.[107]

An example of the casual attitude with which a pregnancy could be treated was mentioned above in the discussion of Marie-Anne Carrerot and Michel de Gannes. In that instance, the unmarried woman seems to have been relatively unconcerned about her condition until she was in the fifth month of pregnancy, at which point she began to worry that her lover and presumed fiancé was not going to marry her.[108] As it turned out, he did not marry her and her child was born illegitimate, but in a number of other cases couples did wed after having waited through five, six, seven, or even eight months of pregnancy.

Compared to eighteenth-century Port Royal, with an illegitimacy rate of 0.6 per cent and a prenuptial conception rate of 1.4 per cent, the Louisbourg figures seem high. Yet when the comparison is made with some other contemporary towns the picture is quite different. In Bristol, Rhode Island, an important centre of commerce of around 1,000–1,200 residents, the rate after 1740 was considerably higher than that in Louisbourg. In the period 1720–40, 10 per cent of Bristol's brides were pregnant at the time of their marriage, or slightly fewer than was the case in Louisbourg for almost the same period. In 1740–60, however, the figure for prenuptial conception in Bristol climbed to 49 per cent, while Louisbourg's recorded rate dropped to less than 10 per cent. In 1760–80 the Bristol rate remained high at 44 per cent. The situation appears to have been much the same in rural England, where it is estimated that between one-third and one-half of the brides were "great with child" on their wedding day.[109]

One might have thought that in Louisbourg, a major fishing and trading centre as well as a military stronghold, premarital sexual activity would have surpassed that of Bristol or of the English countryside. Yet, notwithstanding the reputation of seaports and garrison towns, Louisbourg does not fit the stereotype. The rate of prenuptial conception in the town was only slightly higher than in seventeenth- and early eighteenth-century Canada (where the rate ranged from 4.5 to 8 per cent) and in Saint André-d'Hébertot, a rural parish in Normandy with 700–800 inhabitants (where the rate was 9.8 per cent).[110]

To what can one attribute the relatively high "moral" standards of Louisbourg brides and grooms? To the influence of the town's Récollet curés or of the Roman Catholic faith in general? Perhaps, but to avoid the temptation of over-hastily judging Louisbourg to have been a particularly virtuous community it is worth looking briefly at some of the "immoral" aspects of life in the town. Reference has already been made to the fondness a number of the inhabitants had for alcohol, to the point of preferring cabarets to church services. Another weakness, likewise a common one in this era, was a passion for gambling. Despite clerical and royal injunctions to the contrary,[111] all levels of Louisbourg society played cards, used dice, and enjoyed board games. Nowhere was the attraction to gaming stronger than at the highest social levels. One observer noted that the Louisbourg ladies always had "cards in their hands," while another lamented that he was a "useless member of society" because he neither knew how nor wanted to play. Reports of Commissaire-ordonnateur Prévost's gambling parties during the 1750s even reached the ears of the minister of marine in Versailles, who urged the colonial official to stop before his reputation was hurt.[112] Swearing was another common failing among the people of Louisbourg. The slightest provocation could sometimes touch off an outburst of profanities and derogatory remarks. With men, the most common insults were that they were thieves or less than honest (*fripon, voleur*, and *coquin*). With women, the attacks were usually on their morality, with slut or whore (*putain, garce*, and similar terms) being the most typical epithets.[113] Owing to the low court costs of the era many of the defamers ended up in court as the men or women slighted sought public apologies and restoration of their honour.

Sexual misconduct was also not unknown at Louisbourg. During the first few years of the colony there was a woman in the settlement identified as "une fille dangereuse par la Colonie" and two others described as "filles de mauvaise vie." The first avoided arrest by sailing to France with her accomplice, a Basque ship captain, and the other two escaped from actual custody with the complicity of their guards. In another instance, local royal officials considered deporting a man and his wife because the latter had "the reputation of a debauched person."[114] Similar vigilance by the state was shown toward males who deviated from the norms of public morality. A surgeon was sent back to France in 1722 for the libertine life he was leading; several years later an ordinance was issued in France forbidding libertines from emigrating to the colonies because of the disruption they caused.[115] By the 1750s there seems to have been some relaxation of the state's watchdog role over public morality. In 1751, just outside the walls of the town, one of the blockhouses erected by the English during their occupation was being used as a retreat for ne'er-do-wells of both sexes. Worse yet, the comte de Raymond, commandant of the colony from

FIGURE 8
Baptisms, Burials, and Marriages at Louisbourg (1722–45; 1749–58)

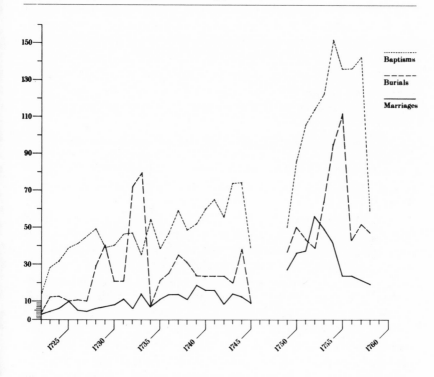

1751 to 1753, was accused of having impregnated his servant and of allowing both the Brothers of Charity and one of his senior officers to keep women of easy virtue. In a separate charge, a Sieur Brécon, an engineer, and his two sons were reported living with a "loose woman" and were awaiting the arrival of a second. That this ménage was in the governor's wing of the King's Bastion barracks was especially shocking to the commissaire-ordonnateur. Elsewhere in the barracks an ordinary soldier was sharing a room with another "femme de mauvaise vie." Though moral standards seem to have slipped, they had not disappeared for three women of this description and several other unwanted individuals were deported from the colony around the same time.[116] Such indications of various types of immoral behaviour suggest a slightly different picture than that presented by the relatively low rate of prenuptial conception at Louisbourg. Further research, especially using comparative data from similar contemporary communities, is necessary before any definite conclusions can be drawn about sexual morality at Louisbourg.

To return to marriage, the process of getting married in Louisbourg was an act, or rather a series of acts, both sacred and profane, which were charged with economic, emotional, religious, and social significance. For the majority of couples, especially relatively young ones, entry into holy matrimony represented a turning point in their lives, a step which entailed the taking on of major responsibilities as husband, wife, and parent. In the eyes of the church the next pivotal moment in one's life came at the time of death.

Death and Burial

Death was much more a part of life in the eighteenth century than it is in modern society.[117] Not only was the mortality rate then several times higher than it is now, but death itself, both as a grim reality and as a concept, had a far greater "presence" two centuries ago. Most individuals, young and old, did not die in hospitals or other institutions, but in the households in which they normally resided, often surrounded by relatives and friends. There were no funeral parlors, so corpses were kept at home until it was time for burial. Then, in what amounted to a sombre public pageant, a procession of mourners accompanied the remains from the deceased's house to the church and on to the graveyard. Cemeteries of that era were not located on the outskirts of town but in conspicuous locations within the community (frequently beside or around the parish church) where they stood as poignant reminders to everyone of their own mortality. In short, death in the eighteenth century was neither hidden nor cosmeticized as it often is today. Rather, it was a familiar and visible fact of life. The popular attitude towards dying seems to have been characterized by the view expressed in all of the Louisbourg wills, that nothing was more certain than death, only the hour of its coming was unknown.[118]

In the view of the Roman Catholic Church, of course, death was far more than just an inevitability. It was also divinely ordained. When Adam and Eve ate the forbidden fruit in the Garden of Eden they did so in defiance of God's clear warning: "but of the tree of knowledge of good and evil you shall not eat, for in the day that you eat of it you shall die." Though a punishment for the sinfulness of human nature, death also held out the possibility of ultimate salvation. According to the teachings of the church the end of earthly existence marked the transition into a new state of being, of either celestial bliss (heaven) or terrible punishment (purgatory or hell, depending on whether the punishment was to be limited or perpetual). Whether or not God granted salvation was determined by the extent to which one adhered to the tenets of the Catholic faith while on earth.

For sinners, and who was not, the last opportunity for reconciliation to God and the faith came just before death.[119] Therefore, in a very real sense, death was the most important event in a person's life.

Because of the importance of death in the Christian context, the church encouraged its faithful to reflect as often as possible on their own mortality. Bedtime was thought to be a particularly appropriate time for such reflection. The bishop of Québec suggested in his *Catéchisme* that people should go to bed each night with the attitude that they were getting into their tombs; that is, with the sober realization that they might die before the night was over.[120] Needless to say, not everyone thought of death as often or with the same equanimity as the church hoped. Nor did every person fear his or her own death in the same fashion. There were a few individuals at Louisbourg whom the parish records describe as having expired showing "a perfect resignation to the will of God."[121] Generally, however, the parish record entries are silent on the subject of how people died.

That individual reactions to death, or rather the prospect of death, varied widely is quite clear from the Chevalier de Johnstone's account of his storm-tossed voyage to Louisbourg in 1750. As described by Johnstone, each man on board the ship responded differently to the situation. While one raged, another wept, a third made exultant jokes, and a fourth quietly composed himself. Johnstone himself was "resigned to die." Yet, in spite of his appearance of tranquillity, he admitted that his mind was "lacerated and tormented to imagine what would be the last fall of the curtain." The only hope of the crew and passengers on the battered ship was thought to be divine intervention. To save themselves from being "swallowed up by the sea" they prayed to Saint Nicholas (patron saint of mariners) and vowed to pay for a high mass at Louisbourg if they were spared. The storm eventually did subside and when the ship arrived in the capital of Ile Royale the crew made a procession to the barracks chapel, "where grand mass was chanted, without sparing any expense, in consequence of their vows during the storm."[122]

Though not everyone went through the terrifying experience of a storm at sea, most people did have to face the fact of their own mortality at some point in their lives. Illness was the most common reminder but there were others, such as the signs of ageing or the death of a close friend or relative. Religious writers of the era hoped that once one grasped the inevitability of death one would do what was necessary "to die well."

The concept of a "good death" was still an important one during the first half of the eighteenth century, as it had been in the sixteenth and seventeenth centuries. The ideal experience, as described in many books and tracts[123] and depicted in many more engravings, drawings, and paint-

TABLE 8
Testators at Louisbourg: Reasons for Their Wills

Testators			Reasons		
Wills	Men	Women	Illness	Voyage	Not Indicated
58	46	12	41	4	13

SOURCE: Most Louisbourg wills are in AN, Outre Mer, G3; some
are in G2. There are selection lists for these series in the AFL.

ings, was one in which the dying individual performed a series of devotional acts before passing away. There were sacraments (confession,
communion, and extreme unction) to participate in, a last will and testament to be drawn up, reflections to be made, final words offered, and last
temptations resisted. Ideally, all of these steps were to take place in one's
own room (with a crucifix and lighted candle) in the presence of a priest
and surrounded by close friends and relatives.[124]

There were two main reasons why the drawing up of a will (testament)
was included on the list of things to be done in order "to die well." First,
the legal and carefully thought-out distribution of one's estate was looked
upon as a Christian obligation for all clerics, debtors, and heads of households. Wealthy people, in the opinion of the bishop of Québec, had a
special responsibility to bequeath sizeable sums of money to the church
and the poor.[125] The church appealed to people to draft wills while they
were still in good mental and physical health, but very few people followed that advice.[126] In Louisbourg, a clear majority forty-one of the fifty-
eight extant wills were dictated by individuals who were seriously ill (see
Table 8).

The second reason why the church considered wills to be important
was because they generally reflected an individual's spiritual concerns.
Each of the Louisbourg wills began with statements declaring the testator's
desire for salvation. The wording varied but every testament expressed
the hope that the testator's soul would go to heaven immediately upon his
death, and that thereafter his body would be buried in consecrated ground.
The statements followed a basic format, but they were not a meaningless
formula. Most wills were dictated by people who felt that they might die
soon, so salvation was very much on their minds. The local officials
(notaires royales) who drew up and certified the wills in Louisbourg may
have put the testator's remarks in standard phraseology, but there is no
reason to think that they simply added items not mentioned by the testa-

tor, particularly since the will had to be read back to the testator to make sure that the wording was as desired.

With regard to the sections where the distribution of the estate was outlined, the *Rituel* for the diocese of Québec stressed that people were to dispose of their earthly possessions in Christian fashion. First, all debts had to be paid and the needs of one's family taken into consideration. Once those basic requirements were taken care of, a true Christian was to give "indications of his piety toward the Church, & of his charity to the poor." In addition, the testator was to consider leaving money for prayers to be said for the repose of his soul and those of his dearest relatives and friends.

The amount of money which one could leave to the church or to charity was of course determined more by one's economic and social position than by one's religious feelings. Where some artisans at Louisbourg left only a few dozen *livres* for masses and prayers, there were wealthier inhabitants who could afford to leave several hundred *livres*, or more, for the same purpose (see Table 9). Predictably, the greatest benefactor of the cause of religion was from the colony's highest social level. As we have seen, in 1740 Governor Isaac-Louis de Forant left practically his entire estate, later adjusted to a 32,000 *livres* settlement, to the Louisbourg community of the Sisters of the Congregation of Notre-Dame.[127]

It may appear from Table 9 that less than half of the fifty-eight people whose wills have survived felt any desire to leave money to the church for posthumous services and prayers for their souls. Yet that was not the case. Virtually everyone who left a will expressed a desire to have masses and prayers said after their death. However, where some left the amount to be spent on such things up to surviving family members, others identified specific sums to be expended. It is this latter, smaller group which is recorded in Table 9. In almost every case they were either unmarried or widowed, and without close family relations in Louisbourg. The only way in which they could be reasonably certain of receiving the kind of burial and memorial services they wanted was by allocating a set portion of their estate for that purpose. Thus, Julien Gery, a fisherman from France, left 50 *livres* to the Récollets of Brittany to cover his burial in the Louisbourg parish cemetery and the saying of mass and prayers on his behalf. To the same end, though with more money, André Angr, a soldier in the Karrer Regiment, bequeathed 300 *livres* to the Récollets, 200 *livres* to the Brothers of Charity, and 100 *livres* to the Sisters of the Congregation.[128] By way of contrast, residents of Louisbourg who had heirs to succeed them usually felt no need to spell out such details in their wills. It was sufficient to state, as the prosperous merchant, Guillaume Delort, did, that he was leaving "the repose of his soul ... entirely to his wife and the executors of his will."[129]

TABLE 9
Wills at Louisbourg: Bequests to Church and Charity

Wills	Bequests		Charity (poor)
	Church (masses, prayers, etc.)		
58	99 livres or less	6	1
	100–500 livres	9	5
	501–1,000 livres	3	
	Over 1,000 livres	3	
	TOTALS	21	6

SOURCE: AN, Outre Mer, G3 and G2.

That having close heirs made a substantial difference in what one put in a will is perhaps most clear in the case of Anne de Galbarret. In 1727, at which point she was a widow without any children of her own, Galbarret had a will drawn up leaving a total of 1,080 livres to various churches in France and to the Louisbourg Récollets. In return, memorial services and prayers were to be said on behalf of herself, her late husband, and her late brother. Fifteen years later, at which point she had been remarried for four years, she drew up a new will. This time she left it almost entirely to her husband to decide how much should be spent on posthumous services. The only specific commitment she made was for a 100 livres endowment to go to the Louisbourg parish church. She asked in return that a requiem mass be celebrated each Thursday between four and five o'clock in the afternoon, with a "De Profundis at the end of the said Mass for the benediction and repose of her soul."[130]

The number of Louisbourg residents who had wills drawn up was relatively small. With most people, a "good death" consisted principally of receiving the final sacraments from the attending priest. Provided there was time, dying individuals were first confessed and then given communion and extreme unction. In cases where the person expired quickly, there was often only time for the last sacrament. Very young children generally did not receive any sacraments at the time of death, unless they were newborn, in which case they were "sprinkled" (ondoyé) before they died. Once a child reached the age of seven, which was considered to be the age of reason, they could be given extreme unction. Confession and communion were not administered until about the age of twelve.[131]

Analysis of the burial entries in the Louisbourg parish records provides a picture of mortality in the town, according to age and sex (see Table 10).

TABLE 10

Burials in Louisbourg Parish Records, 1722–45 and 1749–58

Age	Males	Females	Sex Not Indicated	Total
less than 1 year	116	108	4	228
1 to 5 years	72	65		137
6 to 12 years	18	17		35
13 to 24 years	94	41		135
25 to 44 years	157	67		224
45 to 64 years	121	31		152
65 and over	29	13		42
adults, age not indicated	178	47		225
TOTALS	785	389	4	1,178

SOURCE: Louisbourg parish *registres*, AN, Outre Mer, GI; baptisms, burials, and marriages were sometimes kept in separate *registres*, at other times in the same one.

The first point to be made about these figures is that they do not reflect every death and burial in Louisbourg during the time periods in question. Individuals who passed away in the Hôpital du Roi were rarely if ever recorded in the town's parish *registres* because there was a different burial ground as well as separate records kept for deceased hospital patients. Since detailed records of the Hôpital du Roi are not extant, it is impossible to know exactly how many people died there over the years. However, it is known that between 1719 and 1742 at least 148 men (the vast majority of whom were soldiers) passed away in the hospital.[132] It is likely that another 100 to 200 men died there during the remaining years (1743–5 and 1749–58) of the French occupation. Therefore in examining the figures in Table 10 it is important to remember that they do not include an additional 200 to 400 adult males who died in the Hôpital du Roi.

Where Table 10 is most useful is in its reflection of overall civilian mortality rates.[133] The figures for adults, for instance reveal quite clearly that average life expectancy in the eighteenth century was much lower than it is today. There were relatively few men and women who lived to the age of sixty-five or older; most died in what is now regarded as middle age. Also noteworthy is the fact that the second highest total for women was in the 13 to 24 age range, not in the 45 to 64 range as was the case for men. The principal cause of that high mortality rate among very young women was more than likely death due to complications at time of child-

TABLE 11
Survival Rate among Children at Louisbourg, 1722–45 and 1749–58

Burials		Baptisms:	2,233	Survival Rate per 1,000	
		surviving to:		(a)	(b)
within 1st month	104	1 month	2,129	953	
1–12 months	124	1 year	2,005	898	767
1–5 years	137	6 years	1,868	837	
6–12 years	35	13 years	1,833	821	
13–19 years	50	20 years	1,783	798	502

(a) Louisbourg
(b) France (1700–1800)

SOURCES: The format is based on the table in François Lebrun, *Les hommes et la mort en Anjou aux 17e et 18e siècles*, 180. The figures in column (b) come from the same table, those in column (a) from surviving baptismal and burial records.

birth. This explanation seems to be supported by the fact that women at Louisbourg married at a relatively young age for the era, with the mean age for first-time brides being 19.9 and the modal age 18.0 (see above and Fig. 5).

As to the figures for children, it is obvious that infant and juvenile deaths represented a significant proportion of the total number of burials in Louisbourg. Every fifth burial (228 of 1,178, 19.2 per cent) was of a child less than one year old; almost every third burial (365 of 1,178, 30.8 per cent) was of a child five or younger. High as those figures may appear by twentieth-century North American standards, the mortality rate among Louisbourg children actually appears to have been remarkably low when compared with figures in eighteenth-century France.

It is possible that a number of children's deaths in Louisbourg went unrecorded, and that therefore the figures in Table 11, column (a), are slightly inflated. The fact that only ten children's deaths were entered in the parish records for the entire period from 1741 to 1745, suggest that possibility. Did the parish priests in the 1740s neglect to record some children's burials? Possibly, but even if that was the case, one could be justified only in adding another forty or fifty burials to the Louisbourg totals. The survival rate for the town's children would still be well above the figures for France.

How does one explain the wide margin between the Louisbourg and French survival rates? Were the diets of Louisbourg residents (and their children) better balanced and more nutritious than their counterparts in

France? Were they as a result less liable to become seriously ill or to contract diseases or infections? Or was the economy of Ile Royale such that there was relatively little poverty by eighteenth-century standards, and that as a result one of the attendant ills of poverty, a high infant mortality rate, was greatly reduced.[134] These are major questions which deserve further study beyond the scope of this book.

Returning to the concept of the "good death," it was noted above that under ideal circumstances this was to occur with close friends and relatives in attendance. These witnesses would provide comfort and consolation to the dying individual, listen to his prayers and final thoughts, and, for their own sake, gain insight into the hidden world of death and the hereafter.[135] Depending on where the people concerned were from there were also certain customs to be followed at this time, though the specific practices adopted at Louisbourg are unknown. In Brittany, one sprinkled the dying person's bed with holy water and lit a special candle, with which one made the sign of the cross three times, as soon as the person expired. Practices in other regions included stopping clocks and watches at the time of death, covering mirrors or turning them to the wall, and sprinkling holy water around the deceased's room. Some people believed that the room should not be swept or dusted immediately after someone died because by doing so one might expel from the house the person's lingering soul.[136]

Unless a person died of a contagious disease, or following a lengthy illness, the church asked that the remains not be buried for at least twenty-four hours, just in case the individual revived.[137] Thereafter, if at all possible, the person was to be interred in consecrated ground. Burial in consecrated ground was extremely important, both to the church and to the dying individual. On a personal level, the wish to be buried in the Louisbourg parish cemetery was so strong that it was specifically mentioned in a number of wills. Similarly, it is likely that the dozen or so deathbed conversions to Roman Catholicism made by Protestants at Louisbourg were motivated as much by a desire to be buried in proper fashion, with respect and in consecrated ground, as they were by a deep-seated preference for Catholic theology.[138]

As for the church, there was a long list of the types of people (heretics, schismatics, unbaptized infants, duellists, unrepentant sinners, suicides, and others) who were never to be given "Ecclesiastical Burial."[139] Interment of someone from an expressly forbidden category was thought to profane consecrated ground. Thus, at Louisbourg, an effort was sometimes made to ascertain the religion of individuals whose bodies were found washed ashore. On occasion, a crucifix or a rosary might be found on a corpse, in which case it was assumed the man had been a Catholic, and he was buried accordingly. If the drowned man's ship was known, inquiries might be made among the crew and chaplain, if there was one, as to whether or not he had been a practising Roman Catholic. And yet, when there was no way to determine the identities of cadavers, as in 1754 when six unidentifiable bodies were washed ashore, the local clergy appear to have given them the benefit of the doubt for they buried each one in the parish cemetery.[140]

Another occasion on which someone was given the benefit of the doubt occurred in September 1757, when the drowned body of Pierre de Montalembert de Cers, an officer in the Louisbourg garrison, was buried in the town's cemetery. Three months earlier Montalembert had disappeared into the woods of Ile Royale, apparently in great depression over his wife's affair with another officer in the garrison. It was widely suspected that Montalembert had taken his own life while in the wilderness, in which case he should not have been buried in consecrated ground. However, the judge of the court of the Bailliage in Louisbourg apparently felt that the evidence was not conclusive, and he ordered that Montalembert's remains be interred in the parish cemetery.[141]

Considerably less charity had been shown several weeks earlier to another suspected suicide, significantly one from much farther down in the social structure of the town. In that case, a local servant named Payen was found dead in his prison cell, "Strangled by a Handkerchief," on the evening of the day on which he had been arrested on suspicion of theft. Following a brief investigation, the verdict was that the servant had committed suicide. In accordance with the standard practice of the era, the suicide's body was punished severely, so that his memory would be condemned in perpetuity for his crime against church and state. Payen's cadaver was dragged behind a cart, face down, through the main street of Louisbourg and then hung upside down for twenty-four hours from a gallows erected in front of his former master's house.[142] Where Payen's body was buried when it was taken down is not known, but it certainly was not in the parish cemetery.

In the course of Louisbourg's four decades as a French settlement there were a succession of different official cemetery locations in the community. The initial burial ground was in Block 3, beside the building which housed the town's first church. For a decade Louisbourg's dead were buried in that harbourfront location. Then in 1722–3 royal officials decided to relocate the graveyard and concede the cemetery land in Block 3 to a few private citizens (with some but not all of the remains being exhumed and reinterred elsewhere). Two new burial grounds were established, one in Block 34, which was to serve as a parish cemetery, and one in Block 40, which was reserved for the use of the hospital. The Block 34 site was quickly judged to be a poor location for a cemetery, and by 1726 the parish burial ground had been relocated to Block 40, adjacent to the hospital graveyard. The two cemeteries probably remained in that area until 1744, though proposals to shift them both surfaced on several occasions during the late 1730s and early 1740s. Sometime in 1744 interments in Block 40 seem to have stopped. One and possibly two new burial grounds may have been established outside the town walls at that time. Certainly during the English occupation of Louisbourg (1745–9) the main graveyard was on Rochefort Point. When the French returned to the town they seem to have used two cemeteries, one on Rochefort Point for "soldiers" and one between the Princess Demi-Bastion and Cap Noir for the "inhabitants."[143]

In addition to the official cemeteries, there were a number of other locations where people were buried in Louisbourg. Poor weather conditions or fear of bringing a contagious disease into town prompted the interment of several bodies in relatively isolated spots, from wilderness sites to Pointe Rosse to Battery Island. The most noteworthy of the "emergency" burial grounds was that established on the Jean Martin habitation in the faubourg during the smallpox epidemic of 1732–3, when the town's annual mortality rate doubled to more than seventy. Nineteen people, all of whom undoubtedly lived in the vicinity, were buried on the Martin property during the eight-month period that the disease was at its peak.[144]

A few individuals were buried in special locations, not out of necessity but because they requested it or others deemed it to be appropriate. In 1729 Marie-Magdelaine Noel, the novice who had aspired to join the Congregation of Notre-Dame, was buried on the lot in Block 3 reserved for the construction of Louisbourg's parish church. Three years later two Récollets, Ignace Audren and Narcisse Varin, were interred in the same lot. In 1740 *major de place* Michel le Neuf de la Vallière may have been buried in the same general area; the parish record entry simply describes the location as the Récollet convent cemetery. No other Récollet is known to have been buried in Block 3. The bodies of all the other friars who died in Louisbourg, except one, were placed in whatever parish cemetery was being used at the time. The exception was Candide Fournier, who in 1752 was buried in the chapel of the Hôpital du Roi, where he had served as chaplain for a number of years.

The most prestigious place to be buried in Louisbourg was unquestionably beneath the Chapelle de Saint-Louis, which from the mid-1720s served as the town's parish church. The first person to be interred there was Governor de Forant, in 1740. As it seemed likely at the time of his death that the parish cemetery in Block 40 would soon be relocated, Commissaire-ordonnateur François Bigot felt that it would be inappropriate to bury a governor there. Instead, he decided that Forant was to be placed beneath the chapel floor. That precedent having been set, the only other governor to die in Louisbourg, Jean-Baptiste Louis Le Prévost Duquesnel, was also buried in the chapel, in 1744. The next interment was that of the remains of duc d'Anville, brought to Louisbourg in 1749 from Halifax where the ill-fated naval commander had died in 1746. The final official burial in the chapel was of *major de place* Michel de Gannes de Falaise, a longtime resident of the town. A fifth and unexplained burial in the chapel, discovered by archaeologists, is that of a young child.[145]

For burials at Louisbourg bodies were either placed in coffins or wrapped in shrouds. During the early years of the settlement, and perhaps throughout the entire history of the town, shrouds seem to have been more common.[146] Archaeological excavation in 1974 of several Block 3 properties uncovered twenty-three graves dating from 1713 to 1723. In only three cases was there evidence that a coffin had been used. The other interments were apparently of the bodies in shrouds. Another finding was that most individuals seem to have been buried without any personal possessions. There was no indication of rosaries, crucifixes, or shoe leather. As for clothes, the only evidence found was of a single button, which is thought to have been from a shirt collar.

A final point about the Block 3 graves is that all of them were relatively shallow, being less than a foot below the eighteenth-century ground level.[147] Since the soil in that area is not particularly difficult to remove, one must conclude that the inhabitants did not think it important to have deep graves for their dead. As a result of such shallow burials, particularly when many of the bodies were wrapped in shrouds, skeletal remains occasionally came to the surface. Several New Englanders who occupied Louisbourg after the first siege remarked on that aspect of the town's burial grounds:

> I saw whare ye Ennemy used to Bury there Dead there I saw Sculs & other Bones Lay upon ye Ground.[148]

> I went to see the Place where they Buried their Dead. and the french Having Occasion for Earth to fortife them-Selves and it being Easiest Digging there, They had taken Earth from that place which uncover'd Many Coffins. and Bones etc.[149]

The practice apparently changed little during the second French occupation. In 1759 an English visitor wrote that French cadavers had been "buried very shallow, so that there were many bones to be seen above ground, and pieces of coffins."[150] That such things did not bother the

French suggests that the medieval idea that it mattered little what "the exact destination of one's bones was" so long as the "body was entrusted to the Church" was still alive among the inhabitants of the town.[151] By way of contrast, when the British occupied Louisbourg they apparently hoped to prevent the same thing from happening to their dead by specifying that all graves were to be at least three feet deep. Notwithstanding the regulation, Governor Knowles complained in 1746 that the New Englanders "buried their dead under the Floors ... rather than go out of Doors in the Cold."[152]

To return to the subject of shrouds and coffins, the only other graves which have been archaeologically excavated at Louisbourg were those beneath the Chapelle de Saint-Louis. In that location, all four men had been put in coffins (three in wooden coffins, one in a lead casket), while the child had apparently been wrapped in a shroud.[153] As for documentary evidence, there are a number of references to coffins (ranging from 3 to 8 *livres* in cost, presumably varying according to the quality of wood and workmanship) in estate inventories of the 1730s and 1740s, but the sample is too small to draw any general conclusions.[154] It is probable, however, that in interments of the poor or of most children, shrouds were used, with coffins and caskets being reserved for those who could afford the additional cost.

Just as wealth and social position could influence how one was buried, so they could determine the number of memorial services and prayers which were said for an individual. Where 21 *livres* was spent on services for fisherman Etienne Guerard, 89 *livres* was expended for Anne Guion Després (*veuve* Chevalier) and 300 *livres* for Governor Duquesnel.[155] The most costly service was undoubtedly that given the duc d'Anville. When his remains were interred at Louisbourg in 1749, funeral expenses were slightly over 1,000 *livres*, with additional money being spent on an elaborate artillery salute.[156]

The standard funeral service, to which everyone was entitled regardless of how much money was involved, was as follows:[157] At the time set for the ceremony to begin (usually in the morning, except on Sundays and feast days), the priest(s), lay assistants, and mourning parishioners assembled in church, generally the parish church. From there, at the signal of a tolling bell and led by the clergy, the group proceeded to the house where the body rested. While the curé was in the house blessing the body and chanting the appropriate antiphons, candles and torches were distributed to those who waited outside. When the remains were brought out the people formed an orderly procession, with the assistant who carried the cross leading the way. The clergy came next, with the curé walking directly in front of the coffin. The mourners followed the remains. Along the route to the church a series of psalms were sung "distinctly, with devotion and gravity."

At the church, the deceased, if a lay person, was placed in the middle of the nave with his feet towards the altar; in the case of a priest or other ecclesiastic the body was put in the choir with his head towards the altar. Lighted candles surrounded the body throughout the service, which in most cases included mass. Following the service there was a procession from the church to the cemetery (with the clergy chanting the antiphon *In Paradisum*), where the curé sprinkled holy water and incense on both the grave and the remains. After interment the clergy returned from the cemetery, saying aloud the antiphon *Si iniquitates* and the psalm *De profundis*. Graves at Louisbourg were likely marked by wooden crosses.[158]

There were variations in the standard funeral service if the deceased's body was not present (such as in a drowning at sea) or if the person to be buried was a child. In the former case, the service was shortened but was to be repeated on the third, seventh, and thirtieth days after a disappearance, and then again at the end of a year. As for children, the *Rituel* for the Diocese of Québec recommended that a special section of each cemetery be reserved for the burial of boys and girls who had not yet reached the age of discretion (around seven years old). It also suggested that if church bells were to be rung at all for the burial of a child, the tolling should express joy rather than sadness. At the burial itself, the custom was to place a crown of flowers, or of sweet-smelling herbs on the child's head, "to mark the 'integrity' of his flesh and his virginity." In some areas of France, and perhaps also at Louisbourg, only a priest and a sacristan were present at the burial of very young children (less than four to five years old).[159] In the case of older children, however, with whom a stronger family attachment had been formed, relatives attended as well.[160]

In many instances of course, burial did not signify the end. Throughout the year, or years, which followed there were often masses and prayers to be said for the repose of the deceased's soul. And, among surviving loved ones, there were the memories. The following extract from a 1749 letter of Madame Bégon, a resident of Montréal, to her son-in-law expresses both the sense of loss which she still felt one full year after her husband's death as well as her concern that his soul be granted eternal rest: "It is one year today, my son, since I lost M. Bégon. You are right in thinking that the preparations leading up to the anniversary are for me a redoubling of the sorrow. Tomorrow we must have a service at the parish church. I hope that wherever you will be, you will not forget to add your prayers to ours. In that way we will give him our best effort."[161] Doubtless there were many individuals in contemporary Louisbourg who had similar feelings over the loss of a loved one. Like Madame Bégon they found solace, and perhaps a meaning for their existence, in their religious faith.

Conclusion

In secular terms, Ile Royale was not a typical part of New France. Not only was there no seigneurial regime but its fur trade was an insignificant factor in the colonial economy, which was based instead on fish, trade, and government expenditure. These sectors made Louisbourg, the island's economic and administrative centre, a prosperous and, by North American standards, well-defended port. Yet the geographic isolation of the settlement from both France and the rest of New France, combined with its dependence on imports of food and other commodities, rendered it extremely vulnerable to any concerted enemy attack. Twice within its short lifespan it was captured, and the second time meant the virtual end of the French presence on Cape Breton for decades.[1] Therefore, though Ile Royale was a sizeable and expensive undertaking, it remained a marginal colony like its seventeenth-century predecessors in the region.[2] Because of the "newness" of Ile Royale there were also some demographic differences between it and the rest of New France. The most important differences were a marked imbalance in the sexes (a standard feature of new colonies) and the fact that a majority of the inhabitants were either French-born or the children of French-born settlers. All of these factors, economic, geographic, and demographic, affected many areas of life in the colony, not the least of which was the sphere of religion.

Institutionally, the church was never strongly established at Louisbourg. To begin with, there was no clerical representative on the Conseil Supérieur and no higher clergy; the island was but part of the vast diocese of the bishop of Québec. The prolonged absences in France of several of the bishops were a problem for the church in Canada. At Louisbourg, which was never even visited by a bishop, the situation was worse. Those named as vicars-general lacked power and influence on the local level and had always to work through either the bishop or Abbé de l'Isle-Dieu in France, a process that could take months or years. Moreover, because the colony was judged to be in its infancy there was no formal requirement for parishioners to pay the standard tax to the church: the tithe (not even the half-tithe demanded by their counterparts in Canada). Voluntary contributions to the church were of course made, but not enough to give the religious a measure of independence from the state. Rather, they relied on annual salaries (400 to 500 *livres* each) and expense payments from the Ministry of Marine simply to maintain their establishments in the colony. With their hands tied economically, and without a local figure of sufficient status and power to battle for them, the Louisbourg religious were at a distinct disadvantage in their dealings with royal officials. Whenever disputes arose, whether between civil and religious authorities or between different religious groups, the issues were invariably settled by representatives of the king.

The relative weakness of the church as an institution at Louisbourg undoubtedly affected the way in which some of the religious carried out their responsibilities. Had there been a strong and independent representative of the higher clergy in the town (such as a bishop or a coadjutor) he would certainly have put an early stop to such things as the erratic behaviour of Récollet Benin Le Dorz and the rumours of sexual activity among a few of the Brothers of Charity. Presumably he would also have either defended the local religious when critics like Abbé de l'Isle-Dieu castigated them for their alleged failings, or, if the criticism was well founded, taken action to rectify the situation.

It is clear that each of the three groups that served at Louisbourg did so under severe handicaps. With the Sisters of the Congregation of Notre-Dame most of the hardships they endured arose from a single cause: they were almost never on a sound financial footing. Consequently, they were often beset with worries over money and on occasion reduced to making straw ticks (*paillasses*) for the soldiers' barracks to generate income. During the 1750s they were unable to admit more than a few students to their school. Notwithstanding the difficulties, the sisters earned the respect of virtually everyone who has left an assessment of their educational and moral impact on the Louisbourg community.

In contrast with the Sisters of the Congregation, the Brothers of Charity did not suffer from any major funding problems. Their difficulties lay rather in the areas of staff shortages, over which only their provincial in France had any control, and jurisdictional conflicts with the royal officials who administered the Louisbourg hospital. Both complications made life at times difficult for the brothers' superiors. Yet although there were disputes over the quality and cost of the health care they provided, and occasional calls for another medical order to take over the Hôpital du Roi, it seems that the brothers offered, on balance, a satisfactory level of medical service.

The group that received the most criticism at Louisbourg was the Récollets of Brittany. At different times and by different people they were described as being poorly educated, complacent, negligent, and generally of little worth. They had their defenders, however, who described them as hard-working, beloved, and entirely suitable for the arduous parish work found in a developing colony like Ile Royale. The truth probably lies somewhere between the two assessments. What is undeniable is that many of the Récollets' difficulties were due to conditions beyond their control, or at least beyond the control of the friars sent to Louisbourg. For instance, the responsibility for the dispute between the Brittany and Paris Récollets over who would serve where in the colony really lay with royal officials and the bishop, who had created the situation of dual representation and inevitable rivalry. Similarly, the Récollets' inability to serve all the parishes on the island stemmed from the failure of their provincial in France to send out enough *religieux*, not from any innate weaknesses among the local friars. As it was, given the small number of Récollets in the colony, that they could meet the needs of most of the several thousand parishioners was a considerable achievement.

That is not to say that the Récollets of Brittany were not deserving of some criticism. Whether they were as negligent as Abbé de l'Isle-Dieu stated, failing to visit the sick, listen to confessions, and so on, is difficult to say given the paucity of supporting documentary evidence in that regard. But it is clear from quantitative analysis of the parish records that the Récollets were lax in some areas of their ministry. To cite three examples, they allowed young children to act as godparents, generally allowed marriages to go ahead with only one or no bann having been read, and did not insist on a formal betrothal. Each of these practices was in contravention of the bishop's guidelines in his *Rituel* for the Diocese of Québec. In more serious matters, however, such as the prohibition of marriages during Lent and Advent and the desirability of baptizing children as soon as possible after birth, the Récollets followed the standard practice of the era.

The Louisbourg parish must not have been an easy one for the Récollets to serve, and to direct. As a garrison town and seaport Louisbourg had both a large transient population and a gross imbalance in the sexes, with males greatly outnumbering females. Notwithstanding the stereotypes, however, Louisbourg does not seem to have been a particularly immoral place, perhaps due in part to the influence of the religious. There are references to prostitutes ("femmes de mauvaise vie") and a couple of court cases of sexual violence or molestation. Yet neither the illegitimacy rate (4.5 per cent) nor the number of brides pregnant at time of marriage (11.2 per cent) was particularly high for the period. The greatest vices in the community seem to have been gambling and drinking (there were always more than twenty cabarets in business), but the popularity of those recreational pursuits was likely due more to isolation and boredom than to a lack of religious or moral sentiment among the population.

Where the Louisbourg parishioners seem to stand apart from their contemporaries in Canada or Acadia is in their profound parsimony. Cornelius Jaenen has shown how in other parts of New France there was often reluctance on the part of the inhabitants to contribute toward the building of a new church or to pay the tithe on time. At Louisbourg there was an absolute refusal to do either. (By way of contrast, parishioners in smaller communities on Ile Royale did get together to erect their own parish churches.) It is difficult to say what lay behind this attitude in Louisbourg. Conceivably, the mercantile atmosphere within the town played a role, as did the presence of large numbers of transients without deep roots in the community. Probably of even greater importance was the fact that Louisbourg was largely a royal creation. From its fortifications to its lighthouse to its many royal buildings, all the major structures in the town were constructed out of funds from the king's treasury. The inhabitants seem to have expected Louis XV to build them a church as well.

As in any study, so in this one of religion at Louisbourg there remain unanswered questions and new avenues for research. More work needs to be done on literacy and therefore on the impact of the Sisters of the Congregation. Further research could be undertaken on drinking and gambling with an eye to finding out more about the morals and morale of the community. Most of all, what is called for are other studies of the religious life in contemporaneous settlements so that the representative and unusual qualities of the Louisbourg experience will stand out more clearly. Only through further research will we acquire a more complete understanding of the role religion played in the disparate regions of New France.

Appendix A

RÉCOLLETS OF BRITTANY[1]

The dates below show the years in which the various Récollets of Brittany are known to have been in Louisbourg, even if only for a few days. They may have visited or stayed there during parts of other years as well, but their names are not mentioned elsewhere in the extant sources. The names of a number of other priests who officiated at baptisms, marriages, and burials in the town, including the local missionaries to the Micmacs, ship's chaplains, and others, are not included in this listing.

	At Louisbourg	Comment
Juvenal ADAM	1735–7	Identified as "vicaire de Louisbourg"; apparently on Ile Saint-Jean, 1745; in 1745–8 at Québec, where he died
Ambroise AUBRÉ	1741–5 1749–52 1755–8	Served at Port Lajoie (Ile Saint-Jean), 1739–41; chaplain of Royal Battery, Louisbourg, 1741–2; at Port Lajoie, 1752–4; curé of Louisbourg, mid-1755 to mid-1757; at Baleine, 1757; in Louisbourg, 1758
Ignace AUDREN	1731–2	Buried in 1732 in the lot set aside for the Louisbourg parish church
Urbain BOURDON	1737–43	Chaplain of Royal Battery, 1739–40
Pierre d'Alcantara CABARET	1753–8	At La Baleine, 1754–5 and 1756–7; in 1759, in France, still on the royal payroll and serving as military chaplain to the soldiers who had been on Ile Royale
Zacharie CARADEC	1728–34 1737–9	Curé of Louisbourg, mid-1728 to mid-1733; returned to France in 1734 following lengthy controversy; during second stay served as commissaire but not curé; again recalled to France
Isidore CAULET	1723–7 1730–45 1749–54	Returned to France during the Le Dorz controversy; identified as "aumonier des troupes" several times during 1720s–40s; at Port Lajoie in 1752; interim curé of Louisbourg after the deaths of Guégot and Fournier, 1752–3; died at Louisbourg in June 1754

	At Louisbourg	Comment
Angélique COLLIN	1743,1745	Served at Port Lajoie, 1736–7, and at La Baleine and Petit Lorembec, 1741–5
Luc COTTIN	1749–52 1754–7	Missionary and curé of La Baleine and Lorembec, 1751–4 and 1755–6
Joseph-Marie DE SÉGUR	1741	
François-Célestin DIANET or DIARET	1723, 1725, 1728	Curé of La Baleine, 1716–20 and 1726–7; curé of Niganiche, 1725
Eugène DORÉ		Missionary at La Baleine, 1714 and 1716
Alexis DUBURONS		At Port Lajoie, 1751
Antoine de Pade DULAURENS	1752, 1755–7	
Candide FOURNIER	1734–45, 1752	Chaplain of Royal Battery, 1734; chaplain of Hôpital du Roi, 1736 and 1738; curé of La Baleine and Lorembec, 1738–9; curé of Louisbourg, 1752 until his death; buried in the hospital chapel, 1752
Athanase GUÉGOT	1732–3, 1735 1737–45 1749–52	Sailed to the colony in 1731; served at Port Lajoie, 1733–6; curé of Louisbourg, mid-1737 to mid-1745, and again from mid-1749 until his death in February 1752
Alexis GUILLOU	1727–8, 1730–1, 1740–5	Curé of La Baleine and Lorembec, 1728–30; at Scatary, 1734; chaplain at Port Toulouse, 1736; chaplain at Royal Battery, 1741; chaplain at hospital, 1741, 1744–5; acting curé after Guégot's departure, 1745
Martial HAREL	1737	
Hippolyte HERP	1733–5	Curé of Louisbourg, mid-1733 to mid-1735
Calixte KERRIOU	1744–5	
Elie KERVICHE		Served at Port Lajoie, 1741–4; at St Pierre-du-Nord, 1745
Patrice LAGRÉE	1752–4, 1756–8	Served at Port Lajoie, 1749–52; at La Baleine in 1754
Eugène LEBRETON	1734, 1743–4	Missionary at Port Dauphin, 1734
Jean-Bertrand LEBRETON	1743	Missionary and curé at St Esprit, 1733–7 and 1741–3
Bénin LE DORZ	1724–7	Curé of Louisbourg, mid-1724 until the fall of 1727 when he was recalled to France
François LE DROGOFF	1723–4	
Michel-Ange LE DUFF	1724, 1726–8	Missionary at La Baleine, 1721–5; military chaplain then curé of Louisbourg from the fall of 1727 until mid-1728
Hyacinthe LEFEBVRE	1753–4	Served at Port Dauphin in 1754
Etienne LE GOFF	1729–31 1735–7 1739–40	Missionary at La Baleine, 1730–1; at St Esprit, 1732; curé at Niganiche, 1734; curé of Louisbourg, mid-1735 to mid-1737; provincial of Récollets of Brittany, 1742–5

	At Louisbourg	Comment
Gabriel LEMOIGN	1744	Missionary at Port Lajoie, 1737–9; missionary and curé at St Pierre du Nord (Ile Saint-Jean), 1739 and 1744
Mathieu-François LEPAIGE	1731	Missionary at Port Lajoie, 1731–6, 1737
Paulin LOZACH	1743–5 1749 1752–3	Chaplain at Royal Battery, 1743; missionary at St Esprit; 1743–5; chaplain at Royal Battery, 1749–50; missionary at La Baleine and Petit Lorembec, 1750–1; chaplain at Hôpital du Roi, 1752
Chérubin MEZIÈRE	1729–30	At Scatary, 1729; missionary at La Baleine, 1730; curé at La Baleine and Lorembec, 1731–3
Julien MOISSON	1752–5	
Marcellin MOYSAN	1722–3	Missionary at Scatary, 1723–4; at La Baleine, 1727, 1728 and 1731
Félix NIZAN	1744–5	Missionary and curé of Lorembec and La Baleine, 1734–8
Aubin PIGERON	1752	Chaplain aboard La Fidèle
Gratien RAOUL	1754	On Ile Royale in 1714–15, then in France until 1754; on Ile Saint-Jean, 1754–8
Samuel RIOU		At Malpec, Ile Saint-Jean, 1745
Chérubin ROPERT	1752–3 1756–7	
Clément ROSSELIN	1753–5	Curé of Louisbourg, mid-1753 to mid-1755
Claude SANQUER	1722–4	Curé of Louisbourg, 1722 to mid-1724
Bruno SAUVÉ	1720	At La Baleine, 1716
René SERVEL	1731, 1734	Chaplain and curé at Port Toulouse, 1731–3
Constantin SOUBEN	1754, 1756–8	Chaplain at Hôpital du Roi, 1756; curé of Louisbourg from the fall of 1757 until July 1758
Narcisse VARIN	1727–8 1732	Buried in 1732 in the lot set aside for the Louisbourg parish church
Felix [?]	1744	Chaplain of the Caribou, buried eleven of the crew at Louisbourg

Appendix B

BROTHERS OF CHARITY

OF SAINT JOHN OF GOD[2]

There were more Brothers of Charity at Louisbourg than those listed below, but the absence of either detailed hospital records or the correspondence exchanged between the superior in the colony and his provincial in France makes it impossible to learn their names. Royal officials who discussed the comings and goings or activities of the brothers usually stated simply that a certain number of "Religieux de la Charité" were arriving or leaving. The names that have been ascertained were listed in a census or financial document, mentioned in official correspondence, entered in the parish records as witnesses to conversions that took place in the Hôpital du Roi, or recorded in the necrology of the order in France. As with the list of Récollets, the dates given represent only the years in which there is evidence that the brothers were in Louisbourg. They may have been there during other years as well.

	At Louisbourg	Comment
Felicium ANCLET	1758	Came out in 1758
Jacques-Louis AYLNARD	1742	Signed an act of abjuration
Claude BARRÉ	1720, 1730	Died at Louisbourg, 1730, aged 46
Potentin BERNARD	1758	Came out in 1758, following Alexis de la Rue's death in 1757, to become the new superior
Odilon BONET	1758	A priest, died at Louisbourg, 1758, aged 48
Félix CAMAX	1733–8	A "père Felix" served at Port Dauphin in 1717 and 1719; superior at Louisbourg, 1733–8
Grégoire CHOMEY	1740–2; 1745	In 1749, a "frère Gregoire" who was familiar with Louisbourg was serving in a hospital in Saintes (Charente-Maritime); Chomey died at Metz in 1758
Félix CLAMART		Died at Paris, 1748; identified as having once served at Louisbourg

	At Louisbourg	Comment
Agricole COTREUIL	1757	Died at Louisbourg, 1757, aged 29
Constance DAMBEC	1734–6	Identified as the sacristan in 1734; died at Léogane, 1751
Achille DANTIER	1757	Died at Louisbourg, 1757, aged 46
[?] DE LA CROIX	1744	
Alexis DE LA RUE	1738, 1740–1, 1745, 1749–50, 1752–4, 1757	Surgeon, 1749–50 and probably from about 1740; superior of the Louisbourg brothers, 1752–7; died at Louisbourg in 1757, aged 57
Florentin DESBOTS	c.1732	In France in 1732, where he was identified as the brothers' superior in Louisbourg
Josaphat GENDARME	1757	Died at Louisbourg, 1757, aged 27
[?] GUERRARD	1749–50	Identified as the "dépensier" in the census
Pasteur HARRAULT	1758	Killed during the siege, 1758, aged 28
Marcellin JACQUOT	1732	Died at Louisbourg, 1732, aged 32
Charles Boromée LE BEGUE	1757	Died at Louisbourg, 1757, aged 32
[?] LEOPOL	1755	Returned to France, 1755
Procope LOY	1732	Died at Louisbourg, 1732
Maurice MEIGNEY	1752	Died at Louisbourg, 1752, aged 36
Gerard MINET	1749–50	Identified as the sacristan in the census
Eugène MOLLIMAN	1738	Signed an act of abjuration
Hugues NODON	1732	Died at Louisbourg, 1732, aged 36
Contron NOEL	1745	Died at sea, 1745, aged 35
Martial PERIGORT	1734, 1736	Identified as a nurse in 1734 census; signed an act of abjuration, 1736; died at Fort St Pierre, 1739
Anaclet PRÉVOST	1720	Superior at Port Dauphin, 1717; superior at Louisbourg, 1720; died at Paris, 1726
Marcellin SOULIER	1726	Died at Louisbourg, aged 26 or 56
Prothais TORAILLE	1736, 1738, 1740–2	Signed various acts of abjuration; died at Brest, 1744
Boniface VIMEUX	c.1731–45 1749–52	Probably the "very good Surgeon" who arrived in 1731; surgeon of the Hôpital du Roi, 1734–9 or longer; superior of the same hospital, c.1740–5 and 1749–52; returned to France 1752
Adolphe [?]	1758	
Eloy [?]	1731	Sailed to the colony, 1731
Girard [?]	1751	A disruptive presence at Louisbourg, he was sent back to France in 1751 or early 1752
Gratay [?]	1734	Identified as the "dépensier" in the census
Gratien [?]	1758	
Marcellin [?]	1731	Sailed to the colony, 1731
Maximin [?]	1749–50	Identified as a nurse in the census

Appendix C

LOUISBOURG MISSION OF THE

SISTERS OF THE CONGREGATION

OF NOTRE-DAME[3]

	At Louisbourg	Comment
Marguerite Roy (1674–1749) Sœur de la Conception	1727–34	Established the mission by herself; *de facto* superior, returned to motherhouse in 1734
Marguerite Trottier (1678–1744) Sœur Saint-Joseph	1733–44	Superior for the entire period; died near Québec on the voyage to the motherhouse in Montréal
Marie-Joseph-Lefebvre Belle-Isle (1693–1769) Sœur Saint-Benoît	1733–44	Cousin of Marguerite Trottier; returned to motherhouse, 1744
Marie-Marguerite-Daniel Arnaud (1699–1764) Sœur Saint-Arsène	1733–58	Superior from 1744 to 1764; in 1745–9 and 1758–64 in France, where she died
Françoise Boucher de Montbrun (1701–45) Sœur Saint-Placide	1734–45	Died in France after the first deportation
Marie-Geneviève Hervieux (1686–1753) Sœur Sainte-Gertrude	1734–51	Struck with paralysis after the return to Louisbourg in 1749; recalled to the motherhouse
Catherine Paré (1698–1778) Sœur Saint-Louis-des-Anges	1734–51	Came to Louisbourg as a novice; made her profession in 1736; accompanied Hervieux to Montréal in 1751
Marie Patenôtre (1720–58) Sœur Sainte-Thècle	1751–8	Replacement for Hervieux; died during the voyage to France after the second siege
Marie Robichaud (d.c.1766) Sœur Saint-Vincent-de-Paul	1751–8	Replacement for Paré; died in France in 1766
Marie-Magdelaine Noël (c.1704–29)		Religious profession made as she lay dying, in the presence of Zacharie Caradec, vicar-general, buried in the emplacement for the Louisbourg parish church
Marie Labauve [?]	1751?	Identified as a lay assistant
Geneviève Henry (d.c.1792)	1751–8	Identified as a lay assistant; still alive in France in 1792

Notes

AAQ   Archives de l'archidiocèse de Québec
ACND   Archives de la congrégation de Notre-Dame, Montréal
AD, C-M   Archives départementales, Charente-Maritime
AD, F-Q   Archives départementales, Finistère-Quimper
AFL   Archives of the Fortress of Louisbourg
AN, Colonies   Archives nationales, Archives des Colonies, Paris
AN, Outre Mer   Archives nationales, Archives d'Outre Mer, Paris
ASQ   Archives du séminaire de Québec
ASSM   Archives du séminaire de Saint-Sulpice de Montréal
CTG   Archives du Comité Technique du génie, Paris
DCB   *Dictionary of Canadian Biography*
MSRC   *Mémoires de la Société royale du Canada*
PAC   Public Archives of Canada, Ottawa
RAPQ   *Rapport de l'archiviste de la province du Québec*
SHA   Archives du Service historique de l'armée, Paris

INTRODUCTION

1   Francis Parkman's material on Louisbourg in *A Half Century of Conflict*, published in 1892, set the tone and approach which many later historians followed. The best all-round study remains J.S. McLennan's *Louisbourg from Its Foundation to Its Fall, 1713–1758*, first published in 1918. McLennan devoted considerable space to the two sieges, but he also wrote at great length on the importance of fishery and commerce to Ile Royale, as well as on other aspects of life in the colonial period.

2   Christopher Moore's recent book, *Louisbourg Portraits*, offers a colourful and well-researched look at virtually all aspects of life in the town. Earlier, Moore published two articles on merchant trade: "The Maritime Economy

of Isle Royale," *Canada, An Historical Magazine* 1, no. 4 (June 1974): 33–46 and "The Other Louisbourg: Trade and Merchant Enterprise in Ile Royale, 1713–58," *Histoire sociale / Social History* 12, no. 23 (1979): 79–96. For a more detailed study see his "Merchant Trade in Louisbourg, Ile Royale" (MA thesis, University of Ottawa 1977). The best study of the fishery is B.A. Balcom's "The Cod Fishery of Isle Royale, 1713–58," AFL, which is to be published by Parks Canada. On French public construction see Frederick J. Thorpe, *Remparts lointains: La politique française des travaux publics à Terre-Neuve et à l'île Royale, 1695–1758* (Ottawa: Editions de l'université Ottawa 1980). On garrison life see Allan Greer, *The Soldiers of Isle Royale, 1720–45*, History and Archaeology, No. 28 (Ottawa: Parks Canada 1979) and Margaret Fortier's forthcoming studies "Fortress Security and Military Justice at Louisbourg, 1720–45" and "The Ile Royale Garrison, 1720–45," AFL. Kenneth J. Donovan has written a number of papers pertaining to family and social life (see Bibliography), including "Social Status and Contrasting Lifestyles: Children of the Poor and Well-to-do in Louisbourg" and "Communities and Families: Family Life and Interior Living Conditions in Eighteenth-Century Louisbourg."

3 Of the few studies which have appeared on religious matters at Louisbourg the most useful are undoubtedly R.P. Hugolin's "Les Récollets de la Province de Saint-Denis et ceux de la Province de Bretagne à l'Ile Royale de 1713 à 1731," *MSRC*, 3e série, 24 (1930): 77–113, and "Table nominale des Récollets de Bretagne, missionnaires et aumôniers dans l'Ile Royale (1713–59)," *MSRC*, 3e série, 25 (1931): 81–100, and [Lemire-Marsolais] *Histoire de la Congrégation de Notre-Dame de Montréal.*

4 McLennan, *Louisbourg*, app. 5, 382; Balcom, "Cod Fishery of Isle Royale," discusses the fishery in detail.

5 McLennan, *Louisbourg*, chap. 12; Moore, "Merchant Trade in Louisbourg."

6 McLennan, *Louisbourg*, app. 2, 370.

7 For a study of Louisbourg's population see Barbara Schmeisser, *The Population of Louisbourg, 1713–58.* Montreal's population for the period 1720–39 ranged from 5,000 to 7,700. Louise Dechêne, *Habitants et marchands de Montréal au XVIIe siècle*, 493. Québec's population was listed as about 4,600 in 1739 and 8,000 in 1754. Schmeisser, *Population of Louisbourg*, 10. New York's population in 1749 was about 13,000 and Boston's in 1764 about 16,500. R.V. Wells, *The Population of the British Colonies before 1776*

8 The comments which follow concerning demographic aspects of Louisbourg are largely based on the data compiled and analysed by Schmeisser in *Population of Louisbourg.*

9 The 1713 census of Louisbourg listed 160 inhabitants, 127 men and 33 women and children. Of the total number 57 were from Placentia, 63 from Canada, 35 from France, and 5 from Acadia. The figures for Canada are mis-

leading, however, as they included military troops. AN, Outre Mer, G1, vol. 466, no. 5, Recensement Général, 1713.

10 The Louisbourg parish records from which these figures on marriage were obtained are located in AN, Outre Mer, G1, vols. 406, 407, 408, and 409.

11 Ibid.

12 Schmeisser, *Population of Louisbourg*, 35–52; Marcel Trudel, *Introduction to New France*, 133; A.H. Clark, *Acadia, The Geography of Early Nova Scotia to 1760*, 399.

13 Balcom, "Cod Fishery of Isle Royale," 77–9. Basque names turn up fairly frequently in the Louisbourg parish and court records, and there are frequent mention of the Basques in reports on the fishery. A good indication of the large number of them who came to Louisbourg is provided by the fact that seventy-seven Basques from a single parish in France (that of Bidart) died in the colony during the period 1715 to 1758. Département des Pyrénnées-Atlantiques, Arrondissement de Bayonne, Mairie de Bidart, Archives, Extraits des Registres des Décès, Côte G-G-10.

14 AN, Colonies, C11B, vol. 7, fols. 14v–16, Saint-Ovide au Ministre, 16 novembre 1724; ibid., B, vol. 48, fols. 959–62, Ministre à Saint-Ovide, 25 juillet 1725; ibid., C11B, vol. 9, fols. 87v.–8, Saint-Ovide au Ministre, 16 décembre 1727. The minister, the comte de Maurepas, was apparently very little bothered by the Protestant faith of some of the Karrer officers and soldiers. In 1729 he wrote to the baron de l'Espérance to say how pleased he was to learn of the latter's marriage to the daughter of one of the French officers in the garrison. The fact that by his marriage, L'Espérance, a Protestant, had broken canonical law did not bother Maurepas. L'Espérance was later, in 1731, to remove the difficulty by converting to Roman Catholicism. AN, Colonies, B, vol. 53, fol. 582v., Ministre au baron de L'Espérance, 19 avril 1729.

15 In "Merchant Trade in Louisbourg," 72–3, Moore concludes that most of the merchants previously thought to be Huguenots were in fact Catholic. As for the conversions, they are scattered throughout the town's parish records. AN, Outre Mer, G1, vols. 406, 407, 408, and 409. For a study of Protestants within the larger context of New France see Marc-André Bédard, *Les Protestants en Nouvelle-France*.

16 Byrne is mentioned several times in different groups of correspondence. See, for instance, AN, Colonies, C11B, vol. 14, fols. 54–61v., Saint-Ovide et Le Normant au Ministre, 15 octobre 1733; ibid., vol. 15, fols. 139–48, Saint-Ovide au Ministre, 1 novembre 1734; ASQ, Lettres M, no. 82, 18 octobre 1733. Lynch acted as the curé on 3 October 1754, AN, Outre Mer, G1, reg. I, fol. 35. He is also listed in Hugolin, "Table nominale des Récollets," 95. The names of the Irish priests in Louisbourg in 1744 are not known, but they were deceived by several English prisoners into revealing secret informa-

tion about the departure date of some valuable cargo ships. Public Record Office, Admiralty 1, vol. 3817, no. 6, 21 September 1744; ibid., no. 8, 19 September 1744.

17 A.A. MacKenzie, *The Irish in Cape Breton*, 21–2.

18 The baptisms are recorded in the parish records. Vincent Vinette was the apprentice baker (AN, Outre Mer, G3, 2047–suite, pièce 29, 5 décembre 1752) and Jean-Baptiste Cupidon the man who purchased his wife's freedom (AN, Outre Mer, G3, 2041–suite, pièce 78, 1 mars 1753).

19 Olive Patricia Dickason, *Louisbourg and the Indians: A Study in Imperial Race Relations, 1713–1760*; B.A. Balcom, "Micmacs at Louisbourg, A Training Manual for Animators" (1979, rev. 1982), AFL. Information on the Micmacs' stay in 1757 is available in AN, Colonies, C11C, vol. 14, fols. 67–75 and 111–12v., Bordereaux ... 1757, 16 décembre 1757, and AN, Marine, B4, vol. 76, no. 3, Mémoire Concernant les Sauvages ... en 1757.

20 As for instance with the thirty-four Récollet letters located in AD, F-Q, série 23 H14.

CHAPTER ONE

1 In the original French this traditional verse is "Mariage de bon devis / De l'Eglise et des fleurs de lis. / Quand l'un et l'autre partira, / Chacun d'eux si s'en partira." Quoted in Joseph LeClerc, "Le roi de France, 'Fils Aîné de l'Eglise'," *Etudes* 214 (1933): 24. The lily is the symbol of the French monarchy.

2 McLennan, *Louisbourg*, 11, 12. On the question of the cross as a typical feature in the founding of new colonies see Olive Patricia Dickason, "Europeans and Amerindians: Some Comparative Aspects of Early Contact," *Historical Papers / Communications historiques*, 182–202, and Charles Edwards O'Neill, *Church and State in French Colonial Louisiana: Policy and Politics to 1732*, 1.

3 For the economic and commercial reasons behind the founding of Ile Royale see Christopher Moore, "The Maritime Economy of Isle Royale," *Canada, An Historical Magazine* 1, no. 4 (June 1974): 33–46.

4 Statements to that effect were made repeatedly in instructions to governors and commissaires-ordonnateurs and in memoirs relating to the purpose of the colony. See for example: AN, Colonies, B, vol. 63, fol. 556, Mémoire du Roi à Saint-Ovide et Le Normant, 5 mai 1735; ibid., vol. 89, fol. 307v., Mémoire du Roi, 28 mars 1749.

5 AN, Colonies, B, vol. 35, fols. 253v.–5, Pontchartrain à Vaudreuil, 29 mars 1713; ibid., fol. 263v., Pontchartrain au Supérieur des Récollets au Canada, 8 avril 1713; ibid., fols. 84v.–5, Pontchartrain à Saint-Ovide, 10 avril 1713.

6 AN, Marine, A2, article 24, fols. 65–8, Règlement et Lettres patentes, Le Roi, Paris, 5 et 8 juin 1718.

7   AN, Colonies, C11B, vol. 20, fol. 87v., de Bourville, 3 octobre 1738.

8   Ibid., B, vol. 36, fols. 450v.–1, Instructions pour le Sr Soubras, 10 avril 1714.

9   Ibid., C11B, vol. 5, fol. 169, Saint-Ovide, 22 juin 1720.

10 Dictionnaire encyclopédique Quillet (Paris, 1962), 2381; Encyclopedia Britannica, 15th ed., 9: 1100; R.R. Palmer and Joel Colton, A History of the Modern World to 1815 (New York: Alfred A. Knopf 1971), 52, 71–4, 90, 136; D. Diderot and J.L. d'Alembert, eds., Encyclopédie, ou dictionnaire raisonné des sciences, des arts et des métiers 9: 474–5.

11 Jean Quéniart, Les hommes, l'Église et Dieu dans la France du XVIIIe siècle, 26.

12 Cornelius J. Jaenen, The Role of the Church in New France, 39, 42.

13 Guy Frégault, Le XVIIIe siècle canadien: Études, 88.

14 Trudel, Introduction to New France, 157. For examples of this regulation being applied at Louisbourg see AN, Colonies, B, vol. 56, fols. 145–45v., Lettre du Roi, 11 mars 1732; ibid., vol. 61, fols. 624v.–5, Commission d'Huissier de l'Amirauté, 27 avril 1734; ibid., C11B, vol. 7, fol. 378, Certificat signé par Athanase Guégot, 20 août 1738.

15 Frégault, Le XVIIIe siècle, 90–1. For a similar assessment see W.J. Eccles, Canada under Louis XIV, 1663–1701, 22.

16 Frégault, Le XVIIIe siècle, 148.

17 Diderot, Encyclopédie 3: 379; ibid., 16: 396. The kings of Spain and Portugal were known respectively as "Le Roi très Catholique" and "Le Roi très fidèle." See also LeClerc, "Le Roi de France."

18 O'Neill, Church and State in French Colonial Louisiana, 2.

19 Jean de la Croix de Saint-Vallier, Catéchisme du diocèse de Québec ..., 408–10.

20 AN, Colonies, C11B, vol. 32, fols. 169–70v., Prévost, 30 septembre 1752; ibid., fols. 309–12v., Ste Marie, 30 septembre 1752.

21 John McManners, French Ecclesiastical Society under the Ancien Régime: A Study of Angers in the Eighteenth Century, 110–11.

22 AN, Colonies, B, vol. 41, fols. 575, 575v., Lettre du Roy, 24 juin 1719; ibid., vol. 4, fol. 191, Saint-Ovide au Conseil, 24 novembre 1719; ibid., B, vol. 61, fol. 619, Ministre à Saint-Ovide, 28 juillet 1734; Boston Weekly News-Letter, 29 June 1744; AN, Colonies, C11B, vol. 37, fol. 115, Prévost au Ministre, 30 septembre 1757; ibid., fol. 58, Drucourt au Ministre, 4 octobre 1757.

23 AN, Colonies, B, vol. 44, fol. 579, Te Deum, 12 août 1721; ibid., fol. 579v., Ministre à Mézy, 12 août 1721; ibid., vol. 45, fols. 433–5, Ministre à Mézy et Saint-Ovide, 26 octobre 1722; ibid., vol. 50, fol. 607v., Ministre à Saint-Ovide,19 août 1727; ibid., Ministre à Mézy, 19 août 1727; ibid., C11B, vol. 11, de Bourville au Ministre, 30 novembre 1730; ibid., vol. 32, fols. 33–33v., Raymond au Ministre, 16 juin 1752.

24 AN, Colonies, B, vol. 63, fols. 579–79v., Reglement sur les honneurs, 5 mai
    1735.
25 Ibid., C11B, vol. 32, fols. 33–33v., Raymond au Ministre, 16 juin 1752; ibid.,
    vol. 33, fols. 67–8, Raymond au Ministre, 20 juin 1753.
26 Henri Têtu and C.-O. Gagnon, eds., Mandements, lettres pastorales et cir-
    culaires des évêques de Québec ... 1: 335–6.
27 Jean Baptiste Thiers, Traité des jeux et des divertissemens, 413–4.
28 Têtu and Gagnon, eds., Mandements 1: 489.
29 AN, Colonies, C11B, vol. 24, fols. 37–40v., Duquesnel et Bigot, 30 octobre
    1742; ibid., vol. 36, fols. 130–3v., Prévost, 11 août 1756; ibid., vol. 1–suite,
    fol. 484, Sur l'Isle Royalle, 1718; ibid., vol. 4, fols. 66–8, Conseil, 24 janvier
    1719.
30 Têtu and Gagnon, eds., Mandements 2: 40–3, 24 novembre 1744; H.H.
    Walsh, The Church in the French Era, From Colonization to the British
    Conquest, 195.
31 Christopher Moore, "Street Life and Public Activities in Louisbourg: Four
    Studies for Animators" (1978), AFL.
32 [Louis-Sébastien Mercier], Tableau de Paris, nouvelle édition 4: 94–5.
33 Olwen Hufton, The Poor in Eighteenth-Century France, 1750–1789 364;
    Jaenen, Role of the Church, 123–4.
34 AN, Colonies, C11B, vol. 4, fol. 269v., Soubras, 14 juillet 1719.
35 Ralph G. Lounsbury, "Yankee Trade at Newfoundland," New England Quar-
    terly 3 (1930): 612.
36 Gilles Proulx, Aubergistes et cabaretiers de Louisbourg, 1713–1758.
37 AN, Outre Mer, G2, vol. 198, dossier 182, fol. 30, 7 juin 1743; AD, C-M, B,
    liasse 6113.
38 Moore, "Street Life and Public Activities"; AN, Outre Mer, G2, vol. 197,
    dossier 134, pièce 10, 12 août 1740.
39 McManners, French Ecclesiastical Society, 111.
40 Gilles Proulx, Les bibliothèques de Louisbourg.
41 See, for example, AN, Outre Mer, G2, vol. 202, dossier 287; vol. 205, dossiers
    388, 395.
42 ASSM, Côte 544, 4.32, mandement du 9 février 1756.
43 Auguste Gosselin, L'église du Canada, depuis Monseigneur de Laval jus-
    qu'à la conquête 2: 264; RAPQ (1935–6), 273–4. Isle-Dieu served as the
    bishop of Québec's vicar-general until 1777, two years before his death.
44 AN, Colonies, C11B, vol. 2, fols. 30–3, Conseil, 2 mars 1717.
45 Ibid., vol. 1, fols. 257v., 258, Inventaire des Maisons, 30 septembre 1715;
    ibid., fol. 255v., Estimation des Maisons, 19 octobre 1715. Information on
    Dominique de La Marche comes from DCB 2: 339.
46 Ibid., B, vols. 443v.–4, Pontchartrain à Costebelle, 22 mars 1714.
47 Gosselin, L'église du Canada 1: 375.

48 AN, Colonies, C11B, vol. 1, fols. 163v., 164, Costebelle, 28 novembre 1715.

49 This idea comes out clearly in another letter of the governor's: ibid., C11A, vol. 106, fol. 409, Costebelle, 1717.

50 Ibid., B, vol. 38, fol. 25v., Conseil à l'evesque de Bethléèm, 31 mars 1716; ibid., fol. 261v., Conseil de Marine à Costebelle et Soubras, 22 avril 1716.

51 Ibid., fols. 246–7, Lettres pattentes pour l'Etablissement, May 1716.

52 Ibid., C11B, vol. 2, fols. 54–5, Soubras' letter of 28 novembre 1717 (sic) considered by the Conseil on 20 April 1717. Soubras' words of praise for Dominique de La Marche are quoted in DCB 2: 339.

53 Lengthy extracts from those letters are transcribed in Hugolin, "Les Récollets de Saint-Denis et de Bretagne," 77–113. The extracts concerning the 1716–17 debate over which province should serve on Ile Royale are on pp. 82–90.

54 Têtu and Gagnon, eds., Mandements 1: 489, 490, 25 août 1716.

55 AN, Colonies, B, vol. 39, fols. 214v–16, Conseil de Marine à l'Evesque de Québec, 31 mai 1717; ibid., fols. 264v.–5v., Lettres patentes, mai 1717.

56 Ibid., vol. 38, fol. 22v., Conseil au Supérieur des Frères de la Charité, 17 mars 1716; ibid., fols. 264, 264v., Conseil à Costebelle et Soubras, 22 avril 1716.

57 For a description of the hospital at Louisbourg at this time see AN, Colonies, C11B, vol. 1, fol. 258, Inventaire des Maisons, 30 septembre 1715; ibid., fol. 256, Estimation ... des Maisons du Roi, 19 octobre 1715.

58 Ibid., B, vol. 38, fols. 282v.–4v., Lettres patentes, avril 1716.

59 Ibid., fols. 143v.–4v., Conseil à Beauharnois, 27 juin 1716.

60 Ibid., C11B, vol. 1, fol. 409v., Costebelle, 26 octobre 1716.

61 Ibid., vol. 2, fol. 17, Conseil, 6 janvier 1717; ibid., B, vol. 39, fol. 285, Conseil à Soubras, 26 juin 1717.

62 Ibid., B, vol. 39, fol. 292v., Mémoire du Roi, juin 1717; ibid., C11B, vol. 2, fol. 166v., Saint-Ovide et Soubras, 13 novembre 1717.

63 Ibid., C11B, vol. 4, fols. 94v.–5, Conseil à Saint-Ovide et Soubras, 19 mars 1719; ibid., fol. 132, Mémoire du Roi, 10 juillet 1719; ibid., B, vol. 41, fols. 598v., 599, Conseil à Saint-Ovide et Mézy, 19 juillet 1719.

64 Ibid., C11B, vol. 5, fols. 119–24, Conseil, 13 août 1720; ibid., fols. 136–43, Saint-Ovide et Mézy, 10 novembre 1720; ibid., fols. 324–24v., Conseil, 4 mars 1721; ibid., fol. 153v., Saint-Ovide et Mézy, 7 décembre 1721.

65 Ibid., C11B, vol. 11, fols. 16–22, Bourville et Mézy, 3 décembre 1730.

66 In the 1715 census there was a man described as a "Me Descolles et Commis." AN, Outre Mer, G1, vol. 466, pièce 51, Recensement des habitants, 14 janvier 1715. There is no other mention of any maîtres d'école until 1730.

67 AN, Colonies, B, vol. 47, fol. 1116, Maurepas à l'évêque de Québec, 30 mai 1724.

68 Ibid., C11B, vol. 7, fols. 171–5, Saint-Ovide et Mézy, 17 décembre 1725; ibid., B, vol. 49, fols. 716v.–18v., Ministre à Saint-Ovide et Mézy, 25 juin 1726.

69 AN, Outre Mer, G1, vol. 466, pièce 68, Recensement, 1726.

70 Ibid., G2, vol. 190, fols. 17v.–18v., Saint-Vallier à Sœur de la Conception, 28 juillet 1727.

71 Ibid.

72 AN, Colonies, C11B, vol. 9, fol. 37, Saint-Ovide et Mézy, 15 décembre 1727.

73 Abbé Amédée Gosselin, L'instruction au Canada sous le régime français, 116.

74 AN, Colonies C11B, vol. 14, fols. 39v.–41v., Saint-Ovide et Le Normant, 11 octobre 1733.

75 Ibid., C11C, vol. 11, fol. 87, Bordereau, 1734, 20 septembre 1736.

76 Ibid., C11A, vol. 107, fols. 282–5, Beauharnois et Hocquart au Ministre, 12 octobre 1733; AN, Outre Mer, G1, vol. 466, pièce 69, Recensement de l'Isle Royalle, octobre 1734.

77 SHA, A1, Reg. 3393, pièce 38, janvier 1752; ASQ, Lettres P, no. 63, Maillard, 29 septembre 1738.

78 [Lemire-Marsolais], Histoire de la Congrégation de Notre-Dame de Montréal, pt. 1, XVIIIe siècle 5: 97–9. An earlier history of the Congregation gives 1765 as the date of the last sister's death. E.-M. Faillon, Vie de la Sœur Bourgeoys 2: 401–4.

CHAPTER TWO

1 Peter Kalm, Travels into North America ... 3: 140.

2 Abbé Brasseur de Bourbourg, Histoire du Canada, de son église et de ses missions 1: 29.

3 At the head of all the ministres provinciaux was a ministre générale. For general information on the Récollets see P. Gratien, Histoire de la fondation et de l'evolution de l'Ordre des Frères Mineurs au XIIIe siècle, vii–x; Pierre Trépanier, "Les Récollets et l'Acadie (1619–1759): Plaidoyer pour l'histoire religieuse," Les cahiers de la société historique acadienne 10, no. 1 (mars 1979): 4–5; Diderot, Encyclopédie 13: 857; Jean Boudriot, Le Vaisseau de 74 canons 4: 155.

4 Hugolin, "Les Récollets de Saint-Denis et de Bretagne," 77–113.

5 Brasseur de Bourbourg, Histoire du Canada 1: 207; AN, Colonies, C11B, vol. 1, fols. 163–63v., Costebelle, 28 novembre 1715; ibid., C11A, vol. 106, fol. 409, Costebelle, 1717; Trépanier, "Les Récollets et l'Acadie," 5; Boudroit, Le vaisseau de 74 cannons, 4: 155.

6 AN, Colonies, C11C, vol. 11, fol. 15, Costebelle au Ministre, 6 novembre 1714; ibid., vol. 15, fol. 210, Saint-Ovide et Mézy, 7 décembre 1721 [lettre du sup. des Récollets, 30 novembre 1720].

7 Kalm, Travels into North America 3: 147–8.

8 AN, Colonies, C11B, vol. 2, fols. 54–5, Conseil, 20 avril 1717.

9 [Thomas Pichon], *Genuine Letters and Memoirs, Relating to the Natural, Civil and Commercial History of the Islands of Cape Breton and Saint John ...*, 200. Abbé de l'Isle-Dieu's correspondence is filled with negative assessments of the Récollets. See *RAPQ* (1935–6), (1936–7), and (1937–8).

10 Quéniart, *Les hommes, l'église et Dieu*, 43–6.

11 AN, Colonies, C11B, vol. 4, fols. 84–5, Conseil, 4 mars 1719; Hugolin, "Les Récollets de Saint-Denis et de Bretagne," 93–4.

12 AN, Colonies, C11B, vol. 5, fols. 300–5, Conseil de Marine, 28 janvier 1721, au sujet de la lettre de Mézy du 3 décembre 1720.

13 Ibid., fols. 151–51v., Saint-Ovide et Mézy, 7 décembre 1721.

14 Ibid., C11C, vol. 15, fol. 210, Saint-Ovide et Mézy, 7 décembre 1721.

15 Ibid., B, vol. 44, fols. 557–9v., Mémoire du Roi à Saint-Ovide et Mézy, juin 1721; ibid., vol. 45, fols. 925–9, Ordonnance pour l'établissement du droit d'un quintal de morue, 12 mai 1722.

16 Ibid., C11B, vol. 6, fols. 251–2, Mézy, 25 novembre 1723.

17 Ibid.; ibid., fols. 152–62v., Saint-Ovide et Mézy, 29 décembre 1723.

18 Linda Hoad, "Reports on Lots A and B of Block 3" (June 1971), 2, AFL; AN, Colonies, C11A, vol. 126, fol. 237 (in the larger numbers), Estat des Emplacements, 1723, no. 3, Lot D.

19 AN, Outre Mer, G1, vol. 406, reg. I, baptême du 12 avril 1724. The curé wrote that the child in question had been "baptisé dans notre chapelle conv. de Ste. Claire."

20 Hoad, "Report on Lots A and B of Block 3," 2.

21 Blaine Adams, "The Construction and Occupation of the Barracks of the King's Bastion at Louisbourg," *Canadian Historic Sites: Occasional Papers in Archaeology and History*, 101.

22 AN, Colonies, C11A, vol. 107, fols. 271–3, Mémoire à Maurepas, février 1736; Lyon's biography is in *DCB* 3: 413–4.

23 AN, Colonies, B, vol. 65, fols. 3v.–4, Ministre au Père Maurice Godefroy, 14 janvier 1737; ibid., fols. 445v.–6v., Ministre à de Brouillan et Le Normant, 16 avril 1737; ibid., C11B, vol. 20, fols. 222–3, Verrier, 2 janvier 1738; ibid., fols. 111–2, Le Normant, 26 janvier 1738.

24 Ibid., B, vol. 66, fols. 297–8, Ministre à Bourville et Le Normant, 6 mai 1738; ibid., C11B, vol. 20, fols. 52–9, Bourville et Le Normant, 21 octobre 1738.

25 *RAPQ*, 1936–7, 435, Isle-Dieu à Pontbriand, 28 mai 1756; see also *RAPQ*, 1936–7, 397, Isle-Dieu à Pontbriand, 25 mars 1755.

26 Schmeisser, *Population of Louisbourg*, 56. During the 1730s in Québec, when its population was between 4,000 and 5,000 inhabitants, there were complaints that its parish church (which was the cathedral for the diocese, built in 1666) was too small for the town. The governor and intendant pro-

posed that a second parish church be erected. Needless to say, the cathedral at Québec, whatever its size limitations, was far larger than the chapels which were used as the parish church in Louisbourg. Gosselin, *L'église du Canada*, 2: 125–6, 337n1.

27 AN, Colonies, C11B, vol. 24, fol. 319, Saint-Ovide et Le Normant, 10 septembre 1736; ibid., vol. 31, fols. 6–6v., 27 janvier 1751; ibid., fols. 7v.–8, 27 janvier 1751. The meeting of parishioners to decide what each should contribute was the standard approach to church construction in Canada. Jaenen, *Role of the Church*, 91.

28 AN, Colonies, C11A, vol. 56, fols. 180–1, Dosquet, 8 septembre 1731. Dosquet also asserted that Niganiche generated more than 1,000 *écus* a year in parish revenue.

29 For studies of these two aspects of the colonial economy see Balcom, "Cod Fishery of Isle Royale"; Moore, "Merchant Trade in Louisbourg"; and idem, "The Other Louisbourg."

30 Hugolin, "Table nominale des Récollets," 92.

31 AN, Outre Mer, G1, vol. 406, reg. I, II, and III, parish records entries for September and October 1724 when Le Dorz's name and title appear for the first time.

32 Hugolin, "Table nominale des Récollets," 92–3.

33 AN, Colonies, B, vol. 50, fols. 18–18v., Maurepas à Saturnin Dirop, 18 février 1727.

34 AD, F-Q, 23 H 14: Lettres des Récollets, pièce 14, Saint-Vallier au Provincial des Récollets, 15 juillet 1727.

35 AN, Outre Mer, G1, vol. 406, reg. II, fol. 4, mariage du 21 février 1725.

36 Ibid., reg. IV, abjuration du 2 mars 1731.

37 Jean de la Croix de Saint-Vallier, *Rituel du diocèse de Québec*, 286–7.

38 AD, F-Q, 23 H 14: Lettres des Récollets, pièce 14, Saint-Vallier au Provincial des Récollets, 15 juillet 1727.

39 Ibid.

40 Official papers were drawn up for two priests, Joachim Fornel and Jean-Baptiste Brault, to go to Louisbourg as *grands-vicaires*. AAQ, Côte 12A, Reg. des insinuations ecclesiastiques, B, vol. 269, lettres de grand-vicaire pour Louisbourg à Joachim Fornel, 2 septembre 1726; ibid., fol. 270, lettres de grand-vicaire à M. Jean-Baptiste Brault, 2 septembre 1726. In the documents concerning the subsequent events at Louisbourg, Brault's name is never mentioned. Thus he may have never made the voyage to Ile Royale, although that does not necessarily follow. The intention certainly was to send them both. AAQ, Copies de Lettres, vol. II, p. 268–9, Saint-Vallier à Maurepas, 10 septembre 1726.

41 AAQ, Copies de Lettres, vol. II, pp. 268–9, Saint-Vallier à Maurepas, 10 septembre 1726.

42 AD, F-Q, 23 H 14: Lettres des Récollets, pièce 8, 24 octobre 1726.
43 AN, Colonies, C11B, vol. 10, fols. 190–2v., Fornel à Saint-Ovide et Mézy, 28 octobre 1726.
44 Ibid., vol. 8, fols. 43–6v., Saint-Ovide au Ministre, 8 novembre 1726.
45 Saint-Vallier's description of the Récollets as reprehensible is in AD, F-Q, 23 H 14, Lettre des Récollets, pièce 13, Saint-Vallier à Dirop, 15 juillet 1727. For other opinions of the bishop see AN, Colonies, B, vol. 50, fol. 535v., Maurepas à l'évêque de Québec, 13 mai 1727. Maurepas mentioned that he had received five letters from the bishop written in September and October 1726.
46 AN, Colonies, C11B, vol. 8, fols. 104–6, Mézy, 5 décembre 1726.
47 AD, F-Q, 23 H 14: Lettre des Récollets, pièce 11, le Provincial au Ministre, 1727.
48 AN, Colonies, C11B, vol. 4, fols. 125–25v., habitans de Louisbourg, 1 décembre 1726; ibid., fols. 127–27v., habitans de Scatary et L'Indienne, 1 décembre 1726.
49 Mézy maintained that most of those who signed the petitions did not understand the issues involved, that they were duped into lending their support to the Récollets. AN, Colonies, C11B, vol. 8, fols. 104–6, Mézy, 5 décembre 1726.
50 Ibid., B, vol. 50, fols. 535v.–8, Ministre à l'évêque de Québec, 13 mai 1727; ibid., fol. 588v., Ministre à Mézy, 10 juin 1727.
51 Ibid., fols. 18–18v., Ministre à Dirop, 18 février 1727.
52 See DCB 2: 328–34, "Saint-Vallier."
53 Trudel, Introduction to New France, 234.
54 Hugolin, "Table nominale des Récollets," 93.
55 DCB 2: 176.
56 AD, F-Q, 23 H 14: Lettres de Récollets, pièce 17, Le Duff à Dirop, 3 novembre 1727.
57 AN, Outre Mer, G1, vol. 406, reg. II: mariages 1722–8, fols. 11–13.
58 AD, F-Q, 23 H 14: Lettres des Récollets, pièce 17, Le Duff à Dirop, 3 novembre 1737. Le Duff's name does not appear in the Louisbourg parish records after June 1728.
59 AN, Colonies, B, vol. 51, fols. 11–11v., Ministre à Dirop, 10 février 1728.
60 AD, F-Q, 23 H 14: Lettres des Récollets, pièce 19, Dirop à Saint-Ovide, 20 février 1728; ibid., pièce 18, Dirop à Mézy, 21 février 1728. Raoul may have come out to the colony, if only briefly, as a chaplain aboard L'Eléphant. Hugolin, "Les Récollets de Saint-Denis et de Bretagne," 106. Raoul appears to have been back in France in October 1728. Hugolin, "Table nominale des Récollets," 97.
61 AD, F-Q, 23 H 14: Lettres des Récollets, pièce 18, Dirop à Mézy, 21 février 1728; ibid., pièce 19, Dirop à Saint-Ovide, 20 février 1728.

62 *RAPQ* (1941–2), 242; AN, Colonies, C11B, vol. 7, fols. 324–6v., Verrier au Ministre, 13 novembre 1725.

63 Caradec added *vicaire-générale* to his list of titles for the first time on 10 octobre 1728. AN, Outre Mer, G1, vol. 406, reg. IV, baptême du 10 octobre 1728.

64 AN, Colonies, C11B, vol. 5, fol. 304v., Conseil, 28 janvier 1721: lettre de Mézy du 3 décembre 1720. In Canada there were generally three *marguilliers du banc* in each parish, except at Québec where there were four. Trudel, *Introduction to New France*, 249. The first *marguillier* mentioned in the correspondence or other records of Louisbourg was a Sr Lasson, in 1724. AN, Colonies, C11B, vol. 7, fol. 54v., 18 novembre 1724.

65 In October 1742 a royal official in the town had it recorded in a local case that he was acting on behalf of the "fabrique de l'Eglise paroissialle de cette ville a déffaut de marguilliers." AN, Outre Mer, G2, vol. 198, dossier 168, De Par le Roy, 13 octobre 1742.

66 AN, Outre Mer, G3, pièce 132, Procès verbal de visite du grand vicaire dans l'église de parroise à Louisbourg, 13 février 1730. The four laymen who signed this document were most likely the *marguilliers*. They were DeLort (Guillaume), Carrerot (Pierre was identified as a warden in 1732), Daccarrette le jeune (Michel was identified as a warden in 1730, 1731, and 1732) and another whose name has not yet been deciphered.

67 For more details on this subject see the discussion in the next chapter. The documentary sources are given in the notes.

68 Jaenen, *Role of the Church*, 85.

69 Frégault, *Le XVIIIe siècle Canadien*, 139–40.

70 AN, Colonies, C11B, vol. 11, fol. 22, Bourville et Mézy, 31 décembre 1730; ibid., vol. 12, fols. 22–4, Saint-Ovide, juin 1731; ibid., vol. 13, fols. 24v.–5v., Mézy, 17 mars 1752; ibid., B, vol. 59, fols. 544–7, Ministre à Saint-Ovide et Le Normant, 16 juin 1733.

71 Ibid., B, vol. 55, fols. 569–72, Ministre à Saint-Ovide et Mézy, 10 juillet 1731.

72 Ibid., fol. 1v., Ministre au Provincial des Récollets de Bretagne, 9 janvier 1731; ibid., fol. 575v., Maurepas à Caradec, 11 juillet 1731.

73 Ibid., C11B, vol. 12, fol. 185, Caradec, 30 novembre 1731.

74 Ibid., B, vol. 57, fols. 773v.–4, Ministre à Caradec, 27 juin 1732.

75 Ibid., C11B, vol. 12, fols. 23v.–4, Saint-Ovide, juin 1731.

76 Ibid., vol. 14, fol. 112, Saint-Ovide, 20 octobre 1733.

77 See for example the receipts for payment of the *dîme* in the accounts of Anthoine Perré. AN, Outre Mer, G2, vol. 195, pièce 83, Partage des biens de la succession d'Anthoine Peré, 1735.

78 Jaenen, *Role of the Church*, 85–90.

79 AN, Colonies, C11B, vol. 13, fol. 25v., Mézy, 17 mars 1732.

80 Ibid., vol. 14, fols. 27v.–8, Saint-Ovide et Le Normant, 10 octobre 1733; ibid., fols. 31–41v., Saint-Ovide et Le Normant, 11 octobre 1733.

81 Ibid., B, vol. 58, fol. 47, Ministre à Godefroy, 2 juin 1733. The comte de Maurepas' explanation of Zacharie Caradec's character flaws was spelled out in a 1735 letter to the provincial of the Récollets de Bretagne. AN, Colonies, B, vol. 62, fols. 37–37v., Ministre à Godefroy, 11 avril 1735.

82 AN, Outre Mer, G1, vol. 406, reg. IV: Louisbourg 1728–38, fols. 49v.–55.

83 Ibid., G2, vol. 190, reg. 4, fols. 1–2, Lettres patentes, juillet 1731.

84 AN, Colonies, B, vol. 54, fols. 50v.–1, Ministre à Godefroy, 10 juillet 1730; ibid., vol. 55, fol. 577v., Ministre à Saint-Ovide et Mézy, 17 juillet 1731; Hugolin, "Les Récollets de Saint Denis et de Bretagne," 107–10; AN, Colonies, C11B, vol. 13, fols. 26–26v., Mézy, 17 mars 1732.

85 Hugolin, "Les Récollets de Saint Denis et de Bretagne," 109.

86 AN, Colonies, C11A, vol. 56, fol. 85–7, Dosquet, 8 septembre 1731.

87 Ibid., vol. 106, fols. 309v.–10, Beauharnois et Hocquart au Conseil, 4 octobre 1731.

88 Ibid., B, vol. 57, fols. 630v.–1, Ministre à l'évêque de Samos, 8 avril 1732.

89 AN, Outre Mer, G2, vol. 194, pièce 55, Procedure criminelle ... contre Pierre Santier et Servanne Bonnier, 8 septembre 1734.

90 AN, Colonies, B, vol. 36, fols. 330v.–1, Ministre à l'évêque de Bayonne, 19 décembre 1714; ibid, vol. 37, fols. 231v.–2, Ministre à Costebelle et Soubras, 4 juin 1715; ibid., vol. 38, fols. 18–18v., Conseil de Marine à Laudreau, 3 mars 1716; ibid., vol. 40, fol. 517v., Conseil à Saint-Ovide, 4 mai 1718.

91 Ibid., vol. 59, Ministre à Saint-Ovide et Le Normant, 16 juin 1733; ibid., C11B, vol. 14, fols. 38–9, Saint-Ovide et Le Normant, 11 octobre 1733.

92 AN, Outre Mer, G2, dossier 119, Procedure sur la plainte du Sr Miquets St Martin, 1737.

93 AN, Colonies, B, vol. 67, fol. 36, Ministre à Godefroy, 9 avril 1738; ibid., vol. 69, fol. 43v., Ministre à Godefroy, 4 janvier 1739; ibid., vol. 67, fols. 45–45v., Ministre à Godefroy, 29 avril 1739; ibid., vol. 71, fol. 72, Ministre au Provincial des Récollets de Bretagne, 2 avril 1740.

94 Hugolin, "Table nominale des Récollets," 94. As for Le Goff's administrative abilities he later (1742–5) went on to become the *ministre provincial* of the Récollets de Bretagne.

95 AN, Colonies, C11B, vol. 19, fols. 126–8, Le Normant, 26 décembre 1737.

96 Ibid.; ibid., B, vol. 62, fol. 27, Ministre a Godefroy, 8 mars 1735; ibid., fols. 37–37v., Ministre à Godefroy, 11 avril 1735.

97 Ibid., B, vol. 65, fol. 9v., Ministre à Godefroy, 28 janvier 1737; ibid., fol. 75v., Ministre à Godefroy, 30 juillet 1737.

98 Ibid., C11B, vol. 19, fols. 126–8, Le Normant, 26 décembre 1737.

99 ASQ, Lettres P, no. 63, Maillard, 29 septembre 1738.

100   D.C. Harvey, *The French Régime in Prince Edward Island*, 76–8; Jill Mac-Lean, *Jean Pierre Roma of the Company of the East of Isle St. Jean*, 16, 17.

101   AN, Colonies, C11B, vol. 19, fols. 67–8, Roma, sans date; ibid., fols. 248–9v., Roma, 14 octobre 1737; *DCB* 3: 566; MacLean, *Jean Pierre Roma*, 24.

102   AN, Colonies, B, vol. 66, fols. 284v.–5v., Ministre à Le Normant, 29 avril 1738.

103   Ibid., fol. 202, Ministre à Godefroy, 3 novembre 1738.

104   Ibid., vol. 67, fols. 45–45v., Ministre à Godefroy, 29 avril 1739.

105   Ibid., vol. 58, fol. 47, Ministre à Godefroy, 2 juin 1733.

106   Ibid., vol. 66, fols. 284v.–5v., Ministre à Le Normant, 29 avril 1738; Frégault, *Le XVIIIe siècle canadien*, 139–40.

107   Archives Maritimes, Archives du Port de Rochefort, série 1R28, Liste des Passagers ... sur Le Plafond, 2 août 1731; Hugolin, "Table nominale des Récollets," 90, states that Guégot was first in the colony in 1732.

108   *DCB* 3: 416.

109   AN, Outre Mer, G1, vol. 407, regs. I et II, passim.

110   ASQ, Lettres P, no. 63, Maillard, 29 septembre 1738.

111   AN, Colonies, B, vol. 77, fol. 64, Ministre à Isle-Dieu, 2 mars 1743; ibid., fols. 66–66v., Ministre à l'abbé de Combes, 12 mars 1743; AAQ, 1W, Eglise du Canada, I, pp. 235–6, Duquesnel et Bigot, 7 novembre 1743.

112   *RAPQ* (1935–6), 276–7, Isle-Dieu à Pontbriand, 4 mai 1743; AAQ, 1W, Eglise du Canada, I, pp. 236, 237, Pontbriand au Supérieur des Récollets, 15 septembre 1743; AN, Colonies, C11B, vol. 78, fols. 392–92v., Ministre à Duquesnel et Bigot, 17 avril 1744; ASQ, Séminaire 14, liasse 6, no. 3, L'Evêque au Ministre, 20 octobre 1743.

113   AN, Colonies, B, vol. 82, fol. 59v., Ministre à Godefroy, 10 février 1745; ibid., fols. 105–5v., Ministre à Isle-Dieu, 3 avril 1745.

114   G.M. Wrong, ed., *Louisbourg in 1745: The Anonymous Lettre d'un Habitant de Louisbourg*, 40; AN, Colonies, Dépôt des Fortifications des Colonies, Amérique Septentrionale (hereafter cited as AN, Colonies, DFC, AS), no. d'ordre 216, fols. 6v–7, Journal de Girard La Croix, 16 juillet 1745.

115   AN, Colonies, DFC, AS, no. d'ordre 216, fols. 11v. et 13v., Journal de Girard La Croix, 16 juillet 1745.

116   G.A. Rawlyk, *Yankees at Louisbourg*, 151; Louis Effingham DeForest, ed., *Louisbourg Journals, 1745*, 34–5. The totals for the baptisms and marriages are from AN, Outre Mer, G1, vol. 407, reg. II, fols. 51v.–6.

117   AD, F-Q, 23 H 14: Lettres des Récollets, pièce 20, Valérien Gaulin à Godefroy, 13 octobre 1745; ibid., pièce 23, Simple Bocquet au Provincial des Récollets de Bretagne, 27 octobre 1748.

118   AN, Colonies, DFC, AS, no. d'ordre 216, fols. 24–5, Journal de Girard La Croix, 16 juillet 1745; Hugolin, "Table nominale des Récollets," 91; AN, Outre Mer, G1, vol. 406, reg. IV, fol. 70v., 22 juillet 1745.

119 Peter Bower, "Louisbourg: A Focus of Conflict, 1745–48" (1970), 178–9 AFL. The quotation is from a 1746 letter of William Pepperrell and Peter Warren to Newcastle.

120 Francis Parkman, "Capture of Louisbourg by the New England Militia," *Atlantic Monthly* 54 (May 1891): 627; *DCB* 3: 471; DeForest, ed., *Louisbourg Journals*, 32–3.

121 Bower, "Louisbourg: A Focus of Conflict," 202–45; DeForest, ed., *Louisbourg Journals*, 42; Rawlyk, *Yankees at Louisbourg*, 155–7.

122 Adams, *Construction and Occupation of the Barracks*, 88.

123 *RAPQ* (1935–6), 277–8, M. L'Evêque de Québec, 3 novembre 1745; ASQ, Séminaire 14, liasse 6, no. 11, lettre de l'évêque, 7 novembre 1748; AN, Colonies, C11B, vol. 27, fols. 280–4, Bigot, 7 septembre 1748.

124 AN, Outre Mer, G1, vol. 466, pièce 76, Dénombrement Général des familles, 1749.

125 AD, F-Q, 23 H 14, pièces 28, 29, and 34. Hervé Martin quotes from this material in "Les Franciscains bretons et les gens de mer: De Bretagne en Acadie (XVe–début XVIIIe siècle)," *Annales de Bretagne et des pays de l'Ouest* 87, no. 4 (décembre 1980): 641–77.

126 Louisbourg parish records for 1749 are found in AN, Outre Mer, G1, vol. 408, 1e registre.

127 Ibid., fols. 56v.–65, 113–5v., 149–52v.

128 PAC, MG 18, F12, vol. 1, Tableau de l'Etat actuel des missions, 252.

129 AD, F-Q, 23 H 14, pièce 34.

130 *RAPQ* (1935–6), 301, Isle-Dieu à Pontbriand, 4 avril 1750. The only Récollet Isle-Dieu seems to have praised was Ambroise Aubré. See for example *RAPQ* (1936–7), 356, Isle-Dieu à Pontbriand, 29 mars 1754.

131 Ibid., 313–15, Isle-Dieu à Pontbriand, 23 mai 1751.

132 Ibid., 310–13, Mémoire à ... M. Rouillé ... de la Part de M.L'Evêque de Québec, 23 mai 1751.

133 SHA, A1, reg. 3393, pièce 38, janvier 1752.

134 AN, Colonies, B, vol. 94, fol. 179v., Ministre au R.P. Abgrall, 6 novembre 1751; ibid., vol. 96, fol. 43, Ministre à Abgrall, 13 février 1752; ibid., fol. 73, Ministre au Provincial des Récollets, 10 avril 1752; *RAPQ* (1935–6), 341–4, Isle-Dieu à Pontbriand, 26 avril 1752.

135 Hugolin, "Table nominale des Récollets," 90. Abbé de l'Isle-Dieu stated that Fournier had been forced out of the colony for "mauvaise conduite" but there is no other evidence to support that remark. *RAPQ* (1935–6), 353, Isle-Dieu au Président du Conseil de Marine, 24 juillet 1752.

136 AN, Outre Mer, G1, vol. 408, reg. I, fol. 162.

137 Ibid., reg. II, fols. 38v., 39, et 41.

138 His name first appears in the parish records in a 6 September 1752 marriage. AN, Outre Mer, G1, vol. 408, reg. II, fol. 41v.

139 Ibid., fols. 42–5v., 2 octobre 1752.

140 Gaston Du Boscq de Beaumont, ed., *Les derniers Jours de l'Acadie (1748–1758): Correspondance et mémoires ...*, 74. Raymond à Rouillé, 24 novembre 1752.

141 AN, Outre Mer, G1, vol. 408, reg. II, fol. 69v., 9 novembre 1752.

142 Du Boscq de Beaumont, ed., *Les derniers jours*, 74, Raymond à Rouillé, 24 novembre 1752.

143 Margaret Fortier, "Fortress Security and Military Justice at Louisbourg, 1720–45" (1980), AFL.

144 AN, Outre Mer, G2, vol. 189, fols. 148–269, Procès contre Le Bon, 1753–4; Adams, *Construction and Occupation of the Barracks*, 102.

145 PAC, MG18, F12, vol. 1, Tableau de l'Etat actuel, 251–7; *RAPQ* (1935–6), 384–6, Isle-Dieu à Pontbriand, 1 avril 1753; P. Albert David, "Les missionnaires du séminaire du Saint-Esprit à Québec et en Acadie au XVIIIe siècle," *Nova Francia* 1, no. 3 (1925): 104–5.

146 AN, Colonies, B, vol. 98, fol. 131, Ministre au Provincial des Récollets de Bretagne, 29 avril 1753.

147 AN, Outre Mer, G1, vol. 408, reg. II, fol. 56, mariage du 8 juillet 1753.

148 Hugolin, "Table nominale des Récollets," 85, 97.

149 *RAPQ* (1936–7), 341, Isle-Dieu à Pontbriand, 5 septembre 1753; ibid., 356, Isle-Dieu à Pontbriand, 29 mars 1754.

150 Du Boscq de Beaumont, ed., *Les derniers jours*, 112–3; AN, Outre Mer, G2, vol. 189, fols. 270–360, Procédure relative au mariage de Jules Caesar Foelix de la Noue, 1754–5.

151 *RAPQ* (1936–7), 378, Isle-Dieu à Pontbriand, 20 juin 1754.

152 AN Outre Mer, G1, vol. 409, reg. I, fol. 18v., 21 juin 1754.

153 Hugolin, "Table nominale des Récollets," 96.

154 Ibid., 85; *RAPQ* (1936–7), Isle-Dieu à Pontbriand, 25 mars 1755.

155 *RAPQ* (1936–7), 417, Isle-Dieu au Secrétaire d'Etat à la Marine, 8 octobre 1755.

156 The friar named *vicaire* was Anthoine de Pade Dulaurens. Hugolin, "Table nominale des Récollets," 90; AN, Colonies, C11B, vol. 35, fol. 221, Prévost, 14 novembre 1755. Along with Rosselin went Julien Moisson. Evidence of Rosselin continuing as curé in the fall is found in AN, Outre Mer, G1, vol. 409, reg. I, fol. 70, 7 septembre 1755.

157 ASSM, Côte 544, 4.32, Mandement du 9 février 1756.

158 *RAPQ* (1936–7), 435, Isle-Dieu à Pontbriand, 28 mars 1756.

159 This statement is based on the fact that for a parish priest Aubré officiated at a relatively small percentage of the total number of marriages, baptisms, and burials in 1756 and 1757.

160 Hugolin, "Table nominale des Récollets," 99.

161 AN, Outre Mer, G1, vol. 409, reg. II, fol. 39, 14 mars 1758.

162 Ibid., reg. III, fols. 1v.–2v.

163 CTG, Manuscrit 66, Journal de Poilly, 82.

164 Ibid., 96; McLennan, *Louisbourg*, 281–2.

165 [Thomas Pichon], *Lettres et memoires pour servir à l'histoire ... du Cap Breton* (The Hague 1760), 311.

166 Among the loose ends cleared up during this period was a 509 *livres* debt paid to the Récollet superior Constantin Souben. AN, Outre Mer, G3, 2045, pièce 107, 1 août 1758.

167 AN, Colonies, C11B, vol. 38, fol. 269v., Liste généralle des familles ... à La Rochelle, 28 avril 1759.

168 Ibid., fols. 247v., 248, auteur inconnu, 22 juillet 1759.

169 The best statement to that effect is Governor Costebelle's remark that the Récollets de Bretagne had "un zelle apostolique populaire et inimitable pour les courses assidues et fatiguants quils sont obligés de fair dans tous les havres repandus sur la Coste." AN, Colonies, C11B, vol. 1, fols. 163v., 164, Costebelle, 28 novembre 1715.

CHAPTER THREE

1 Diderot et D'Alembert, eds., *Encyclopédie*, 7: 301. The entry on the Brothers of Charity of Saint John of God was written by D'Alembert.

2 Jaenen, *Role of the Church*, 95.

3 Joseph-G. Gélinas, "Des oubliés," *La revue dominicaine* (1922): 218–29.

4 Diderot, *Encyclopédie*, 7: 301; [Louis-Sébastien Mercier], *Tableau de Paris* 12: 21–2.

5 AN, Colonies, B, vol. 38, fols. 129v.–30, Conseil à Beauharnois, 7 juin 1716.

6 *Histoire générale de la marine*, vol. 3, "Code des Armées Navales ou Recueil des Edits, Declarations, Ordonnances et Reglemens ...," Ordonnance de 1689, 324–31.

7 See for instance, AN, Colonies, B, vol. 63, fols. 556–9v., Mémoire du Roi à Le Normant, 5 mai 1735.

8 *DCB* 3: 98; AN, Colonies, B, vol. 59, fol. 526v., Ministre à Le Normant, 26 mai 1737.

9 AN, Colonies, B, vol. 47, p. 1267, Ministre à Saint-Ovide, 26 juin 1724.

10 John McManners describes hospitals as "ecclesiastical institutions" in *French Ecclesiastical Society under the Ancien Régime*, 99–100. Regulations and ordinances on hospitals are located in *Etat militaire de France, pour l'année 1758* (Paris 1758), 299–313, and *Code militaire ou compilation des ordonnances des roys de France*, vol. 2 (Paris 1728), 401–26. The specific customs and rules of the Brothers of Charity are mentioned in Gélinas, "Des oubliés," 223.

11 AN, Colonies, C11B, vol. 1, fol. 409v., Costebelle, 26 octobre 1716; ibid., vol. 4, fols. 94v.–5v., Conseil à Saint-Ovide et Mézy, 19 mars 1719; ibid., B, vol. 41, fol. 598v., Conseil à Saint-Ovide et Mézy, 19 juillet 1719; ibid., C11B, vol. 5, fols. 119–24, Conseil, 13 août 1720.

12   Ibid., C11B, vol. 8, fols. 76–7v., Saint-Ovide, 2 décembre 1726; ibid., B, vol. 50, fol. 31, Ministre au Provincial des Rx de la Charité, 1 avril 1727.

13   Ibid., C11B, vol. 11, fols. 24–5, Bourville, 30 novembre 1730; ibid., fols. 99–100v., des Pensens, 30 novembre 1730; ibid., vol. 13, fol. 22, Mézy, 17 mars 1732.

14   Ibid., vol. 14, fols. 227–9v., Le Normant, 19 octobre 1733. For a list of furniture, tools, and other articles in the hospital at the end of 1733 see ibid., fols. 238–41v., Carrerot à Fèlix Camax, 31 décembre 1733.

15   Ibid., vol. 13, fol. 22, Mézy, 17 mars 1732; ibid., fols. 138–38v., Le Normant, 5 février 1732; ibid., B, vol. 57, fol. 777v., Ministre à Saint-Ovide et Le Normant, 27 juin 1732.

16   Hermas Bastien, L'Ordre Hospitalier de Saint-Jean-de-Dieu au Canada, 59.

17   AN, Outre Mer, G1, vol. 466, pièce 69, Recensement de l'Isle Royale, octobre 1734.

18   AN, Colonies, B, vol. 59, fols. 521–2, Ministre à Saint-Ovide et Le Normant, 19 mai 1733; ibid., fols. 526–7, Ministre à Le Normant, 26 mai 1733.

19   Ibid., B, vol. 65, fols. 460–61, Ministre à Saint-Ovide et Le Normant, 30 avril 1737; ibid., C11B, vol. 19, fols. 20–2v., Saint-Ovide et Le Normant, 24 octobre 1737.

20   For a favourable assessment of how the hospital was being run see AN, Colonies, C11B, vol. 14, fols. 260–2v., Sabatier, 1 janvier 1739. One complaint which did surface was made by Franz-Joseph Cailly, commander of the Karrer Regiment detachment at Louisbourg. The details of Cailly's criticism were not recorded but he alleged that his men were not being well treated. AN, Colonies, B, vol. 67, vol. 272, Ministre à Karrer, 9 avril 1738.

21   AN, Colonies, C11B, vol. 22, fols. 168v.–9v., Bigot au Ministre, 17 octobre 1740. Folie is not a precise clinical description but simply a popular term for a condition characterized by changeable and unusual behaviour.

22   Ibid.

23   Ibid., vol. 15, fols. 93–7v., Saint-Ovide et Le Normant, 5 novembre 1734; ibid., B, vol. 62, fol. 136v., Ministre à Beauharnois, 8 février 1735. On the treatment of the affliction with mercury see Diderot, Encyclopédie 17: 1–2.

24   [Mercier], Tableau de Paris 8: 11–14.

25   AN, Colonies, B, vol. 64, fols. 475v.–6v., Ministre à Saint-Ovide et Le Normant, 8 mai 1736.

26   Ibid., C11B, vol. 23, fols. 133–33v., Bigot, 26 novembre 1741.

27   Ibid., B, vol. 76, fols. 479–79v., Ministre à Bigot, 12 juin 1743; ibid., C11B, vol. 25, fols. 115–16, Bigot, 19 octobre 1743.

28   Ibid., C11B, vol. 29, Prévost, 14 novembre 1750; ibid., B, vol. 91, Ministre à Prévost, 19 mai 1750.

29   Ibid., vol. 36, fol. 456v., Instruction pour le Sr Soubras, 10 avril 1714; ibid., C11B, vol. 5, fols. 150–1, Saint-Ovide et Mézy, 7 décembre 1721.

30 Ibid., C11B, vol. 3, fols. 193–5, Bordereau, 1715.

31 Ibid., B, vol. 37, fol. 218v., Ministre à Soubras, 4 juin 1715; ibid., C11B, vol. 1, fols. 317–20, Droits sur les Pescheurs pour l'hopital, 14 mars 1716; ibid., B, vol. 38, fol. 264, Conseil de Marine aux Srs Costebelle et Soubras, 22 avril 1716.

32 Ibid., C11B, vol. 5, fols. 148–55v., Saint-Ovide et Mézy, 7 décembre 1721; ibid., B, vol. 45, fols. 925–9, Ordonnance pour l'Etablissement du droit, 12 mai 1722.

33 Ibid., C11B, vol. 6, fols. 251–2, Mézy, 25 novembre 1723.

34 Jacques Ducharme, "Les revenus des Hospitalières de Montréal au XVIIIe siècle," in L'Hôtel-Dieu de Montréal, 1642–1973 (Montréal 1973), 244.

35 Boston Weekly News-Letter, 20 September 1744.

36 For an example from the 1720s of the sick off ships being treated by the Brothers of Charity see AN, Colonies, C11B, vol. 7, fols. 211–12, Mézy, 16 août 1725. The situation in 1732 is discussed in ibid., vol. 13, fols. 37–9, Le Normant, 15 août 1739; ibid., fol. 120, Le Normant, 10 août 1732; ibid., vol. 12, fols. 243–4, Saint-Ovide, 20 août 1732; ibid., B, vol. 56, fols. 275v.–6v., Ministre à Beauharnois, 23 septembre 1732.

37 Ibid., C11B, vol. 15, fols. 52–9, Saint-Ovide et Le Normant, 23 janvier 1734.

38 See plan designated 754–8, AFL.

39 AN, Colonies, C11B, vol. 35, fols. 236–8v., Prévost, 6 décembre 1755.

40 Renée Haynes, Philosopher King: The Humanist Pope Benedict XIV, 76.

41 Jaenen, Role of the Church, 115. For an example of a Louisbourg civilian being treated at home see AN, Outre Mer, G2, vol. 197, dossier 151, papiers ... de la deffunct veuve Desgoutins, 17 mai 1741.

42 The first two entries, totalling 6,000 livres, were not paid for out of the Ile Royale budget but out of funds in the "Domaine d'Occident." See for example AN, Colonies, C11A, vol. 115, fols. 135–8, Marine 1744 Sur le fonds du Domaine d'Occident. For an example of other allocations see AN, Colonies, C11C, fol. XI, fols. 108–12, Estat des fonds necessaires ... pour 1736, 20 octobre 1735.

43 Frégault, Le XVIIIe siècle canadien, 110.

44 AN, Colonies, B, vol. 59, fols. 521–2, Ministre à Saint-Ovide et Le Normant, 19 mai 1733. The religieux had requested 20 sols per day per soldier; ibid., C11B, vol. 13, fols. 42–3, Mézy, 17 mars 1732.

45 Ibid., C11B, vol. 18, fols. 92–4, Le Normant, 11 novembre 1736.

46 Ibid., B, vol. 65, fols. 458v.–9v., Ministre à Le Normant, 22 avril 1737.

47 Ibid., fols. 460–1, Ministre à Saint-Ovide et Le Normant, 30 avril 1737; ibid., vol. 66, fols. 291v.–2v., Ministre à Le Normant, 6 mai 1738; ibid., C11B, vol. 19, fols. 98–101, Le Normant, 4 décembre 1737.

48 John J. Heagerty, Four Centuries of Medical History in Canada ... 1:271.

49 AN, Colonies, C11B, vol. 24, fols. 140–1v., Bigot, 12 octobre 1742; ibid., B, vol. 76, fols. 479–79v., Ministre à Bigot, 12 juin 1743.

50 AN, Colonies, DFC, AS, no. d'ordre 216, fols. 13v., 24–5v., Journal de Girard la Croix, 16 juillet 1745.

51 DeForest, ed., *Louisbourg Journals*, 50–1.

52 *RAPQ* (1935–6), 277–8, Mgr L'Evêque de Québec, 3 novembre 1745; AN, Colonies, C11B, vol. 27, fols. 280–4, Bigot, 7 septembre 1748; AN, Outre Mer, G1, vol. 466, pièce 76, Denombrement Général, 1749; Gélinas, "Des oubliés," 225; ASQ, Séminaire 14, liasse 6, no. 11, lettre de l'Evêque, 7 novembre 1748.

53 AN, Colonies, C11B, vol. 28, fols. 303–20, Boucher, 30 août 1749.

54 Ibid., fol. 75v., Desherbiers, 9 août 1749.

55 Ibid., vol. 30, fols. 259–61v., Prévost, 11 novembre 1751; ibid., vol. 31, fols. 118–21v., Boucher, 20 novembre 1751.

56 Ibid., vol. 32, fols. 193–7, Prévost, 15 novembre 1752.

57 Ibid., vol. 37, fols. 172–5, Prévost, 16 octobre 1757.

58 Du Boscq de Beaumont, ed., *Les derniers jours*, 186, Des Bourbes à Surlaville, 18 avril 1756.

59 Heagerty, *Four Centuries of Medical History*, 271. For another patient's account of treatment see Madame Bégon's entry in her journal. *RAPQ* (1934–5), Mme Bégon, 11 mai 1749.

60 AN, Colonies, C11B, vol. 36, fols. 86–92, Prévost, 10 avril 1756.

61 Ibid., vol. 37, fols. 172–5, Prévost, 16 octobre 1757.

62 Ibid., vol. 30, fols. 259–61, Prévost, 11 novembre 1751; ibid., vol. 32, fols. 193–7, Prévost, 15 novembre 1752.

63 Ibid., vol. 33, fols. 123–7v., Prévost, 6 juin 1753; ibid., fols. 269–74v., Prévost, 27 octobre 1753.

64 SHA, A1, reg. 3393, pièce 39, Mémoire sur l'hôpital, janvier 1752.

65 ASQ, Polygraphie 56, no. 64, Sotises, no. 65 [sic].

66 [Pichon], *Genuine Letters and Memoirs*, 200–3.

67 Ibid., SHA, A1, reg. 3393, pièce 39, Mémoire sur l'hôpital, janvier 1752.

68 AN, Colonies, C11B, vol. 28, fol. 148, Bigot, 20 août 1749; ibid., fol. 34v., Desherbiers et Prévost, 16 octobre 1749.

69 Ibid., vol. 29, fols. 165–7, Prévost, 14 novembre 1750.

70 Ibid., vol. 34, fols. 110–13, Prévost, 20 octobre 1754.

71 Bastien, *L'Ordre Hospitalier de Saint-Jean-de-Dieu*, 59; Gélinas, "Des oubliés," 228.

72 AN, Colonies, B, vol. 104, fol. 511, Ministre à de Ruis, 5 mai 1756. As for there being seven, the death of five *religieux* in 1757 reduced their numbers to two. Ibid., C11B, vol. 37, fols. 201–4, Prévost, 27 novembre 1757.

73 Ibid., C11B, vol. 37, fols. 201–4, Prévost, 27 novembre 1757; Gélinas, "Des oubliés," 228; Bastien, *L'Ordre Hospitalier de Saint-Jean-de-Dieu*, 59.

74 AN, Colonies, B, vol. 107, fol. 342, Ministre à Drucours et Prévost, 11 janvier 1758.

75 Gélinas, "Des oubliés," 228; Bastien, *L'Ordre Hospitalier de Saint-Jean-de-Dieu*, 59.

76 AN, Colonies, C11B, vol. 38, fols. 36–8v., Prévost, 7 juillet 1758; CTG, Manuscrit 66, Journal de Poilly, 77–9.

77 AN, Colonies, C11B, vol. 38, fols. 104–6, juillet 1758.

78 Ibid., B, vol. 112, fol. 468, Ministre à de Ruis, 2 mai 1760; ibid., fol. 215, Ministre au Procureur syndic de l'ordre des frères de la Charité à Paris, 30 mai 1760.

79 Ibid., C11B, vol. 38, fol. 248, auteur inconnu, 22 juillet 1759. The names of the four remaining brothers are given in AN, Colonies, C11B, vol. 38, fol. 269v., 28 avril 1759.

80 "Notice sur les Frères Hospitaliers de la Charité de l'Ordre de St-Jean-De Dieu, au Canada, de 1713 à 1758," *Bulletin des recherches historiques* 33, no. 9 (September 1927): 522–4.

81 Albert Almon, *Rochefort Point, A Silent City in Louisbourg*, 13–15.

CHAPTER FOUR

1 Kalm, *Travels into North America* 3: 304–5.

2 M. DuClos, *Considérations sur les mœurs de ce siècle*, 27.

3 *Dictionnaire universel François et latin ... (Dictionnaire de Trevoux)*, 7 vols. (Paris 1743), 2: 1562. Other definitions along the same basic lines can be found in Diderot, *Encyclopédie* 5: 397–403, and Antoine Furetière, *Dictionnaire universel, contenant généralement tous les mots françois*, vol. 1 (1690; reprint, Geneva, 1970), entries on "Education."

4 Saint-Vallier, *Rituel*, 300.

5 L'Abbé Sicard, *L'ancien clergé de France, vol. 1, Les évêques avant la Révolution*, 437.

6 Trudel, *Introduction to New France*, 260; RAPQ (1941–2), 260.

7 The minister of marine, the comte de Pontchartrain, adopted a policy in 1713–14 of discouraging the sending of women and children to the colony. AN, Colonies, B, vol. 36, fols. 104–04v., Pontchartrain à Beauharnois, 7 mars 1714; ibid., fols. 155–5v., Pontchartrain à Beauharnois, 4 avril 1714.

8 McLennan, *Louisbourg*, app. 3, 371.

9 AN, Colonies, B, vol. 47, p. 1116, Maurepas à L'évêque de Québec, 30 mai 1724; ibid., C11B, vol. 7, fols. 171–5, Saint-Ovide et Mézy, 17 décembre 1725; ibid., B, vol. 49, fols. 716v.–18v., Ministre à Saint-Ovide et Mézy, 25 juin 1726.

10 Ibid., C11B, vol. 5, fols. 300–3v., Conseil, 28 janvier 1721.

11 Ibid., F3, vol. 50, fols. 497–8v., Raymond, 8 janvier 1753.

12 Francis Parkman, *The Old Régime in Canada* , pt. 4, 432. Parkman's source was *Mémoire de 1736; Détail de toute la colonie* (Historical Society of Québec).

13 SHA, série A1, reg. 3457, pièce 66, Objets d'Observations que le Sr Magellon, 1757.

14 Peter N. Moogk, "Manual Education and Economic Life in New France," *Studies on Voltaire and the Eighteenth Century* 167 (1977): 125–68. For more information on military cadets, see Margaret Fortier, "The Ile Royale Garrison, 1713–1745," AFL.

15 AN, Outre Mer, G1, vol. 466, pièce 51, Recensement des habitants, 14 janvier 1715. In 1730 Zacharie Caradec, in his capacity as vicar-general, announced his intention of examining the *maîtres d'école* of the town. None of the teachers was mentioned by name. AN, Outre Mer, G3, dossier 2037, pièce 132, 13 février 1730.

16 AN, Outre Mer, G2, vol. 203, dossier 361, Testimony of Pierre Boziac, mai 1755.

17 Antoine Perré's upbringing is discussed at length in Kenneth J. Donovan, "Social Status and Contrasting Life Styles: Children of the Poor and Well-to-do in Louisbourg."

18 See, for instance, Kalm, *Travels into North America* 3: 147–8.

19 *RAPQ* (1935–6), 311–13, Mémoire à M. Rouillé, 23 mai 1751.

20 The quoted extracts are from Saint-Vallier and Dosquet. AAQ, Registre C, Lettre d'établissement pour ... Sœurs Congréganistes, 20 août 1735; AN, Outre Mer, G2, vol. 190, reg. IV, fols. 17v.–18v., Saint-Vallier à Sœur de la Conception, 28 juillet 1727.

21 Gosselin, *L'église du Canada* 2: 138.

22 Trudel, *Introduction to New France*, p. 243.

23 Louis Franquet, *Voyages et mémoires sur le Canada en 1752–53*, 31–2. For European perspectives on the possible dangers of over-education, see Harvey Chisick, *The Limits of Reform in the Enlightenment: Attitudes toward the Education of the Lower Classes in Eighteenth-Century France*.

24 See sources in note 9.

25 *DCB* 3: 574–5; AN, Outre Mer, G2, vol. 190, fols. 17v.–9v., Saint-Vallier à Sœur de la Conception, 28 juillet 1727.

26 *DCB* 3: 574–5.

27 AD, F-Q, série 23 H 14: Lettres des Récollets, pièce 15, Saint-Vallier au Père Joseph Denys, 6 septembre 1727; ibid., pièce 17, Le Duff à Saturnin Dirop, 3 novembre 1727.

28 AN, Colonies, C11B, vol. 9, fol. 37, Saint-Ovide et Mézy, 15 décembre 1727.

29 AN, Outre Mer, G1, vol. 406, reg. IV, fol. 9, Sépulture du 19 janvier 1729.

30 AN, Colonies, C11B, vol. 9, fols. 108–9, Mézy, 10 décembre 1727.

31 Ibid., B, vol. 54, fol. 433v., Mémoire du Roi à Beauharnois et Hocquart, 11 avril 1730.

32 AN, Outre Mer, G2, vol. 190, reg. IV, fols. 9–14, 3 octobre 1733.

33 AN, Colonies, C11B, vol. 9, fol. 37, Saint-Ovide et Mézy, 15 décembre 1727.

34 Ibid., B, vol. 57, fols. 756–56v., Ministre à Sœur de la Conception, 19 juin 1732.

35 Dosquet quoted in *DCB* 3: 575.

36 AN, Colonies, C11B, vol. 12, fols. 214–5, Saint-Ovide et Le Normant, 22 décembre 1732.

37 AN, Outre Mer, G2, vol. 191, fols. 48v–9v.

38 AN, Colonies, C11A, vol. 107, fols. 227–8v., Sœur Marguerite Le Roy à Monseigneur, 23 décembre 1732; Gosselin, *L'église du Canada* 2: 235; AN, Colonies, B, vol. 59, fols. 398v.–99, Ministre à L'évêque de Samos, 24 mars 1733.

39 AN, Colonies, B, vol. 59, fols. 424–32, Ministre à Saint-Ovide et Le Normant, 26 mai 1733; ibid., C11B, vol. 14, fols. 39v.–41v., Saint-Ovide et Le Normant, 11 octobre 1733.

40 ACND, 4A/11, no. 3 (2220), Extrait du Registre des Nominations, 24 août 1733.

41 Gosselin, *L'église du Canada* 2: 235; AN, Colonies, B, vol. 59, fol. 422v., Ministre à Beauharnois et Hocquart, 14 avril 1733.

42 AN, Colonies, C11C, vol. XI, fol. 87, Bordereau, 1734, 20 septembre 1736.

43 *DCB* 3: 574–5.

44 The only person at Louisbourg who left behind a criticism of Sister Marguerite Le Roy was the Récollet Michel-Ange Le Duff. Shortly after her arrival in town in 1727, Le Duff wrote to his provincial that the sister only feigned indifference to worldly concerns while at the same time she was making strides in an affected manner toward setting up her new establishment. Part of Le Duff's resentment towards the sister was undoubtedly due to the fact that the bishop had placed her under the spiritual direction of Le Duff's religious rival, Joseph Denys of the Récollets of Paris. AD, F-Q, pièce 17, Le Duff à Dirop, 3 novembre 1727.

45 ASQ, Lettres P, no. 63, Maillard, 29 septembre 1738.

46 [Pichon], *Genuine Letters and Memoirs*, 203

47 Previous writers were unaware of the entry in the parish records concerning the profession of Marie-Magdelaine Noel and maintained that Catherine Paré's profession was Cape Breton's first. See, for instance, [Faillon], *Vie de la Sœur Bourgeoys* 2: 347; [Lemire-Marsolais], *Histoire de la Congrégation de Notre-Dame* 4: 33; Sister Saint Miriam of the Temple, "The Congregation of Notre Dame in Early Nova Scotia" (Paper read at the 20th Annual Meeting of the Canadian Catholic Historical Association 1953).

48 AN, Outre Mer, G2, vol. 194, pièce 77, 20 avril 1735; AN, Colonies, C11B, vol. 18, fols. 5–5v., Conseil, 23 janvier 1736.

49 AN, Colonies, C11C, vol. XI, fol. 88, Bordereau, 1734, 20 septembre 1736; ibid., fols. 104, 104v., Bordereau, 1735, 30 octobre 1736.

50 [Faillon], *Vie de la Sœur Bourgeoys* 2: 351; AN, Colonies, C11A, vol. 107, fols. 271–3, Lyon de St Ferréol, février 1736. In August 1735 Bishop Dosquet had issued his own "lettre d'établissement" for the Louisbourg sisters. AAQ, Reg. C, Lettre d'établissement, 20 août 1735.

51 AN, Colonies, B, vol. 64, fol. 476, Ministre à Saint-Ovide et Le Normant, 8 mai 1736.

52 Ibid., C11B, vol. 19, fols. 14v.–15, Saint-Ovide et Le Normant, 23 octobre 1737.

53 Ibid., B, vol. 66, fols. 297–8, Ministre à Bourville et Le Normant, 6 mai 1738.

54 Ibid., C11B, vol. 20, fols. 52–9, Bourville et Le Normant, 21 octobre 1738.

55 Ibid., vol. 14, fols. 260v.–1, Sabatier, 1 janvier 1739; ibid., B, vol. 68, fols. 362–3, Ministre à Sabatier, 22 juin 1739.

56 Ibid., B, vol. 68, fols. 355–55v., Ministre à Forant et Bigot, 22 juin 1739. The 3,000 *livres* came out of the budget of Canada not that of Ile Royale.

57 *DCB* 2: 224–6; AN, Colonies, B, vol. 73, fol. 52, Ministre à Mlle de Forant, 25 février 1741; ibid., vol. 72, fol. 418, Ministre à Duquesnel et Bigot, 20 mai 1741; ibid., vol. 74, fols. 553–53v., Ministre à Duquesnel et Bigot, 1 juin 1742; bid., fol. 599v., Ministre à Bigot, 11 août 1742; ibid., vol. 76, fols. 479–79v., Ministre à Bigot, 12 juin 1743.

58 AN, Colonies, C11B, vol. 23, fols. 170 et 172, Bordereau, 1741, 18 octobre 1741.

59 *RAPQ* (1935–6), 300, Isle-Dieu à Pontbriand, 4 avril 1750.

60 *DCB* 3: 629–30.

61 *Histoire de la Congrégation de Notre-Dame* 4: 100; [Faillon], *Vie de la Sœur Bourgeoys* 2: 360.

62 *Histoire de la Congrégation de Notre-Dame* 4: 162.

63 AN, Colonies, C11A, vol. 107, fols. 269–70v., Les Sœurs de la Congrégation de Louisbourg, 18 mars 1746; ibid., B, vol. 84, fol. 382, Ministre à de Ricouart, 31 octobre 1746; *RAPQ* (1935–6), 300–1, Isle-Dieu à Pontbriand, 4 avril 1750; *Histoire de la Congrégation de Notre-Dame* 4: 141–5.

64 ASQ, Polygraphie 7, no. 41, Mémoire sur les fondations du duc d'Orleans; ACND, 4A/11, no. 17 (2234), 4 mai 1756; *RAPQ* (1936–7), 427, Isle-Dieu à Pontbriand, 28 mars 1756.

65 ASQ, Séminaire 14, liasse 6, no. 11, Lettre de l'évêque de Québec, 7 novembre 1748.

66 *Histoire de la Congrégation de Notre-Dame* 4: 151.

67 *RAPQ* (1935–6), 300–1, Isle-Dieu à Pontbriand, 4 avril 1750.

68 AN, Colonies, C11C, vol. 13, fol. 83v., Bordereau, 1749, 13 septembre 1751.

69 Ibid., C11B, vol. 28, fols. 143–43v., Bigot, 20 août 1749; *Histoire de la Congrégation de Notre-Dame* 4: 152.

70 AN, Colonies, B, vol. 91, fol. 335, Ministre aux Srs Desherbiers et Prévost, 19 mai 1750; ibid., fol. 345, Ministre à Desherbiers et Prévost, 31 mai 1750; *Histoire de la Congrégation de Notre-Dame* 4: 152.

71 *Histoire de la Congrégation de Notre-Dame* 4: 152–3. The date of the two sisters' return and the arrival of the replacements comes from AN, Colonies, C11C, vol. 13, fol. 149v., Bordereau, 1751, 15 novembre 1753. Sœur Saint-Louis-des-Anges did not travel with Sœur Sainte-Gertrude but sailed a little later. A secular accompanied the paralytic back to Montréal. The lay assistants who served the mission from 1751 were Marie Labauve and Geneviève Henry. *Histoire de la Congrégation de Notre-Dame* 4: 266.

72 [Pichon], *Genuine Letters and Memoirs*, 203.

73 *Histoire de la Congrégation de Notre-Dame* 4: 154–6; SHA, A1, reg. 3343, pièce 38, janvier 1752.

74 *Histoire de la Congrégation de Notre-Dame* 4: 266–8; *RAPQ* (1935–6), 384, Isle-Dieu à Pontbriand, 1 avril 1753; British Museum, Burney Collection, Burney 463, *Whitehall Evening Post or The London Intelligencer*, 15–17 January 1754, item 1237; AN, Colonies, C11A, vol. 107, fols. 262–4v., Les Sœurs de la Congrégation de Notre Dame au Ministre, 10 octobre 1753.

75 *RAPQ* (1936–7), 362–3, Isle Dieu au Président du Conseil de Marine, 1 avril 1754; *Histoire de la Congrégation de Notre-Dame* 4: 268–9.

76 Du Boscq de Beaumont, ed., *Les derniers jours*, 122, Lettre de Joubert, 10 octobre 1754. Joubert gave the fee as 10 *pistoles*, which has been converted into *livres* according to the equivalency table given in Trudel, *Introduction to New France*, 185.

77 *RAPQ* (1936–7), 435–6, Isle Dieu à Pontbriand, 28 mars 1756; *Histoire de la Congrégation de Notre-Dame* 4: 268–9.

78 AN, Colonies, C11B, vol. 37, fols. 39–43v., Drucourt et Prévost, 28 décembre 1757.

79 Ibid., C11B, vol. 38, fol. 219, Moras à Drucourt et Prévost, 28 avril 1758.

80 *Histoire de la Congrégation de Notre-Dame* 4: 368–75, 407–8.

81 Ibid., 374; ibid., 5: 87–98; ibid., 4: 22–5. Before the 250 *livres* annual royal pension was awarded the members of the Congrégation were paid at the rate of 12 *sols* per day. AN, Colonies, B, vol. 108, fol. 409, Ministre à L'Abbé de l'Isle-Dieu, 11 décembre 1758; ibid., C11B, vol. 38, fol. 269v., Liste generale des familles, 28 avril 1759.

82 *Histoire de la Congrégation de Notre-Dame* 22–5.

83 These texts are the *Reglemens des Sœurs seculiers de la Congrégation de Notre-Dame* (Montréal 1846) and the *Coutumier des Sœurs de la Congrégation de Notre-Dame de Ville-Marie* (Montréal 1875). The archivist, Sister Florence Bertrand, at the Congrégation de Notre-Dame in Montréal, where I consulted these books in January 1979, informed me that much of

the content of these works dated back to the seventeenth and eighteenth centuries, although the Congrégation had not had them published until the nineteenth century.

84 Gosselin, *L'église du Canada* 2: 136.
85 *Reglemens des Sœurs seculiers*, 23, 24; Kalm, *Travels into North America* 3: 304–5.
86 Un Missionnaire, *La civilité puérile, et sonnets pour l'instruction des enfans* (Troyes 1735), 4. See also Robert Mandrou, *De la culture Populaire aux XVIIe et XVIIIe siècles*, 126–30.
87 *Reglemens des Sœurs seculiers*, 99–104. The family names of the six officers' daughters boarding at the Louisbourg school in 1743 were de Couagne, de l'Espérance, Benoît, Chassin de Thierry, Lafresillière, and Loppinot. AN, Colonies, C11B, vol. 25, fols. 58–58v., Duquesnel, 27 octobre 1743. They ranged in age from five to seventeen, according to data in the family reconstitution file, AFL.
88 AN, Outre Mer, G2, vol. 197, dossier 129, pièce 19, 4–5 février 1740.
89 *RAPQ* (1935–6), 399–400, Isle-Dieu au Président du Conseil de la Marine, 9 mai 1753; ibid., 405, Isle-Dieu à Pontbriand, mai 1753.
90 Fernand Porter, *L'institution catéchistique au Canada: Deux siècles de formation religieuse, 1633–1833*, 180–1, 244.
91 *Coutumier des Sœurs de la Congrégation*, 155–66.
92 Haynes, *Philosopher King*, 18–19.
93 *Neptunia*, no 136 (4e Trimestre 1979): 28, research note by René Chartrand.
94 AN, Colonies, F3, vol. 50, fols. 497–8v., Raymond, 8 janvier 1753.
95 *Coutumier des Sœurs de la Congrégation*, 171–5.
96 *Reglemens des Sœurs seculiers*, 104–5.
97 Ibid., 105. In some parts of Italy the school year ran from 1 September to 1 August the following year, with Sundays and feast days as days off and with fifty half-holidays. Haynes, *Philosopher King*, 18–19.
98 AAQ, Copies des Lettres, vol. II, p. 131, Saint-Vallier permet aux Sœurs de la congrégation de Notre-Dame, Ville Marie, 21 avril 1719; *RAPQ* (1941–2), 190.
99 Amédée Gosselin, *L'instruction au Canada sous le régime français (1635–1760)*, 192.
100 AN, Outre Mer, G2, vol. 179, fol. 548, 27 juillet 1728.
101 This figure is obtained by calculating how much was allotted to pay the *pensions* of the eight officers' daughters whose fees were paid out of the Forant estate (annually worth 1,600 *livres*).
102 AN, Outre Mer, G2, vol. 203, dossier 300, reçu daté 30 juillet 1756. Angélique Poinsu, aged fifteen, stayed with the sisters for a little over four months in 1755 and paid at the rate of 250 *livres* per year.

103 AN, Colonies, C11B, vol. 21, fols. 8, 8v., Forant et Bigot, 30 octobre 1739.
104 *RAPQ* (1935–6), 399–400, Isle-Dieu au Président, 9 mai 1753; ibid., 405, Isle-Dieu à Pontbriand, mai 1753.
105 The parish records are located in AN, Outre Mer, G1, vols. 406 et 407.
106 Allan Greer, "The Pattern of Literacy in Québec, 1745–1899," *Histoire Sociale / Social History* 11, no. 22 (November 1978), 299. In fifty-five marriages from 1745 to 1754, 54.5 per cent of the brides signed their own names. In Port Royal, Nova Scotia, the literacy rate dropped to practically zero between 1710 and 1745, but that was due to the English conquest and subsequent departure of teaching orders. Gisa I. Hynes, "Some Aspects of the Demography of Port Royal, 1650–1755," *Acadiensis* 3, no. 1 (Autumn 1973): 7–8.
107 In *Poverty and Charity in Aix-en Provence, 1640–1789*, 167, Cissie Fairchilds states that in Provence in 1700 "barely ten per cent of the population ... could sign their names." The national average for France at that point, she claims, was about 21 per cent. A study of a town in Normandy revealed that in the period 1720–39 only 12 per cent of the brides could sign, while during the period 1740–59 that figure had climbed to 25 per cent. Françoise Becart, "Saint-André-d'Hébertot au XVIIe et au XVIIIe siècles: Etude demographique," *Annales de Normandie* 27, no. 3 (October 1977): 293.
108 Greer, "Pattern of Literacy," 299. The figure for grooms who signed in the period 1745–54 was 49.1 per cent. At Port Royal, the rate for grooms, like that for the brides, fell to zero during this period. Hynes, "Demography of Port Royal," 7, 8.
109 These figures come from an analysis of the Louisbourg parish records. See sources in note 105.
110 For an account of the vigorous economy of Ile Royale see Moore, "The Other Louisbourg."

CHAPTER FIVE

1 Kalm, *Travels into North America* 3: 43–4.
2 [Mercier], *Tableau de Paris* 3: 47; ibid., 4: 94–5; ibid., 6: 56–8. The *fête-Dieu* was also known as the *fête du Saint-Sacrement*.
3 CTG, Manuscrit 66, Journal de Poilly, 36.
4 Ibid.
5 The general lack of sympathy among the Canadiens for various church regulations and attempts to raise money is discussed at length in Jaenen, *Role of the Church*.
6 Marc Venard, "Popular Religion in the Eighteenth century," 138–54, in *Church and Society in Catholic Europe of the Eighteenth Century*, ed. W.J. Callahan and David Higgs, 138–54.

7 O. Perrin, *Galerie Bretonne ou vie des Bretons de l'Amorique* 1: 33; Arnold Van Gennep, *Manuel de folklore français contemporain* 1, pt. 1: 128.

8 Van Gennep, *Manuel de folklore français* 1, pt. 1: 128.

9 Saint-Vallier, *Rituel*, 23–4.

10 AN, Outre Mer, G1, vol. 406, fol. 23v., 27 juillet 1726; ibid., reg. IV, fol. 15, 19 septembre 1729. Ages for the de la Pérelle children are calculated from the genealogical information provided in H. Paul Thibault, *L'îlôt 17 de Louisbourg (1713–1768)*, Travail Inédit 99 (Ottawa: Parcs Canada 1972), 114.

11 Two further examples: In January and December 1741 two children were born to Pierre Martissans, a Louisbourg merchant, and his wife Angélique Chavigny de la Chevrotière. In one baptism Jean François Martissans (aged nine) was the *parrain* for his newborn sister; in the other Martin Martissans (aged eleven) was the *parrain* for his infant brother. AN, Outre Mer, G1, vol. 407, reg. I, fols. 63–4, 19 janvier 1741; ibid., fol. 85, 25 décembre 1741. Ages for the *parrains* are calculated from information in the family reconstitution file, AFL.

12 Saint-Vallier, *Rituel*, 23–4.

13 [Mercier], *Tableau de Paris* 7: 34.

14 Van Gennep, *Manuel de folklore français* 1, pt. 1: 117.

15 AN, Outre Mer, G2, vol. 196, fols. 140v.–1, Audience du bailliage ... 21e janvier 1737, entre Domingo, Cordonnier, et Jean Darraq.

16 [Pichon], *Genuine Letters and Memoirs*, 202–3. Pichon accused the brothers of being overly fond of obstetrics. In 1751 Frère Alexis de la Rue, the surgeon at the Hôpital du Roi, delivered an illegitimate child and "sprinkled" it. The child died three weeks later, at which time de la Rue had still not revealed the mother's identity, though he said he would do so at a later date. AN, Outre Mer, G1, vol. 408, reg. I, fol. 159, sépulture du 13 juillet 1751.

17 For entries naming *sages-femmes* see AN, Outre Mer, G1, vol. 406, baptêmes du 3 et 9 septembre 1735, 3 et 11 juin, 11 août 1736, 14 décembre 1736, 5 octobre 1737, 27 mai 1739; ibid., vol. 407, reg. II, fol. 27, baptême du 17 novembre 1743; ibid., G2, vol. 194, pièce 55, enfant de Servanne Bonnier et Pierre Santier était "accouché" par Madame LeLarge, 3 septembre 1734.

18 A description and analysis of the problems associated with unskilled midwives in France is provided by Mireille Laget, "Childbirth in Seventeenth and Eighteenth Century France: Obstetrical Practices and Collective Attitudes," in *Medicine and Society in France: Selections from the Annales*, ed. R. Forster and O. Ranum, 137–76.

19 AN, Colonies, B, vol. 66, fols. 294v.–5, Ministre à Bourville et Le Normant, 6 mai 1738; ibid., C11B, vol. 20, Bourville et Le Normant, 21 octobre 1738.

20 AN, Colonies, B, vol. 90, fols. 268–68v., Ministre à M. de Givry, 13 janvier
    1749; ibid., C11C, vol. 13, fol. 163v., Etat des fonds, 10 décembre 1751;
    ibid., C11B, vol. 38, fol. 247, auteur inconnu, 22 juillet 1759. Madame Droit's
    maiden name is revealed in AN, Outre Mer, G1, vol. 408, reg. I, fol. 133v.,
    mariage du 5 juin 1751 and ibid., reg. II, fol. 22, baptême du 18 mars 1753.
    The 400 livres salary seems to have been standard in New France. For
    examples in Canada see RAPQ (1941–2), 213; Frégault, Le XVIII siècle
    canadien, 144. Until 1754 the veuve Droit was apparently assisted by a
    female black slave, who died at the age of sixty in March of that year. AN,
    Outre Mer, G1, vol. 409, reg. I, fol. 5v., 3 mars 1754.

21 Saint-Vallier, Rituel, 30–1, 563–4. An example of the election of a midwife
    in Canada can be found in RAPQ (1922–3), 151.

22 Louisbourg parish records for the years 1722–58 are in AN, Outre Mer, G1,
    vols. 406, 407, 408, and 409. For the totals in different categories relating to
    baptisms see Figs. 4, 7, and 8.

23 Perrin, Galerie Bretonne 1: 34.

24 Van Gennep, Manuel de folklore français 1, pt. 1: 135–6.

25 Ibid., 133–5.

26 This conclusion is based on my analysis of baptisms from the period 1722 to
    1745.

27 The Biblical justification of the practice is in Leviticus 12.2 and 12.8.

28 Perrin, Galerie Bretonne 1: 45.

29 Ibid., 45–8; Van Gennep, Manuel de folklore français 1, pt. 1: 119–21;
    Encyclopaedia Britannica, vol. 2 (Edinburgh 1771), 197; Saint-Vallier, Caté-
    chisme, 247–8; Saint-Vallier, Rituel, 313–17.

30 Saint-Vallier, Rituel, 12–44; idem, Catéchisme, 244–7. For lists of accept-
    able names see Rituel, 573–92.

31 Saint-Vallier, Rituel, 45–53.

32 Van Gennep, Manuel de folklore français 1, pt. 1: 136.

33 Jacques Henripin, La population canadienne au début du XVIIIe siècle,
    54–5. Henripin gives the following illegitimacy rates: 1721–30, 7.69 per 1,000
    births; 1731–40, 11.71 per 1,000; 1741–50, 11.71 per 1,000; 1751–60, 12.21
    per 1,000. The illegitimacy rate in two towns (Saint-André-d'Hébertot and
    Crulai) in Normandy in the seventeenth and eighteenth centuries were 1.19
    per cent and 0.66 per cent. Another town, Trousseauville, had a rate of 5.8
    per cent. Becart, "Saint-André-d'Hébertot au XVIIe et au XVIIIe siècles,"
    281–94. The industrial centre of Lille had an illegitimacy rate of 4.5 per cent
    in 1740. Venard, "Popular religion," 149. Olwen Hufton gives the following
    general figures: rural France, 1 to 2 per cent of all births were illegitimate;
    towns under 10,000, about 4 per cent; cities, from 12 to 20 per cent. The
    Poor of Eighteenth-Century France, 320.

34   Saint-Vallier, *Rituel*, 300.

35   Saint-Vallier, *Catéchisme*, xv–xvi.

36   The first quotation is from Quéniart, *Les hommes, l'église et Dieu*, 316; the second from David D. Bien, *The Calas Affair: Persecution, Toleration and Heresy in Eighteenth-Century Toulouse*, 41–2. Isle-Dieu's remark is in *RAPQ* (1935–6), 339, Isle-Dieu à Pontbriand, 19 avril 1752. For Jaenen's comments see *Role of the Church*, 122–4.

37   [William Pote], *The Journal of Captain William Pote Jr. during His Captivity in the French and Indian War, from May, 1745, to August, 1747*, ed. J.F. Hurst and Victor Paltsits, 16. Other references to religion are on pp. 29 and 34. For a comment on the lack of religious sentiment in colonial America see Jon Butler, "Magic, Astrology, and the Early American Religious Heritage," *American Historical Review* 84, no. 2 (April 1979): 317–46.

38   AN, Outre Mer, G2, vol. 203, dossiers 361 and 363. Kenneth Donovan discusses the case in more detail in "Social Status and Contrasting Lifestyles: Children of the Poor and Well-to-do in Louisbourg" (1980), AFL.

39   Brenda Dunn, "The Private Properties in Block 2, Louisbourg" (1978), AFL. Dunn's summary is based on her analysis of AN, Outre Mer, G2, vol. 201, dossier 242, 4 pièces, mai-juin 1752.

40   All three levels of religious instruction are contained in the bishop's *Catéchisme*, cited above.

41   Têtu and Gagnon, *Mandements* 1: 276, Ordonnance du 16 février 1691.

42   *RAPQ* (1935–6), 311–13, Mémoire à A.M. Rouillé, 23 mai 1751.

43   Fernand Porter, *L'institution catéchistique*, 75n33, 232.

44   Saint-Vallier, *Catéchisme*, 483.

45   CGT, Manuscrit 66, Journal de Poilly, 11, 26 février 1758.

46   Antoine Furetière, *Dictionnaire universel*, vol. 1, "discrétion"; Saint-Vallier, *Rituel*, 90.

47   Trudel, *Introduction to New France*, 253.

48   Marie de l'Incarnation of the Ursulines noted in 1668 that the girls of her school were so well instructed that they were allowed to take communion as early as the age of eight. As for confirmation, unusual circumstances sometimes called for unusual action. "Conscious of being on the brink of a great disaster, Bishop Pontbriand administered confirmation to approximately 1,200 persons in the cathedral on 4 September 1757, including a number of young children and even infants in arms." Jaenen, *Role of the Church*, 116.

49   Porter, *L'institution catéchistique*, 208, 213; Trudel, *Introduction to New France*, 251.

50   Porter, *L'institution catéchistique*, 208.

51   Venard, "Popular religion," 154; Van Gennep, *Manuel de folklore français* 1, pt. 1: 185.

52   Porter, *L'institution catéchistique*, 215.

53 Ibid., 215–16.

54 Trudel, *Introduction to New France*, 251; Têtu and Gagnon, *Mandements* 1: 276–7, Ordonnance 16 février 1691.

55 [Pote], *Journal of Captain William Pote, Jr.*, 50n1.

56 Saint-Vallier, *Rituel*, 279–80.

57 Some of the legal aspects of marriage in the eighteenth century are discussed in Kenneth J. Donovan, *Family Life in 18th-Century Louisbourg*.

58 Saint-Vallier, *Rituel*, 282; G.-L. de Buffon, *Histoire naturelle, generale et particulière, avec la description du cabinet du Roy*, (Paris, 1749), 2: 489. Saint-Vallier simply stated that twelve and fourteen were the ages of puberty. Buffon was of the same opinion in so far as southern Europe and the continental cities were concerned, but he thought that puberty came later among the poor and people who lived in the countryside. Climate and nutrition were, in Buffon's opinion, two of the major influences on the time of arrival of puberty.

59 For an example of a parent granting a minor permission to marry see AN, Outre Mer, G3, 2046–2, pièce 67, 21 septembre 1741.

60 Philip J. Greven, *Four Generations: Population, Land and Family in Colonial Andover, Massachusetts*, 16, 74, cited in Donovan, *Family Life in Louisbourg*, 19. For the poor the "period of waiting and saving" for marriage could understandably take years. See Fairchilds, *Poverty and Charity in Aix-en-Provence*, 120–1.

61 In September 1750 Judith Maisonat, widow of Rene Tréguy, formally opposed the marriage of her son Pierre (approximately thirty years old) to Jeanne Clermont. The wedding was delayed for two months but some form of agreement was reached and the couple was married on 16 November 1750, with Judith Maisonat in attendance. AN, Outre Mer, G3, 2047–1, pièce 107, 5 septembre 1750. See also family reconstitution file on Pierre Tréguy, AFL.

62 *RAPQ* (1920–1), 366–7; Têtu and Gagnon, *Mandements* 1: 492–4; Trudel, *Introduction to New France*, 255.

63 In a paper entitled "Coping with Social Change; Some Louisbourg Case Studies," delivered at the 1980 conference of the Atlantic Association for the Study of the Eighteenth Century, Christopher Moore suggested that LeLarge's personal rise in economic and social terms in Louisbourg society "was in itself a rebellion against family expectations, which ... left LeLarge unwilling to be bound any longer by parental rules and conventions."

64 The LeLarge-Sanson case is in AN, Outre Mer, G2, vol. 184, fols. 430–53, Procedure instruite ... Jean LeLarges, Navigateur et Louise Sanson, 1737. The marriage act is recorded in AN, Outre Mer, G1, vol. 406, reg. IV, fol. 66v., 8 juillet 1737. The baptism of their first child is in ibid., G1, vol. 407, reg. I, fols. 6–6v., 18 avril 1738.

65   Sr de Briquet, *Code militaire ou compilation des ordonnances des Roys de France* 1: 213–16.

66   AN, Colonies, C11B, vol. 36, fols. 61–2v., Drucourt au Ministre, 27 janvier 1756.

67   Details of soldiers' marriages are found in Margaret Fortier's "The Ile Royale Garrison, 1713–1745" (1981), AFL.

68   AN, Colonies, B, vol. 55, fols. 703–7, 10 juillet 1731; AN, Outre Mer, G1, vol. 406, reg. IV, fol. 23, mariage du 15 octobre 1730 et baptême du 16 octobre 1730; Fortier, "The Ile Royale Garrison," section on captains.

69   Du Boscq de Beaumont, ed., *Les derniers jours*, 112–13; AN, Outre Mer, G2, vol. 189, fols. 270–360, Procédure relative du mariage de Jules Caesar Foelix de la Noue, 1754–5.

70   Schmeisser, *Population of Louisbourg*, 13–16; AN, Outre Mer, G1, vol. 466, pièce 77, Recensement Général des habitants de la ville de Louisbourg, du Barachois, 1752.

71   Hubert Charbonneau, *Vie et mort de nos ancêtres: Etude démographique*, 158–64. In *The Population of Louisbourg*, Barbara Schmeisser provides a table showing the population of Canada, 14, Table 6. Figures for Port Royal, during the period 1725–39, are given in Hynes, "Demography of Port Royal," 10–11.

72   The ages of Louisbourg brides and grooms at the time of their first marriage is based on an analysis of data in the family reconstitution files, AFL.

73   The youngest bride identified to date was thirteen-year-old Marie-Louise Cruchon de la Tour, who was born in 1729 and married in 1742. AN, Outre Mer, G1, vol. 406, reg. IV, fol. 10v., 15 mars 1729; ibid., vol. 407, reg. II, fol. 5, 31 août 1742.

74   There are numerous cases where at the time of marriage grooms were approximately twice as old as their brides. In a few instances the gap was even wider, such as the 1735 marriage of forty-five-year-old Blaise Cassaignolles to nineteen-year-old Marie-Jeanne Saux. AN, Outre Mer, G1, vol. 406, reg. IV, mariage du 22 février 1735.

75   DesRoches and Galbarrette married in January 1738. Brenda Dunn, "Supplementary Report on the Dauphin Fauxbourg" (1976), 5, AFL. Another example is that of Pierre Boisseau (twenty-six) marrying Marie Douaron (forty-six and a widow) in 1729. AN, Outre Mer, G1, vol. 406, reg. IV, fol. 14v., mariage du 5 septembre 1729.

76   Family reconstitution files on Antoine Paris and Dominique Collonques, AFL, and corresponding parish record entries. On the general topic of remarriages see Natalie Zemon Davis, "The Reasons of Misrule: Youth Groups and Charivaris in Sixteenth-Century France," *Past and Present*, no. 50 (February 1971): 41–75; Trudel, *Introduction to New France*, 255; Thiers, *Traité des jeux*, 288.

77   Hufton, *The Poor of Eighteenth-Century France*, 359.

78   The Marie-Anne Carrerot-Michel de Gannes case is in AN, Outre Mer, G2, vol. 180, pp. 1–61, février 1729.

79   Ibid.; ibid., G1, vol. 406, reg. IV, mariage du 21 novembre 1730.

80   AN, Outre Mer, G2, vol. 178, fols. 759–63, Anthoinette Isabeau *veuve* Plantin versus Sr Claude Auguste de Brise, 27 novembre 1721; AN, Colonies, B, vol. 45, fol. 9, Conseil à Beauharnois, 14 janvier 1722. Virginity was highly valued in eighteenth-century society. It was said of a fifteen-year-old girl who lost hers at Plaisance in 1705 that she had been divested "[of] what is more sacred than anything in religion." *DCB* 3: 454.

81   Between 1722 and 1758, the period for which the Louisbourg parish records exist, there were 565 marriages in the town. During the same period 204 marriage contracts were drawn up, a figure which represents 36.1 per cent of the total number of weddings. Nearly all the contracts are in the various volumes of AN, Outre Mer, G3. A good example of a document which illustrates very briefly and legibly the items which a young woman brought into a marriage as part of her *dot* is in AN, Outre Mer, G2, vol. 198, dossier 180, Etat des Meubles et Nippes et argent ... pour son Dot de Mariage, 24 octobre 1743. Marriage contracts in eighteenth-century Paris are briefly discussed in M.S. Anderson, *Historians and Eighteenth-Century Europe, 1715–1789*, 44–5.

82   AN, Outre Mer, G3, 2041–1, pièce 158, 23 octobre 1752; ibid., pièce 159, 31 octobre 1752.

83   Saint-Vallier, *Rituel*, 289.

84   The only *fiançailles* recorded is that of George François du Boisberthelot and Jeanne DeGoutin on 8 October 1730. AN, Outre Mer, G1, vol. 406, reg. IV, 8 octobre 1730. The couple was married on 15 October 1730.

85   Saint-Vallier, *Rituel*, 289–90.

86   AN, Outre Mer, G3, 2041, pièce 50, 24 septembre 1750 et 25 septembre 1750; ibid., G1, vol. 408, reg. I, fol. 128v., mariage du 16 novembre 1750. On the marriage certificate Isabelle LeMordant is mistakenly called Isabelle Hebert (her mother's family name), but the error was not repeated in subsequent entries in the parish records.

87   Paul-André Leclerc, "Le mariage sous le régime français," *Revue d'histoire de l'Amérique française* 13, no. 3 (December 1959): 400.

88   See for instance *RAPQ* (1936–7), 434–5, Isle-Dieu à Pontbriand, 28 mars 1756; ibid., 450–1; AN, Colonies, C11B, vol. 24, fols. 33–5, Desherbiers, 18 septembre 1750. Dispensations for consanguineous relations are mentioned in a number of other marriage entries in the Louisbourg parish records.

89   AN, Outre Mer, G2, vol. 194, pièce 55, Procedure criminelle ... contre Pierre Santier et Servanne Bonnier accusez d'avoir fait un enfant, 1734.

90 AD, F-Q, 23 H 14: Lettres des Récollets, pièce 6, Joseph Denys, 1726; ibid., pièce 14, Saint-Vallier au Provincial des Récollets, 15 juillet 1727. The Daccarrette-Gonillon marriage was legitimized in 1737, AN, Outre Mer, G1, vol. 406, reg. IV, fol. 70, 29 décembre 1737.

91 Saint-Vallier, Catéchisme, 302.

92 See for instance AN, Outre Mer, G1, vol. 409, reg. I, mariage du 19 mars 1756; ibid., reg. II, mariage du 27 décembre 1756.

93 The fête de Saint-Michel (29 September) was the traditional closing day for the Ile Royale fishery. See Balcom, "Cod Fishery of Isle Royale," 90. Arnold van Gennep states that "au bord de la mer ... c'est à l'automne, à la rentrée au port, que la noce est célébrée de préférence." Manual de folklore français 1, pt. 2: 381.

94 Van Gennep, Manuel de folklore français 1, pt. 2: 379–80.

95 Davis, "The Reasons of Misrule," 45.

96 Saint-Vallier, Rituel, 297.

97 AN, Outre Mer, G1, vol. 409, reg. 2, fol. 32, mariage du 13 décembre 1757.

98 The people who married at night were as follows (wedding dates in parenthesis): Charles-Léopold Ebérard de L'Espérance and Marguerite Dangeac (26 February 1725), Gabriel Rousseau de Villejouin and Barbe Le Neuf de la Vallière (30 December 1753), Joseph Brisson and Geneviève Girardin (7 July 1754), Pierre Montalembert de Cers and Marie Charlotte Chassin de Thierry (7 September 1755), François Du Pont, Chevalier du Vivier de Vane and Anne Magdelaine Lafitte (10 September 1755), Etienne Roche and Anne Fizel (10 January 1756, Louis Joseph Donnadieu de Pelissier, chevalier Du Gres and Louis Marguerite Vallée (13 December 1757), Michel De Couagne and Jeanne de Loppinot (19 February 1758), and Jean Lessenne and Catherine Morin (21 May 1758). Brisson was a négociant, Roche an arpenteur, De Couagne an engineer, and the rest military officers.

99 Van Gennep, Manuel de folklore français 1, pt. 2: 383–4. Van Gennep states that the custom was kept longest in small towns in France. During the first half of the eighteenth century its popularity was more widespread, if the 1723 nighttime marriage in Paris of an illustrious noble described by E.J.F. Barbier was at all typical. Barbier, Journal historique et anecdotique du règne de Louis XV (Paris 1847; reprint 1966), 1: 165–6.

100 RAPQ (1934–5), 35, Journal de Mme Begon, 6 février 1749. The entry reads as follows: "A propos des dames de l'île Royale, il faut que je te réjouisse d'une pointe de Mlle La Ronde, lorsqu'elle s'est mariée. Tu sais, ou ne sais point, que le curé doit, avant d'administrer le sacrement, savoir si les futurs époux sont instruits. Le curé de Québec qui est un jeune homme venu cette année de France, homme très scrupuleux, questionna M. de Bonaventure qui lui répondit sur tout fort sagement. Après quoi, il le pria de faire entrer, comme il avait fait, dans la sacristie, Mlle La Ronde,

à qui il demanda si elle savait ce que c'était que le sacrement de mariage. Elle lui répondit qu'elle n'en savait rien, mais que s'il était curieux, que dans quatre jours, elle lui en dirait des nouvelles. Le pauvre curé baissa le nez et le laissa là. Cette pointe a fait beaucoup rire. En voilà assez."

101   The ceremony before 1767 is described by Saint-Vallier, *Rituel*, 298–313. The changes in wording made by Bishop Briand are located in Têtu and Gagnon, eds., *Mandements* 2: 208, 1 novembre 1767.

102   Compare for instance the weddings of Louis Le Neuf de la Vallière and Marie-Charlotte Rousseau de Souvigny (20 September 1739), with twenty-five signatures, and that of Robert Maié and Marie Le Tourneur Alenard (26 November 1737), with four signatures or marks.

103   Numerous customs are discussed in Van Gennep, *Manuel de folklore français*, vol. 1, pt. 2, and Perrin, *Galerie Bretonne*, vol. 3. See also André Burguière, "Le rituel du mariage en France: Pratiques ecclésiastiques et pratiques populaires (XVIe–XVIIIe siècle), *Annales: Economies, sociétés, civilisations* 33, no. 3 (mai–juin 1978): 637–49.

104   The wedding in question was the controversial one of Jules César Felix Bogard de la Noue and Marguérite Guedry. AN, Outre Mer, G2, vol. 189, fol. 312v., testimony of Jean Le Jeune, 22 novembre 1754.

105   There were four marriages entered in the Louisbourg parish records in which the couples already had children, in two cases up to two years before they decided to marry and have their offspring legitimized. There were also eight couples who had their marriages rehabilitated, that is, officially sanctioned by the Roman Catholic Church. They had either been married previously by a Protestant minister or else had married themselves in front of witnesses without the benefit of any clergy.

106   These figures are taken from the Louisbourg parish records. AN, Outre Mer, G1, vols. 406, 407, 408, et 409. The parish records before 1722 did not survive, while from mid-1745 to mid-1749 the townspeople were in France. The recorded periods stop at mid-1744 and mid-1757 because of sieges in the spring of the following years which interrupted the keeping of parish records. As a result it is not possible to calculate whether the couples who married in the latter half of 1744 and early 1745 or in the latter half of 1757 and early 1758 had children within thirty-six weeks of their marriages.

107   Hufton, *The Poor of Eighteenth-Century France*, 321–33; Burguière, "Le rituel du mariage en France," 645.

108   AN, Outre Mer, G2, vol. 180, fols. 1–61, février 1729.

109   Hynes, "Demography of Port Royal," 14–15; John Demos, "Families in Colonial Bristol, Rhode Island: An Exercise in Historical Demography," in *Quantitative History: Selected Readings in the Quantitative Analysis of Historical Data*, ed. D.K. Rowney and J.Q. Graham, 293–307;

James Axtell, *The School upon a Hill: Education and Society in Colonial New England*, 56. Axtell's estimates cover the broad period from 1540 to 1835, in seventy-seven rural English parishes.

110 Charbonneau, *Vie et mort de nos ancêtres*, 214–15; Henripin, *La population canadienne*, 55; Becart, "Saint-André-d'Hébertot au XVIIe et au XVIIIe siècles," 281–94.

111 Thiers, *Traité des jeux*; AN, Marine, A1, article 60, pièce 75, Ordonnance du Roy pour la Défense des Jeux aux Colonies Françoises; AN, Colonies, C11B, vol. 14, fols. 17–20, Conseil, 15 mars 1732; ibid., B, vol. 59, fols. 530v.–2, Ministre à Saint-Ovide, 26 mai 1733; ibid., C11B, vol. 26, fol. 195, Duquesnel et Bigot, 23 octobre 1742.

112 The first quotation is from James Johnstone, *Memoirs of the Chevalier de Johnstone* 2: 178; the second from Du Boscq de Beaumont, ed., *Les derniers jours*, 182. The reference for Prévost's gambling is AN, Colonies, B, vol. 107, fol. 356, Ministre à Prévost, 11 février 1758.

113 For studies on popular insults, in Canada and at Louisbourg, see André Lachance, "Une etude de mentalité: Les injures verbales au Canada au XVIIIe siècle (1712–1748)," *Revue d'histoire de l'Amérique française* 31, no. 2 (September 1977): 229–38, and Peter Moogk, "'Thieving Buggers' and 'Stupid Sluts': Insults and Popular Culture in New France," *William and Mary Quarterly*, 3rd ser., 36, no. 4 (October 1979): 529–47.

114 AN, Colonies, B, vol. 37, fols. 90v.–1, Ministre à Landreau, 30 avril 1715; ibid., fols. 214v.–15v., Ministre à Costebelle, 4 juin 1715; ibid., C11B, vol. 1, fols. 146v.–7, Costebelle, 5 novembre 1715; ibid., vol. 5, fols. 78–82v., Conseil, 20 août 1720.

115 Ibid., B, vol. 45, fol. 931, 12 mai 1722; ibid., vol. 55, fol. 82, Ministre à M. de Porsemeur Le Bigot, 18 décembre 1731. For an example of the severity with which adulterers could be treated in Canada see Abbé Hermann Plante, *L'Eglise catholique au Canada (1604–1886)*, 135.

116 AN, Colonies, C11B, vol. 30, fols. 338–40, Prévost, 28 décembre 1751; ASQ, Polygraphie 56, no. 64. "Sotises," nos. 29, 65, 65 bis; Adams, *Construction and Occupation of the Barracks*, 118.

117 This point has been made frequently. See for instance, François Lebrun, *Les hommes et la mort en Anjou aux 17e et 18e siècles*, 416; Pierre Chaunu, *La mort à Paris, 16e, 17e, 18e siècles*, 171–5 and Philippe Ariès, *Western Attitudes toward Death: From the Middle Ages to the Present*.

118 See virtually any of the *testaments* drawn up in Louisbourg, for instance, that of Anne de Galbarrer in AN, Outre Mer, G3, 2058 (1727), pièce 7, 26 juin 1727.

119 To illustrate, in 1757 Louisbourg resident Geneviève Allemand lay sick and dying in her bed. When the priest arrived she felt obliged to tell him

that she and her husband (Gabriel Revol) had had their daughter two years before they were married. Allemand died the following day with a clear conscience. AN, Outre Mer, G 1, vol. 409, reg. II, fol. 19, 11 mai 1757.

120 Saint-Vallier, *Catéchisme*, 486–500.

121 For examples see AN, Outre Mer, G1, vol. 406, reg. III, fol. 2v., 22 juillet 1724; ibid., fol. 4v., 17 décembre 1726.

122 Johnstone, *Memoirs* 2: 157–68.

123 Religious books were one of the most common categories of reading material in Louisbourg. For a statistical breakdown and analysis of the kinds of books recorded in inventories after death and in merchants' retail outlets see Gilles Proulx, *Les bibliothèques de Louisbourg*.

124 Pierre Chaunu discusses the concept of "bien mourir" throughout *La mort à Paris*. See especially pp. 275–85.

125 Saint-Vallier, *Rituel*, 564–5.

126 Lebrun, *Les hommes et la mort*, 450–1. The Louisbourg wills are scattered throughout AN, Outre Mer, G3. As in Louisbourg, in most places considerably more wills were drawn up by men than by women. In Paris, however, the situation was the reverse with testaments by women outnumbering those by men. Chaunu, *La mort à Paris*. Wills could be drawn up in any one of three ways: before a *notaire*, with two witnesses; before a curé with three witnesses; or by the testator himself if it was entirely in his own handwriting. *RAPQ* (1920–1), 1. For the bishop of Québec's stand on wills see Saint-Vallier's *Rituel*, 564–9.

127 Deforant's will is in AN, Outre Mer, G2, 2046–1, pièce 81, 10 mai 1740. Though he did not specify in his will how much he was leaving to the Sisters of the Congregation, I have included his bequest in the totals of Table 9.

128 AN, Outre Mer, G3, 2047–1, pièce 53, Testament de Julien Gery, 13 mai 1743; ibid., 2038–1, pièce 55, Testament d'André Angr, 2 janvier 1731.

129 Ibid., 2037, pièce 27, Testament de Guillaume Delort, 12 novembre 1728.

130 Ibid., 2058, pièce 7, Testament d'Anne de Galbarrer, 26 juin 1727; ibid., 2046 suite, pièce 117, Testament d'Anne Galbarret, 7 septembre 1742. Spelling variants are in the original documents.

131 Lebrun, *Les hommes et la mort*, 454. The evidence from the Louisbourg parish records backs up the general rule. Dying children did not receive the sacraments of confession or communion until they were about twelve years old. For two examples see AN, Outre Mer, G 1, vol. 406, reg. IV, 13 octobre 1728; ibid., 15 avril 1733.

132 AN, Outre Mer, G1, vol. 411 (bis), Tables alphabétiques de Haran. There are tables for the period from 1719 to 1735 and from 1736 to 1742, as well as a list of the military officers who died in the hospital during the 1750s.

133 This is true as a generalization only. Some military personnel (officers and enlisted men alike) were buried in the parish cemetery, and hence their

deaths were recorded in the town's parish records. There were also some civilians (fishermen and retired soldiers) buried in the hospital cemetery.

134 On the economy of Ile Royale see Christopher Moore, "The Other Louisbourg"; Balcom, "Cod Fishery of Isle Royale," AFL.

135 As it is expressed by one author, "Chacun se poussait en avant comme pour voir passer la mort et surprendre dans les derniers regards du moribond le secret de ce monde inconnu qu'elle allait lui révéler." Perrin, Galerie Bretonne 3: 155.

136 Ibid., 155–6; Van Gennep, Manuel de folklore français 1, pt. 2: 655–70.

137 Saint-Vallier, Rituel, 242–3.

138 Forty-two conversions, under the designation of either abjuration or profession de foi, were entered in the Louisbourg parish records, twenty-eight in the period 1722–45 and fourteen in the period 1749–58. Many were of individuals who were not gravely ill, but who were probably anxious to become Catholics in order to marry or to be more fully accepted in the community.

139 Saint-Vallier, Rituel, 245.

140 For the burials of unidentifiable cadavers in 1754 see AN, Outre Mer, G1, vol. 409, reg. I, fols. 8, 11v., 26, 26v. et 27v. Of course it is possible that other corpses were found which were not buried in the town's parish cemetery, and of which there was therefore no record of interment.

141 The best source for the Montalembert case is Du Boscq de Beaumont, ed., Les derniers jours, 14, 116, 137, 149, 150, 157, 161, 169, 211, 213, and 215. Discovery of the body is reported in AN, Colonies, C11B, vol. 37, fols. 77–9. For the burial entry see AN, Outre Mer, G1, vol. 409, reg. II, fol. 26, 1 septembre 1757.

142 AN, Outre Mer, G2, vol. 193, reg. IV, Procès contre le cadavre du nommé Payen, 19 juillet 1757; SHA, A1, pièce 89, page 19 bis, Journal de Mr Pontleroy.

143 Christopher Moore, "Cemeteries," in "Historical Memoranda, 1974," and plans 740–3, 742–2, 751–7 and 751–10C, AFL.

144 Moore, "Cemeteries"; the burial records for 1732–3 are in AN, Outre Mer, Série G1, vol. 406, reg. IV, fols. 33v.–49v

145 The identities of the men buried in the chapel are known from the parish records. The analysis of the remains is found in J.E. Anderson, "The Human Skeletons in the King's Chapel" (September 1964), AFL.

146 There were complaints in 1718 that cloth for shrouds was wrongly being used for other purposes, including the lining of officers' rooms. Moore, "Cemeteries," 1.

147 Sonja Jerkic, "Excavations at Fortress Louisbourg of Human Skeletons in the Summer of 1974," AFL.

148 "Journal kept by Lieut. Daniel Giddings," Essex Institute Historical Collections 48, no. 4 (October 1912): 303, 4 July 1745 (O.S.).

149 Louis E. DeForest, ed., *Louisbourg Journals, 1745*, 30, 28 June 1745 (o.s.).

150 Diary of Jacob Haskins, 8 July 1759, Boston Public Library; cited in Moore, "Cemeteries," 11.

151 Ariès, *Western Attitudes toward Death*, 22.

152 Moore, "Cemeteries," 10–11.

153 Anderson, "The Human Skeletons."

154 To date, I have come across fourteen inventories in which burial and / or funeral costs are given. In only five cases is a coffin specifically mentioned, though that obviously does not mean that there was no casket in all of the others. The inventories in question are all found in AN, Outre Mer, G2.

155 AN, Outre Mer, G2, vol. 194, dossier 69, dossier d'Etienne Guerard, 1735; ibid., vol. 199, dossier 187, dossier d'Anne Guion Desprès, 1744–5; Adams, "*Construction and Occupation of the Barracks*," 151. The prescribed costs for different kinds of burials and services in the diocese of Québec are given in Têtu and Gagnon, *Mandements* 1: 272, 9 novembre 1690.

156 AN, Colonies, C11B, vol. 13, fols. 73, 83–83v., 13 septembre 1751; ibid., vol. 27, fol. 266, 30 septembre 1751. When Michel Le Neuf de la Vallière was buried in the Récollet convent cemetery in 1740 seven cannon shots were fired. AN, Colonies, C11B, vol. 22, fol. 166, Bigot, 15 octobre 1740. In 1737 a Micmac Indian chief was buried in or near Louisbourg. Acting commandant Bourville "luy a rendu quelques honneurs," but whether they included cannon or musket firing is not known. A detachment of soldiers led by a sergeant was present at the chief's burial. AN, Colonies, C11B, vol. 19, fol. 56v., Bourville et Le Normant, 27 décembre 1737.

157 This summary is based on the material in Saint-Vallier, *Rituel*, 240–75.

158 No archaeological or literary evidence has been found of the French using stone monuments to mark their graves. In *An Account of the Customs and Manners of the Micmakis and Maricheets ...* (London 1758), 66, there is a reference to crosses on the graves of Micmacs buried in the Port Toulouse area. The relevant section, probably written by Abbé Pierre Maillard, describes the action of the New Englanders in Ile Royale in 1745. "The burying-place of the savages was demolished, and all the crosses, planted on the graves, broke into a thousand pieces."

159 Lebrun, *Les hommes et la mort*, 424.

160 Madame Bégon described in her journal the burial in Canada of a five- to six-year-old girl. In official attendance were four of her father's *écrivains*, four *demoiselles*, two priests, and four choir boys. How many relatives or other lay people were present she did not say. *RAPQ* (1934–5), Journal de Mme Bégon, 4 décembre 1748, 13.

161 *RAPQ* (1934–5), Journal de Mme Bégon, 30 avril 1749, 61.

CONCLUSION

1 Robert J. Morgan, "Orphan Outpost: Cape Breton Colony, 1784–1820" (PHD thesis, University of Ottawa 1972).
2 John G. Reid, *Acadia, Maine, and New Scotland: Marginal Colonies in the Seventeenth Century.*

APPENDICES

1 Appendix A is based on my notes of the Louisbourg parish records, Hugolin's "Table nominale des Récollets," Pineau's *Le clergé français dans l'île du Prince Edouard*, 145, and the research notes in file B156–5/2 in the Archives des Franciscains in Montreal. Hugolin's list mistakenly included a few Brothers of Charity and a Récollet of Paris, omitted here.
2 Appendix B is based primarily on my notes of the Louisbourg parish records, official correspondence, lists of financial payments, and censuses. The names of the fourteen brothers whose ages at time of death are given come from the records of the Order of Saint-John of God in France, as published in Joseph-G. Gélinas, "Des oubliés," *La revue Dominicaine* (1922), 228. The same list, but with a couple of errors, is published in *Bulletin des recherches historiques* 33, no. 9 (September 1927): 522–4.
3 Appendix C is based on my research notes of the Louisbourg documentation and the relevant biographical material scattered throughout several volumes of the *Histoire de la Congrégation de Notre-Dame de Montréal.*

Bibliography

PRIMARY SOURCES

The most important sources for a study of religion at Louisbourg are of course those maintained by the French themselves: parish records, official correspondence, court cases, census data, and so on. After each of the two sieges the voluminous records of the town and its population were shipped to France, with most of the documents eventually making their way into what is now the Archives Nationales in Paris. Additional pertinent documents were deposited in departmental, municipal, or other archives in France.

Although much less remained in Canada vis-à-vis Louisbourg than went to France, there are important collections of documents in the province of Québec, notably in the Archives de l'Archidiocèse de Québec (AAQ) and the Archives du Séminaire de Québec (ASQ), both in Québec City. The archives of the Congrégation de Notre-Dame (ACND) and the Franciscans in Montréal possess only a few items of interest. A number of important items, most notably the correspondence of Pierre de la Rue, Abbé de l'Isle-Dieu, are held in the Archives Nationales (AQ), in Québec City, and have been published in the *Rapport de l'Archiviste de la Province de Québec*.

Since the beginning of the reconstruction project in the early 1960s it has been the policy of the Fortress of Louisbourg National Historic Park to acquire copies of all primary and secondary research material relevant to the history of the eighteenth-century town. To date thousands of pages of research material have been acquired, largely on microfilm. Except for a short visit to Québec and Montréal in 1979, I have consulted all the following sources by using copies in the Archives of the Fortress of Louisbourg.

FRENCH ARCHIVES

Archives nationales, Paris
Archives des Colonies
B   Lettres envoyées (35–110)
C11A   Correspondance générale. Lettres reçues. Canada (106–7, 115, 126)

C11B   Correspondance générale. Lettres reçues. Ile Royale (1–38)
C11C   Amérique du Nord (7–16)
D2C   Troupes des Colonies (47–8, 53, 57–60)
E   Dossiers personnels
F3   Collection Moreau St Méry (50)
F5A   Missions religieuses

Archives de la France d'Outre Mer
G1 Registres de l'état civil, recensements, et documents divers (406–11, 458–9, 462, 466–7)
G2 Greffes des tribunaux de Louisbourg et du Canada, Conseil Supérieur et bailliage de Louisbourg (178–212)
G3 Notariat, greffes des notaires de Louisbourg (2037–47, 2056–58)
Dépot des fortifications des colonies, Amérique septentrionale, No. d'ordre 216

Archives de la Marine
A2 Actes du Pouvoir Souverain (Article 24)
B4 Campagnes, 1640–1782 (Vol. 76)
C7 Personnel individuel

Archives de la guerre, Vincennes
Archives du Service Historique de l'Armée
A1 Correspondance générale (3343, 3393, 3457)

Bibliothèque du Génie
Manuscrit 66   Journal de Poilly

Archives départementales. Charente-Maritime, La Rochelle
B   Cours et jurisdictions, Amirauté de Louisbourg (265–83, 6109–25)

Archives départementales. Finistère-Quimper
23H14   Papiers affaires commerciales, papiers des Récollets

Archives départementales. Pyrénées Atlantiques, Arondissement de Bayonne
Mairie de Bidart, extracts from parish records

Archives Maritimes, Archives du port de Rochefort
Série 1R   Colonies, pays étrangers, consulats, 1684–1775 (28)

Archives municipales et bibliothèques, Bibliothèque municipale de Vire
Pichon Papers (1)

CANADIAN ARCHIVES

Public Archives of Canada, Ottawa
MG18, F12, Vol. I   Tableau de l'Etat

Archives de l'Archidiocèse de Québec, Québec
Copies de Lettres   Vol. II
Côte 12 A   Registre des insinuations ecclésiastiques (B, 268–70); C, 15; C, 131)
Registre B
Registre C
1W, Eglise du Canada

Archives de la Congrégation de Notre-Dame, Montréal
4A/11   Lettres, contrats, reçus, etc. (1–25)

Archives des Franciscains, Montréal
Copies of documents and original research notes of Stanislaus Lemay (R.P. Hugolin) and others

Archives du Séminaire de Québec, Québec
Lettres M   Nos. 52, 82
Lettres N   No. 48
Lettres P   Nos. 63, 70
Lettres S   No. 7
Lettres T   Nos. 57, 59
Polygraphie 7   Nos. 5, 41, 43, 106–8, 113–15, 117–22
Polygraphie 9   No. 29
Polygraphie 22   No. 33
Polygraphie 55   Nos. 1–51
Polygraphie 56   Nos. 1–65
Polygraphie 57   Nos. 1–52
Polygraphie 58   Nos. 1–64
Séminaire 14   liasse 5 (4)
Séminaire 14   liasse 6 (3, 11, 14)
Séminaire 15   No. 66

BRITISH ARCHIVES

British Museum, London
Burney Collection   Burney 463 (*Whitehall Evening Post or The London Intelligencer*)

Public Record Office, London
Admiralty I Vol. 3817

SECONDARY SOURCES

ADAMS, Blaine. "The Construction and Occupation of the Barracks of the King's Bastion." *Canadian Historic Sites: Occasional Papers in Archaeology and History*. Ottawa: Parks Canada 1978.
ALLARD, Michel, et al. *L'Hôtel Dieu de Montréal, 1642–1973*. Montréal: Hurtubise HMH 1973.
ALMON, Albert. *Rochefort Point, A Silent City in Louisbourg*. Glace Bay: McDonald 1940.
ANDERSON, J.E. "The Human Skeletons in the King's Chapel." Report, 1964, Archives of the Fortress of Louisbourg. Typescript.
ANDERSON, M.S. *Historians and Eighteenth-Century France, 1715–1789*. Oxford: Clarendon Press 1979.
ARIES, Philippe. *Centuries of Childhood: A Social History of Family Life*. Translated by Robert Baldick. New York: Knopf 1962.
– *The Hour of our Death*. Translated by Helen Weaver. New York: Knopf 1982.
– *Western Attitudes toward Death: From the Middle Ages to the Present*. Translated by Patricia M. Ranum. 1974. Reprint. Baltimore: Johns Hopkins University Press 1977.
ARSENAULT, Bona. *Louisbourg, 1713–1758*. Québec: Le Conseil de la vie française en Amérique 1971.
AXTELL, James. *The School upon a Hill: Education and Society in Colonial New England*. New York: W.H. Norton 1974.
B, J.-C. *Voyage au Canada fait depuis l'an 1751 à 1761*. Paris: Aubier Montaigne 1978.
BAILYN, Bernard. *Education in the Forming of American Society: Needs and Opportunities for Study*. New York: W.H. Norton 1960.
BALCOM, B.A. "The Cod Fishery of Isle Royale, 1713–1758." Report, 1979, Archives of the Fortress of Louisbourg. Typescript.
BARBER, Elinor G. *The Bourgeoisie in 18th Century France*. Princeton: Princeton University Press 1970.
BASTIEN, Hermas. *L'Ordre Hospitalier de Saint-Jean-de-Dieu au Canada*. Montréal: Les Editions Lumen 1947.
BÉCART, Françoise. "Saint-André-D'Hébertot au XVIIe et au XVIIIe siècles: Etude demographique." *Annales de Normandie* 27, no. 3 (octobre 1977): 281–94.
BÉDARD, Marc-André. *Les Protestants en Nouvelle-France*. Cahiers d'histoire, no. 31. Québec: La Société Historique de Québec 1978.

BELMONT, Nicole. "La fonction symbolique du cortège dans les rituels populaires du mariage." *Annales: Economies, sociétés, civilisations* 33, no. 3 (mai-juin 1978): 650–5.

BIDEAU, Alain. "A Demographic and Social Analysis of Widowhood and Remarriage: The Example of Castellany of Thoissey-en-Dombes, 1670–1840." *Journal of Family History* 5, no. 1 (Spring 1980): 28–43.

BIEN, David B. *The Calas Affair: Persecution, Toleration and Heresy in Eighteenth-Century Toulouse*. Westport, Conn.: Greenwood Press 1979.

BLAYO, Yves, and HENRY, Louis. "Données démographiques sur la Bretagne et l'Anjou de 1740 à 1829." In *Annales de démographie historique* (1967), 91–171. Paris: Editions Sirey 1967.

BOSSY, John. "Holiness and Society." *Past and Present*, no. 75 (May 1977): 119–37.

BOUCHARD, Gérard, and LA ROSE, André. "La réglementation au contenu des actes de baptême, mariage, sépulture, au Quebec, des origines à nos jours." *Revue d'histoire de l'Amérique française* 30, no. 1 (juin 1976): 67–84.

BOUDRIOT, Jean. *Le vaisseau de 74 canons: Traité pratique d'art naval; construction du vaisseau*. 4 vols. Grenoble: Editions des Quatre Seigneurs 1973.

BOURBOURG, Abbé Brasseur de. *Histoire du Canada, de son église et de ses missions*. 2 vols. Paris 1852. Reprint. New York: Johnson Reprint Corporation 1968.

BOWER, Peter. "Louisbourg: A Focus of Conflict, 1745–1748." Report, 1970, Archives of the Fortress of Louisbourg. Typescript.

BRIQUET, Sieur de. *Côde militaire, ou compilation des ordonnances des roys de France concernant les gens de guerre*. vol. 1. Paris 1728.

BURGUIÈRE, André. "Le rituel du mariage en France: Pratiques ecclésiastiques et pratiques populaires (XVIe–XVIIIe siècle)." *Annales: Economies, sociétés, civilisations* 33, no. 3 (mai-juin, 1978): 637–49.

BUTLER, Jon. "Magic, Astrology, and the Early American Religious Heritage." *American Historical Review* 84, no. 2 (April 1979): 317–46.

CALLAHAN, William J., and HIGGS, David, eds. *Church and Society in Catholic Europe of the Eighteenth Century*. London: Cambridge University Press 1979.

Canada, An Historical Magazine 1, no. 4 (June 1974). Complete issue on Louisbourg.

CASGRAIN, Abbé H.R. *Les Sulpiciens et les prêtres des missions-étrangères en Acadie (1676–1762)*. Québec 1897.

CHARBONNEAU, Hubert, ed. *La Population du Québec: Etudes rétrospectives*. Montréal: Boréal Express 1973.

– *Vie et mort de nos ancêtres: Etude démographique*. Montréal: Les Presses de l'Université de Montréal 1975.

CHARRON, Yvon. *Mother Bourgeoys (1620–1700)*. [Montréal]: Beauchemin 1950.

CHAUNY, Pierre. *La mort à Paris, XVIe, XVIIe et XVIIIe siècles*. Paris: Fayard 1978.

CHISICK, Harvey. *The Limits of Reform in the Enlightenment: Attitudes toward the Education of the Lower Classes in Eighteenth-Century France*. Princeton: Princeton University Press 1981.

CIPOLLA, Carlo M. *Literacy and Development in the West*. London: Penguin 1969.

CLARK, A.H. *Acadia, The Geography of Early Nova Scotia to 1760*. Madison: University of Wisconsin Press 1968.

CLICHE, Marie-Aimée. "Les attitudes devant la mort d'après les clauses testamentaires dans le gouvernement de Québec sous le régime français." *Revue d'histoire de l'Amérique française* 32, no. 1 (juin 1978): 57–94.

[CONGRÉGATION DE NOTRE-DAME]. *Coutumier des Sœurs seculiers de la Congrégation de Notre-Dame*. Montréal 1846.

– *Reglemens des Sœurs seculiers de la Congrégation de Notre-Dame*. Montréal 1846.

CORVISIER, André. *Armies and Societies in Europe, 1494–1789*. Translated by Abigail T. Siddal. 1976. Reprint. Bloomington: Indiana University Press 1979.

COURTIN, Antoine de. *Nouveau traité de la civilité qui se pratique en France, parmi les honnêtes gens*. Paris 1671.

CROWLEY, Terence. "Government and Interests: French Colonial Administration at Louisbourg, 1713–58." PHD thesis, Duke University 1975.

– "'Thunder Gusts': Popular Disturbances in Early French Canada." In *Historical Papers / Communications Historiques*, 11–32. Saskatoon: Canadian Historical Association 1979.

CUNNINGTON, Phillis, and LUCAS, Catherine. *Costume for Births, Marriages and Deaths*. 1972. Reprint. London: Adam and Charles Black 1978.

DAVID, P. Albert. "Les missionnaires du séminaire du Saint-Esprit à Québec et en Acadie au XVIIIe siècle." *Nova Francia* 1, no. 1 (1925): 9–14; no. 2, 52–5; no. 3, 99–105; no. 4 152–9.

DAVIS, Natalie Zemon. "The Reasons of Misrule: Youth Groups and Charivaris in Sixteenth-Century France." *Past and Present*, no. 50 (February 1971): 41–75. ·

DECHÊNE, Louise. *Habitants et marchands de Montréal au XVIIe siècle*. Montréal: Plon 1974.

DEFOREST, Louis Effingham, ed. *The Journals and Papers of Seth Pomeroy, Sometime General in the Colonial Service*. New York: Society of Colonial Wars 1932.

– *Louisbourg Journals, 1745*. New York: Society of Colonial Wars 1932.

DEMOS, John. "Families in Colonial Bristol, Rhode Island: An Exercise in Historical Demography." In *Quantitative History: Selected Readings in the Quantitative Analysis of Historical Data*, edited by D.K. Rowney and J.Q. Graham, Jr, 293–307. Homewood, Ill.: Dorsey 1969.

DICKASON, Olive Patricia. "Europeans and Amerindians: Some Comparative Aspects of Early Contact." In *Historical Papers / Communications historiques*, 182–202. Saskatoon: Canadian Historical Association 1979.

– *Louisbourg and the Indians: A Study in Imperial Race Relations, 1713–1760*. History and Archaeology No. 6. Ottawa: Parks Canada 1976.

Dictionary of Canadian Biography. Vols. 2–4. Toronto: University of Toronto Press 1969, 1974, 1979.

DIDEROT, D., et D'ALEMBERT, J.L., eds. *L'encyclopédie, ou dictionnaire raisonné des sciences, des arts et des métiers*. 17 vols. 1751–65.

DINET, Dominique. "Mourir en religion aux dix-septième et dix-huitième siècles: La mort dans quelques couvents des diocèses d'Auxere, Langres et Dijon." *Revue historique* 259 (janvier-mars 1978): 30–54.

DONOVAN, Kenneth J. "Canada's First Astronomical Observatory, 1750." *Canadian Geographic* 100, no. 6 (December 1980–January 1981): 36–43.

– "Communities and Families: Family Life and Interior Living Conditions in Eighteenth-Century Louisbourg." *Material History Bulletin* (Ottawa: National Museum of Man), no. 15 (1982): 33–47.

– "Family Life in 18th-Century Louisbourg." Manuscript Report No. 271. Ottawa: Parks Canada 1977.

– "A Letter From Louisbourg, 1756." *Acadiensis* 10, no. 1 (Autumn 1980): 113–30.

– "Paying One's Way: Dining and Drinking in Louisbourg's Cabarets and Auberges." *Research Bulletin* (Ottawa: Parks Canada) no. 135 (August 1980): 1–16.

– "Rearing Children in Colonial Louisbourg: A Seaport and Garrison Town 1713–1758." Paper delivered at the annual meeting of the Atlantic Society for Eighteenth-Century Studies, Mount St Vincent University, 26–28 April 1979.

– "Social Status and Contrasting Lifestyles: Children of the Poor and Well-to-do in Louisbourg." Paper delivered at the annual meeting of the Atlantic Society for Eighteenth-Century Studies, College of Cape Breton, 1 May 1980.

DORN, Walter L. *Competition for Empire, 1740–1763*. New York: Harper and Row 1940.

DUBOIS, Jacques. "La carte des diocèses de France avant la Révolution." *Annales: Economies, sociétés, civilisations* 20, no. 4 (1965): 680–91.

DU BOSCQ DE BEAUMONT, Gaston, ed. *Les derniers jours de l'Acadie (1748–1758): Correspondances et mémoires; extraits du portefeuille de M. le Courteois de Surlaville ...* Paris, 1899.

DUCLOS, M. *Considérations sur les mœurs de ce siècle*. Paris 1764.

DUNN, Brenda. "The Private Properties in Block 2, Louisbourg." Report, 1978, Archives of the Fortress of Louisbourg. Typescript.

ECCLES, W.J. *Canada under Louis XIV, 1663–1701*. Toronto: McClelland and Stewart 1964.

- *France in America*. New York: Harper and Row 1972.
- "The Social, Economic, and Political Significance of the Military Establishment in New France." *Canadian Historical Review* 52, no. 1 (March 1971): 1–22.
FAILLON, E.-M. *Vie de la Sœur Bourgeoys*. Vols. 1 and 2 of *Mémoires particuliers pour servir à l'histoire de l'église de l'Amérique du Nord*. Paris 1853.
FAIRCHILDS, Cissie C. *Poverty and Charity in Aix-en-Provence, 1640–1789*. Baltimore: Johns Hopkins University Press 1976.
FINCH, B.E., and GREEN, Hugh. *Contraception through the Ages*. Springfield: Charles C. Thomas 1963.
FLEURY, M., and VALMARY, P. "Les progrès de l'instruction elémentaire de Louis XIV à Napoleon III, d'après l'enquête de Louis Maggiolo (1877–1879)." *Population* 12 (1957): 71–92.
FORSTER, Robert, and RANUM, Orest, eds. *Biology of Man in History: Selections from the* Annales: Economies, sociétés, civilisations. Baltimore: Johns Hopkins University Press 1975.
- *Family and Society: Selections from the* Annales: Economies, sociétés, civilisations. Baltimore: Johns Hopkins University Press 1976.
- *Medicine and Society in France: Selections from the* Annales: Economies, sociétés, civilisations. Baltimore: Johns Hopkins University Press 1980.
FRANQUET, Louis. *Voyages et mémoires sur le Canada en 1752–53*. 1889. Reprint. Toronto: Canadiana House 1968.
FRÉGAULT, Guy. *La civilisation de la Nouvelle-France (1713–1744)*. Montréal: Société des Editions Pascal 1944.
- *Le XVIIIe siècle canadien: Etudes*. Montréal: Editions HMH 1968.
- *François Bigot, administrateur français*. 2 vols. Ottawa: Les Etudes de l'Institut d'Histoire de l'Amerique française 1948.
GÉLINAS, Joseph G. "Des oubliés." *La revue dominicaine* (1922): 218–19.
GELIS, Jacques. "Sages-Femmes et accoucheurs: L'obstétrique populaire aux XVIIe et XVIIIe siècles." *Annales: Economies, sociétés, civilisations* 32, no. 5 (septembre-octobre 1977): 927–57.
GOODY, Jack, ed. *Literacy in Traditional Societies*. Cambridge: Cambridge University 1968.
GOSSELIN, Abbé Amédée. *L'instruction Au Canada sous le régime français*. Québec Laflamme et Proulx 1911.
GOSSELIN, Abbé Auguste. *L'église du Canada, depuis Monseigneur de Laval jusqu'à la conquête*. 3 vols. Québec: Laflamme et Proulx 1911–14.
GOUJARD, Philippe. "Echec d'une sensibilité baroque: Les testaments Rouennais au XVIIIe siècle." *Annales: Économies, sociétés, civilisations* 36, no. 1 (janvier-février 1981): 26–43.
GOWANS, Alan. *Church Architecture in New France*. Toronto: University of Toronto Press 1955.

GRATIEN, P. *Histoire de la fondation et de l'évolution de l'Ordre des Frères Mineurs au XIIIe siècle*. Paris: Société et Librairie, St François d'Assise 1928.

GREER, Allan. "The Pattern of Literacy in Québec, 1745–1899." *Histoire Sociale / Social History* 11, no. 22 (November 1978): 295–335.

– *The Soldiers of Isle Royale, 1720–1745*. History and Archaeology No. 28. Ottawa: Parks Canada 1979.

GREVEN, Philip J. *Four Generations: Population, Land and Family in Colonial Andover, Massachusetts*. Ithaca: Cornell University Press 1970.

HARVEY, D.C. *The French Régime in Prince Edward Island*. New Haven: Yale University Press 1926.

HAYNES, Renée. *Philosopher King: The Humanist Pope Benedict XIV*. London: Weidenfeld and Nicolson 1970.

HEAGERTY, John J. *Four Centuries of Medical History in Canada, and a Sketch of the Medical History of Newfoundland*. Vol. 1. Toronto: Macmillan 1928.

HENRIPIN, Jacques. *La population canadienne au début du XVIIIe siècle: Nuptialité-fécondité-mortalité*. Paris: Presses universitaires de France 1954.

HILL, Christopher. "Sex, Marriage, and the Family in England." *The Economic History Review* 31, no. 3 (August 1978): 450–63.

Histoire générale de la marine ... 3 vols. Amsterdam, 1758.

HOAD, Linda. "Report on Lots A and B of Block 3." Report, 1971, Archives of the Fortress of Louisbourg. Typescript.

– *Surgeons and Surgery in Ile Royale*. History and Archaeology No. 6. Ottawa: Parks Canada 1976.

HOUDAILLE, Jacques. "Un indicateur de pratique religieuse: La célébration saisonnière des mariages avant, pendant et après la révolution française (1740–1829)." *Population* 33, no. 2 (mars-avril, 1978): 362–80.

HUFTON, Olwen H. *The Poor of Eighteenth-Century France, 1750–1789*. Oxford: Oxford University Press 1974.

HUGOLIN, R.P. [Stanislaus Lemay]. *L'établissement des Récollets de la Province de Saint-Denis à Plaisance en l'Ile de Terre-Neuve, 1689*. Québec 1911.

– *Le Père Joseph Denis, premier Récollet canadien (1657–1736)*. 2 vols. Québec: Laflamme 1926.

– "Les Récollets de la Province de Saint-Denis et ceux de la Province de Bretagne à l'Ile Royale de 1713 à 1731." *Mémoires de la Société Royale du Canada*, Sec. 1, 3e série, 24 (1930): 77–113.

– "Table nominale des Récollets de Bretagne, missionnaires et aumôniers dans l'Ile Royale (1713–1759)." *Mémoires de la Société Royale du Canada*, Sec. 1, 3e série, 25 (1931): 81–100.

HYNES, Gisa I. "Some Aspects of the Demography of Port Royal, 1650–1755." *Acadiensis*, 3, no. 1 (Autumn 1973): 3–17.

INNIS, Harold A. "Cape Breton and the French Régime." *Transactions of the Royal Society of Canada*, Sec. 2 (1935): 51–87.

JAENEN, Cornelius J. *The Role of the Church in New France*. Toronto: McGraw-Hill Ryerson 1976.

JERKIC, Sonja. "Excavations at Fortress Louisbourg of Human Skeletons in the Summer of 1974." Report, 1974, Archives of the Fortress of Louisbourg. Typescript.

JOHNSON, Micheline Dumont. *Apôtres ou agitateurs: La France missionnaire en Acadie*. Trois-Rivières: Boréal Express 1970.

JOHNSTON. Rev. A.A. *A History of the Catholic Church in Eastern Nova Scotia*. Vol. 1 (1611–1827). Antigonish: St Francis Xavier University Press 1960.

JOHNSTONE, James, Chevalier de. *Memoirs of the Chevalier de Johnstone*. 3 vols. Translated by Charles Winchester. Aberdeen 1870.

JOUVE, Père Odoric. "Franciscains et Acadiens sous la domination anglaise." *Chroniques et documents* 28, no. 2 (juin 1975): 145–54. Province Saint-Joseph Canada.

JUDGE, H.G. "Church and State under Louis XIV." *History* 65 (1960): 217–33.

KALM, Peter. *Travels into North America; Containing Its Natural History, and a Circumstantial Account of Its Plantations and Agriculture in General, with the Civil, Ecclesiastical and Commercial State of the Country ....* Vol. 3. London 1771.

KAPLOW, Jeffry. *The Names of Kings: The Parisian Laboring Poor in the Eighteenth Century*. New York: Basic Books 1972.

KREISER, B. Robert. *Miracles, Convulsions, and Ecclesiastical Politics in Early Eighteenth-Century Paris*. Princeton: Princeton University Press 1978.

LACHANCE, André. "Une étude de mentalité: Les injures verbales au Canada au XVIIIe siècle (1712–1748)." *Revue d'histoire de l'Amérique française* 31, no. 2 (septembre 1977): 229–38.

LANDRY, Yves. "Mortalité, nuptialité et canadianisation des troupes françaises de la guerre de Sept Ans." *Histoire Sociale / Social History* 12, no. 24 (November 1979): 298–315.

LATRIE, M. le comte de Mas. *Trésor de chronologie d'histoire et de géographie pour l'étude et l'emploi des documents du Moyen Age*. Paris 1889.

LAVER, James. *The Age of Illusion: Manners and Morals, 1750–1848*. London: Weidenfeld and Nicolson 1972.

LEBRUN, François. *Les hommes et la Mort en Anjou aux 17e et 18e siècles: Essai de démographie et de psychologie historiques*. The Hague: Mouton 1971.

LECLERC, Joseph. "Le roi de France, 'Fils Aîné de l'Eglise'," *Etudes* 214 (1933): 21–36, 170–89.

LECLERC, Paul-André. "Le mariage sous le régime français." *Revue d'histoire de l'Amérique française* 13, no. 2 (septembre 1959): 230–46; 13, no. 3

(décembre 1959): 374–401; 13, no. 4 (mars 1960): 525–43; 14, no. 1 (juin 1960): 34–60; 14, no. 2 (septembre 1960): 226–45.

[LEMIRE-MARSOLAIS (Sister Sainte-Henriette)]. *Histoire de la Congrégation de Notre-Dame de Montréal*. 9 vols. Montréal: CND 1941

– *Histoire de la Congrégation de Notre-Dame de Montréal: Index onomastique*. Montréal: CND 1969.

MACDONALD, L.R. "France and New France: The Internal Contradictions." *Canadian Historical Review* 52, no. 2 (June 1971): 121–43.

MACKENZIE, A.A. *The Irish in Cape Breton*. Antigonish: Formac 1979.

MACLEAN, Jill. *Jean-Pierre Roma of the Company of the East of Isle St. Jean*. Cornelius Howatt Commemorative Series, no. 4. P.E.I.: Prince Edward Island Heritage Foundation 1977.

MCLENNAN, J.S. *Louisbourg from Its Foundation to Its Fall, 1713–1758*. 1918. Reprint. Sydney: Fortress Press 1969.

MCMANNERS, John. *French Ecclesiastical Society under the Ancien Régime: A Study of Angers in the Eighteenth Century*. Manchester: University of Manchester Press 1960.

[MAILLARD, Abbé Pierre]. *An Account of the Customs and Manners of the Micmakis and Maricheets Savage Nations ...*. London 1758.

MANDROU, Robert. *De la culture populaire aux XVIIe et XVIIIe Siècles: La bibliothèque bleue de Troyes*. Paris: Stock 1964.

MARTIN, Hervé. "Les Franciscains bretons et les gens de mer: De Bretagne en Acadie (XVe-début XVIIIe siècle)." *Annales de Bretagne et des pays de l'Ouest* 87, no. 4 (décembre 1980): 641–77.

[MERCIER, Louis-Sébastien]. *Tableau de Paris, nouvelle édition, corrigée et augmenté*. Amsterdam 1783.

MISSON, M. *Memoirs and Observations in His Travels over England with Some Account of Scotland and Ireland*. Written in French, translated by Mr. Ozell. London 1719.

MITHELL, Allan. "Phillippe Aries and the French Way of Death." *French Historical Studies* 10, no. 4 (Fall 1978): 684–95.

MOIR, John S. *Church and State in Canada, 1627–1867: Basic Documents*. Toronto: McClelland and Stewart 1967.

MOOGK, Peter N. "Manual Education and Economic Life in New France." *Studies on Voltaire and the Eighteenth Century* 167 (1977): 125–68.

– "'Thieving Buggers' and 'Stupid Sluts': Insults and Popular Culture in New France." *William and Mary Quarterly*, 3rd ser., 36, no. 4 (October 1978): 524–47.

MOORE, Christopher. "Cemeteries." Report, 1974, Archives of the Fortress of Louisbourg. Typescript.

– *Louisbourg Portraits: Life in an Eighteenth-Century Garrison Town*. Toronto: Macmillan 1982.

- "Miscellaneous Louisbourg Reports." Manuscript Report No. 317. Ottawa: Parks Canada 1974–8.
- "The Other Louisbourg: Trade and Merchant Enterprise in Ile Royale, 1713–58." *Histoire sociale / Social History* 12, no. 23 (mai / May 1979): 79–96.
MORGAN, Edmund S. "Ezra Stiles: The Education of a Yale Man, 1742–1746." *Huntington Library Quarterly* 17, no. 1 (November 1953): 251–68.
"Notice sur les Frères Hospitaliers de la Charité de l'Ordre de St-Jean-Dieu, au Canada, de 1713 à 1758." *Bulletin des recherches historiques* 33, no. 9 (September 1927): 522–4.
O'NEILL, Charles Edwards. *Church and State in French Colonial Louisiana: Policy and Politics to 1732.* New Haven: Yale University Press 1966.
PARKMAN, Francis. "The Capture of Louisbourg by the New England Militia." *Atlantic Monthly* 54 (March 1891): 314–25; (April 1891): 514–23; (May 1891): 621–30.
- *The Old Régime in Canada: France and England in North America.* Part Fourth. Toronto 1898.
PERRIN, O. *Galerie Bretonne ou vie des Bretons de l'Armorique.* 3 vols. Paris, 1836.
PICART, Bernard. *The Ceremonies and Religious Customs of the Various Nations of the Known World; Together with Historical Annotations, and several Curious Discourses Equally Instructive and Entertaining.* Translated from the French. Vols. 1 and 2. London 1733–4.
[PICHON, Thomas]. *Genuine Letters and Memoirs, Relating to the Natural, Civil and Commercial History of the Islands of Cape Breton and Saint John ....* London 1760.
- *Lettres et mémoires pour servir à l'histoire naturelle, civile et politique du Cap Breton ....* The Hague 1760.
PINEAU, Wilfrid. *Le clergé français dans l'Ile du Prince-Edouard, 1721–1821.* Québec: Les Editions Ferland 1967.
PLANTE, Abbé Hermann. *L'Eglise catholique au Canada (1604–1886).* Trois Rivières: Editions du Bien public 1970.
PORTER, Fernand. *L'institution catéchistique au Canada: Deux siècles de formation religieuse, 1633–1833.* Montréal: Les Editions franciscaines 1949.
[POTE, William]. *The Journal of Captain William Pote, Jr. during His Capitivity in the French and Indian War, from May, 1745, to August, 1747.* Edited by J.F. Hurst and Victor Paltsits. New York 1896.
POTHIER, Bernard. "Acadian Emigration to Ile Royale after the Conquest of Acadia." *Histoire sociale / Social History* 3, no. 6 (November 1970): 116–31.
PRITCHARD, James S. "The Pattern of French Colonial Shipping to Canada before 1760." *Revue française d'histoire d'outre-mer* 63, no. 231 (2e trimestre 1976): 189–210.
PROULX, Gilles. *Aubergistes et cabaretiers de Louisbourg, 1713–1758.* Travail inédit, No. 136. Ottawa: Parcs Canada 1972.

- *Tribunaux et Lois de Louisbourg.* Travail inédit, No. 303. Ottawa: Parcs Canada 1975.
- *Les bibliothèques de Louisbourg.* Travail inédit, No. 271. Ottawa: Parcs Canada 1974.

QUÉNIART, Jean. "Culture et société urbaines dans la France de l'Ouest au 18e siècle." 2 vols. Thèse Présentée devant l'Université de Paris I, 1975. Université de Lille III, 1977.

- *Les hommes, L'église et Dieu dans la France du XVIIIe siècle.* Paris: Hachette 1978.

Rapport de l'Archiviste de la Province de Québec (1920–67).

REID, John G. *Acadia, Maine, and New Scotland: Marginal Colonies in the Seventeenth Century.* Toronto: University of Toronto Press 1981.

ROBERTS, Penfield. *The Quest for Security, 1715–1740.* New York: Harper and Row 1947.

ROCHEMONTEIX, Camille de. *Les Jésuites de la Nouvelle-France au XVIIIe siècle ....* Vol. 1. Paris: Alphonse Picard et fils 1906.

ROY, Raymond, and CHARBONNEAU, Hubert. "Le contenu des registres paroissiaux canadiens du XVIIe siècle." *Revue d'histoire de l'Amérique française* 30, no. 1 (juin 1976): 85–97.

SAINT-VALLIER, Jean-de-la-Croix de. *Catéchisme du Diocèse de Québec ....* Paris 1702. Reprint. Montréal 1958.

- *Rituel du Diocèse de Québec.* Paris 1703.

SAUSSURE, César de. *A Foreign View of England in the Reigns of George I and George II: The Letters of Monsieur César de Saussure to His Family.* Translated and edited by Madame Van Muyden. London: John Murray 1902.

SCHMEISSER, Barbara. "The Population of Louisbourg, 1713–1758." Manuscript Report No. 303. Ottawa: Parks Canada 1976.

SICARD, Abbé. *L'ancien clergé de France: Les éveques avant la Révolution.* Paris 1893.

SMITH, B.G. "Death and Life in a Colonial Immigrant City: A Demographic Analysis of Philadelphia." *Journal of Economic History* 37, no. 4 (December 1977): 863–89.

STANDEN, S. Dale. "Politics, Patronage, and the Imperial Interest: Charles de Beauharnois's Disputes with Gilles Hocquart." *Canadian Historical Review* 60, no. 1 (March 1979): 19–40.

TACKETT, Timothy. *Priest & Parish in Eighteenth-Century France: A Social and Political Study of the Curés in a Diocese of Dauphiné, 1750–1791.* Princeton: Princeton University Press 1977.

TÊTU, Henri, and GAGNON, C.-O., eds. *Mandements, lettres pastorales et circulaires des évêques de Québec.* Vols. 1 and 2. Québec 1887–90.

THIERS, Jean-Baptiste. *Traité des jeux et des divertissemens qui peuvent être permis, ou qui doivent être défendus aux Chrétiens selon les regles de l'Église ....* Paris 1686.

TRÉPANIER, Pierre. "Les Récollets et l'Acadie (1619–1759): Plaidoyer pour l'histoire religieuse." *Les cahiers de la société historique acadienne* 10, no. 1 (mars 1979): 4–11.

TRUDEL, Marcel. *Introduction to New France*. Toronto, Montréal: Holt, Rinehart and Winston 1968.

TRUMBACH, Randolph. *The Rise of the Egalitarian Family: Aristocratic Kinship and Domestic Relations in Eighteenth-Century England*. New York: Academic Press 1978.

VAN GENNEP, Arnold. *Manuel de folklore français contemporain*. 7 vols. Paris: A. Picard 1943–79.

VOVELLE, Michel. "Les attitudes devant la mort: Problèmes de méthodes." *Annales: Economies, sociétés, civilisations* 31, no. 1 (janvier-fevrier 1976): 120–32.

– "The History of Mankind in the Mirror of Death." In *Proceedings of the Sixth Annual Meeting of the Western Society for French History, 9–11 November 1978*, edited by Joyce Duncan Falk, 91–109. Santa Barbara: Western Society for French History 1979.

WALSH, H.H. *The Church in the French Era, From Colonization to the British Conquest*. Toronto: Ryerson Press 1966.

WELLS, Robert V. *The Population of the British Colonies in America before 1776: A Survey of Census Data*. Princeton: Princeton University Press 1975.

WRONG, George M., ed. *Louisbourg in 1745: The Anonymous Lettre d'un Habitant de Louisbourg*. Toronto 1897.

ZOLTVANY, Yves F. "Esquisse de la coutume de Paris." pp. 365–84, *Revue d'histoire de l'Amérique française* 25, no. 3 (décembre 1971): 365–84.

– *The French Tradition in North America*. Vancouver: Fitzhenry and Whiteside 1969.

Index